READING
FREIRE AND HABERMAS

READING
FREIRE AND HABERMAS

Critical Pedagogy
and
Transformative Social Change

RAYMOND A. MORROW
CARLOS ALBERTO TORRES

Teachers College, Columbia University
New York and London

Published by Teachers College Press, 1234 Amsterdam Avenue, New York, NY 10027

Copyright © 2002 by Teachers College, Columbia University

Library of Congress Cataloging-in-Publication Data

Morrow, Raymond Allen.
    Reading Freire and Habermas : critical pedagogy and transformative social change / Raymond A. Morrow, Carlos Alberto Torres.
        p. cm.
    Includes bibliographical references (p.   ) and index.
    ISBN 0-8077-4202-3 (pbk. : alk. paper) — ISBN 0-8077-4203-1 (cloth : alk. paper)
        1. Freire, Paulo, 1921–   2. Habermas, Jèrgen.   3. Critical pedagogy.   4. Social change.
    I. Torres, Carlos Alberto.   II. Title
    LC196 .M67   2002
    370.11′5—dc21   2001060375

ISBN 0-8077-4202-3 (paper)
ISBN 0-8077-4203-1 (cloth)

Printed on acid-free paper

Manufactured in the United States of America

09   08   07   06   05   04   03   02   8   7   6   5   4   3   2   1

We dedicate this book to Paulo Freire in memoriam
*and to his children, Magdalena, Fátima, Christina, Joachim, and Luti
and to his widow, Ana Maria Araujo Freire.*

Contents

Preface

Our primary objective in this book is to bring to a larger audience some of the most important developments in the understanding of the relationship of social theory, education, and educational practice in the 20th century through the writings of the late Paulo Freire and Jürgen Habermas.[1] Their key contributions date from the 1960s and have exercised an immense if often diffuse influence on a number of academic fields and types of professional training. Both authors are difficult to classify in either disciplinary or ideological terms, and their reception in various intellectual and national contexts has been a complex and controversial process. Freire is known primarily in educational circles as a Brazilian adult educator who pioneered a form of literacy training based on breaking down the hierarchical teacher-learner relationship, thus allowing adults to learn to "name" the power relations that define their social world. In contrast, Habermas is best known as a difficult German philosopher who has extended the Frankfurt tradition of critical social theory—which originated in the Weimar Republic in the late 1920s—by defending a critical modernism as a response to the "incomplete" vision of the 18th-century Enlightenment.

We will also occasionally refer to others influenced by their work, especially in domains where they have said little or remained silent. Though this community of researchers is most obvious in the case of Habermas, it has become more apparent recently with the publication of testimonies and commentaries on educational experiments influenced by Freire's theories.

Our strategy is comparative in that we attempt to develop a comparison of these two theorists, stressing the complementarity of their approaches, despite significant differences in focus and style. We view both as working within a shared *critical theory of the dialogical and developmental subject*. Their approach presumes a "dialogical subject" because it rejects a monological and transcendental theory of the subject, that is, one based on an abstract, metaphysical "I" that individualistically "knows" the world. Instead, they locate selfhood and identity formation in contexts

of intersubjective communication. Their strategy is "developmental" because it argues that identity formation has, despite variable cultural contents, directional potential for growth than can be fully realized only
under optimal conditions of socialization. With respect to Habermas,
such concerns are most evident in his preoccupation with a theory of
communicative action, moral development, and emancipatory reason. In
the case of Freire, parallel concerns can be detected in terms of what has
come to be called his pedagogy of liberation and conception of cultural
action.

The arguments of this study are rooted in our previous individual
as well as co-authored works. In *Social Theory and Education* (Morrow &
Torres, 1995) we sought to show how the concept of social reproduction,
originating in efforts to view Marxism in a less economically reductionist
manner, has over the past couple of decades become a key strategy for
attempting to understand the relationship between education and society.
In particular, we show how the traditional base-superstructure model of
Marx's theory is inadequate to deal with the profoundly historical and
relational nature of the type of social theory he proposed. In these discussions, however, we treated Freire and Habermas in separate contexts
(Morrow, 1990; Morrow & Torres, 1994, 1995). Considering them comparatively here allows shifting the focus to the problematic of agency that
complements our previous focus on structure. At the same time, we view
Freire and Habermas in terms of the more general problematic of the
issues of critical social theory and methodology, especially with respect
to Habermas's critique of the human sciences (Morrow, 1982, 1983, 1989,
1991, 1994a, 1994b).

Further, our approach is situated in relation to a long-standing and
intensive concern with Freire's philosophy (Torres, 1978a, 1978b, 1979,
1980, 1994; Torres, 1995a; 1998a; Torres & Freire, 1994), as well as the long
history of his engagement with educational reform, especially in the Latin
American context (Pescador & Torres, 1985; Torres, 1990b; Torres & Puiggrós, 1996; Torres & Rivera, 1994) and elsewhere.

Our primary objective is to introduce Freire and Habermas as complementary thinkers, rather than to develop extensive criticisms. In notes
and asides, however, we also provide points of departure for the further
exploration of issues. Particularly in the case of Habermas there have
been a number of efforts to amend or revise aspects of his work that go
beyond the tasks of the present introduction (Rasmussen, 1996; White,
1995a). For Freire, however, much of this task remains to be done, though
we hope this study may facilitate that process.

We have several types of audiences in mind. Most immediately our
discussion is directed to educators in the professional sense, primarily in

graduate schools of education. Second, we believe that people in communications studies and interpretive social psychology will find our approach of interest. Third, we would hope that those who are educators in the more extended sense of being concerned about transformative social change will find our contribution potentially helpful. Finally, those with general interests in social theory might find useful the issues posed by critical pedagogy for rethinking aspects of critical theory.

1

Introduction

Reading Freire Through Habermas

> All social institutions have a meaning, a purpose . . . to set free and to develop the capacities of human individuals without respect to race, sex, class or economic status . . . the test of their value is the extent to which they educate every individual into the full stature of his possibility. Democracy has many meanings, but if it has a moral meaning, it is found in resolving that the supreme test of all political institutions and industrial arrangements shall be the contribution they make to the all-around growth of every member of society.
> —Dewey, 1957

Paulo Freire (1921–1997), an educator born in Brazil and later forced into exile for many years, is perhaps the best-known figure internationally in postwar adult education. He is known primarily in educational circles as an expert on "Third World" literacy training. His contribution is a methodology based on a distinction between *banking education*, through which knowledge is mechanically accumulated, and *critical education*, in which the learner becomes an active participant in the appropriation of knowledge in relation to lived experience.

In recent years, however, he has been widely cited in the context of the controversial form of curriculum theory linked with *critical pedagogy*, a term associated with teaching strategies sensitive to the effects of relations of power based on race, class, gender, ethnicity, and so forth, on learning and consciousness formation (McLaren, 1996, 1997). As well, his approach has inspired empowerment-oriented research and practice not only in Brazil and Latin America (Gadotti et al., 1996; Gadotti & Torres, 1994), but around the world in such diverse fields as participatory action research, community development, nursing, health promotion, social work, and liberation psychology.[2]

In contrast to Freire's association with Third World adult education and empowerment strategies for marginalized groups, Habermas, born in Germany in 1929, is often acknowledged as the most influential German philosopher and social theorist of the postwar period. A quantitative indicator of Habermas's influence can be found in the fact that by 1981, there were nearly a thousand bibliographical references to his work (Görtzen, 1982, 1990). He is generally regarded as the most important contemporary representative of *critical theory*, a term that alludes to the tradition of critical social theory originating in the Frankfurt School in Germany in the late 1920s. The Frankfurt School's research institute became the basis of the first systematic and autonomous attempt to explore the potential of Marx's historical materialism as a scientifically credible research program. By the end of the Second World War, the members of the Frankfurt School had become disillusioned with the Marxian tradition. In the 1960s, however, Habermas developed a strategy for revitalizing critical theory through its radical reconstruction and engagement with other theoretical traditions. In breaking with key assumptions of both classical Marxism and the older Frankfurt tradition, Habermas's *theory of communicative action* assumed a distinctive form for which the contentious label "Marxist" no longer appears appropriate. Most important, his epistemological strategy is *postfoundationalist* in that it does not base knowledge claims on either "laws of history" (classical Marxism) or direct "correspondence" between theories and empirical reality (e.g., positivism). The term *critical social theory* thus has become a useful way of designating a distinctive body of thought that cannot be subsumed within the older categories (Calhoun, 1995).

Habermas's greatest impact has been in the human sciences, initially among specialists in social and political theory, but now in a number of professional fields. He is not normally known as an educational theorist in the strict sense, though philosophers of education and curriculum theorists have often drawn on his work (Ewert, 1991). The common lament, however, is that Habermas's "neglect of everyday life in schools and classrooms" makes it difficult for teachers because he "appears to inhabit a distant, unfamiliar world; a rarefied region of theory and jargon that does not touch the children and the classrooms that we know" (Gibson, 1986. p. 41). Nevertheless, critical pedagogy as a form of critical theory has now become a well-established orientation that reaches teachers' training programs in accessible forms (e.g., Hinchey, 1998; Kanpol, 1994).

CONVERGENT BIOGRAPHICAL TRAJECTORIES

Our objective is to read Freire and Habermas as complementary thinkers. Our central claim is that they share a conception of the human sciences, the crisis of modern societies, theory of the subject, and pedagogical practice. These commonalities can best be revealed by a strategy of reading that is grounded in an understanding of the shared foundational intuition of their social theories: the origins of thought and action in intersubjective communicative relations of mutual recognition. Our basic claim will be that Habermas and Freire *taken together* provide a framework for further developing and radicalizing the themes relating philosophy, education, and democracy joined in the great American pragmatist John Dewey, who continues to inspire provocative formulations of democratic reform (Steiner, 1994), despite his lack an adequate theory of social psychological domination and societal crisis (Bernstein, 1971; Paringer, 1990).

The influence on Habermas of the work of John Dewey, as well as the fellow pragmatists George Herbert Mead and Charles Sanders Peirce, is relatively well known (Joas, 1993). Though Freire's position develops more directly out of European theory, it was also influenced by a tentative dialogue with Dewey as introduced in Brazil by Anísio Teixeira (1900–1971), who studied with Dewey at Columbia University. After returning to Brazil, in 1935 he became Secretary of Education and Culture in the Federal District (then in Rio de Janeiro) and introduced the idea of the *escola nova* or new school. Influenced by Teixeira, Freire always considered Dewey a key educational philosopher. Ironically, Teixeira was branded a "communist" because of Dewey's influence on Lenin's wife, Krupskaya, who pioneered Soviet educational policy (Freire, 1997b, pp. 118–119).

A number of surprising affinities justify this strategy of comparison. Both Freire and Habermas were influenced early in their careers by existentialist philosophy, and deal extensively with the work of early 19th-century philosopher Hegel in working through problems with Karl Marx's theory of praxis and its relation to democratization. Even more than Dewey's, their political philosophies do not shy away from the recognition that democracy takes place in the context of capitalism, even though they reject simplistic notions of working-class revolution and dogmatic socialist alternatives. The origins of this remarkable degree of convergence can be traced to complementary shifts (revisionist for Habermas, a radicalization for Freire) in their thinking in the 1960s. The outcome was a critical theory of society that seeks to bridge between revolutionary Marxism and reformist liberalism in a manner that was first anticipated by, though not successfully realized in, the work of the sociologist Karl Mannheim in the 1930s in response to Max Weber's critique of historical materialism (Morrow, 1994c). Habermas moved to this position through a revision of historical materialism (and Marx) based on a reflexive theory of knowledge and communicative action. In contrast, Freire moved toward it via a radicalization of his dialogical and Mannheimian point of departure through a new appreciation of Marx as a theorist of praxis.

One immediate consequence of our comparative strategy is to rescue both theorists from ghettoization within their respective intellectual traditions—Habermas as a mandarin, esoteric German philosopher and Freire as a moralistic and rhetorical traditional Latin American *pensador*. Habermas is much more of a passionate and grounded thinker than he is often given credit for, and Freire has a philosophical depth and rigor that is not always apparent in his "conversational" style oriented to teachers. In short, we hope to show how both transcend such stereotypes. In the process, it becomes possible to show when and how Habermas offers Freire arguments that justify, ground, reframe, and further elaborate his positions, and to suggest when and how Freire contributes to the practical and political concerns of Habermas at the level of concrete interactions and practices.

PATTERNS OF RECEPTION

These affinities were long obscured by the disparate contexts of reception of their work. From the late 1960s, Habermas's early work was hailed as an important contribution to educational theory, under the short-lived influence of the West German critical pedagogy movement. There has been a more enduring and visible influence in the English-speaking world, culminating in the early 1980s, prior to the reception of his theory of communicative action. For the most part, reference was made to his early epistemological writings (i.e., the theory of knowledge interests), which is used to legitimate both the hermeneutic foundations of knowledge and the introduction of a socially and politically engaged approach to education (Carr, 1995; Carr & Kemmis, 1986; Comstock, 1994; Giroux, Penna, & Pinar, 1981; Grundy, 1987; Misgeld, 1975, 1981, 1985).

Surprisingly, Habermas has been only a peripheral influence on the more recent American critical pedagogy literature, especially relative to Freire. There are various reasons for this, aside from the complexity of Habermas's work. On the one hand, it reflects the split between adult educators—where Habermas has been very influential—and child educators: "Even the 'critical pedagogy' literature often associated with Henry Giroux and Peter McLaren scarcely references any of the critical adult education literature. Educational theory exists in two solitudes as those who write about children and school remain oblivious to important discussion on the learning of adults" (Welton, 1995c, p. 2). Most important, however, the emergence of the postmodernist problematic has displaced attention from of Habermas's "modernist" approach toward a "critical postmodernism" (Aronowitz & Giroux, 1991). But as demonstrated by

Robert Young (1989) in his *A Critical Theory of Education* and the excellent collection *In Defense of the Lifeworld* (Welton, 1995b), Habermas does indeed continue to provide important insights for rethinking adult education and educational institutions generally. Paradoxically, however, the centrality of educational theory is not evident in the specialized literature on Habermas.[3] This neglect of educational issues has contributed to glossing over some of the key features of his overall project.

Until recently, Freire has not been directly associated with critical social theory. In part this reflects the belated reception of Habermas in Latin America, as well as a tendency for commentators to be baffled by the diverse sources of his educational theory. Despite brief references to Mannheim, Fromm, and Marcuse—individuals associated at some point with the Frankfurt critical theory tradition in the 1930s—Freire's approach has been classified in confusing ways in relation to Marxism, Gramsci, French existentialism, Christian personalism, Hegelianism, and liberation theology. Consequently, the relation between his pedagogy and Habermas's theory of communicative action has not been adequately explored. Moreover, little attention is given to the tension between the vaguely Marxian aspects of Freire's thinking and his defense of a practical moral philosophy, a point implicit in the suggestion that "Paulo Freire dares to tread where even Marx refused to walk—on the terrain where the revolutionary *love* of struggling human beings sustains their faith in each other and keeps hope alive within themselves and in history" (West, 1993, p. xiv).

Though the affinities between Freire and Habermas have been often noted, they have never been explored in sufficient depth (McLaren & Lankshear, 1994; McLaren & Leonard, 1993; Taylor, 1975, 1993). Peter Roberts's otherwise excellent work suffers from not linking him to the critical theory tradition (Roberts, 2000). Most surprisingly, the significant German reception of Freire did not recognize these connections because of a tendency to read him in either overly Marxist or theological terms. Working out of Geneva in the 1970s, Freire had extensive contact with the Christian Left in Germany, especially in relation to the education of guest workers. This association contributed to his reputation as a politically radical Christian existentialist, whereas Marxists routinely dismissed his work as idealist and subjectivist, though holding out some hope of integrating it within a more materialist, Marxist framework (Bräuer, 1985). That Habermas's theory of communicative action might provide the most natural basis for rethinking aspects of Freire appears to have been largely obscured by the blindspots of German academic life. Similarly, the extensive Latin American reception of Freire in the 1970s was preoccupied by his relation to Christian existentialism and Marxism in a context where

Habermas was not then well understood (Torres, 1979). Nevertheless, in Latin America it was generally acknowledged that Freire's methodology implied a philosophy of social science and a theory of society. For example, Julio Barreiro (1974) introduced the theory of popular education and Freire's concept of *conscientization*—a process of becoming aware of social realities—in relation to a theory of society that attempted to combine the social phenomenology of Peter Berger and Thomas Luckmann with the structuralist Marxism. The outcome was a mechanical juxtaposition of fatalistic determinism with the voluntarism of conscientization as a theory of class consciousness (Barreiro, 1974). One of the most sophisticated exceptions to these tendencies was the early efforts of Carlos A. Torres (1978b) to link Freirean methods with a nonempiricist, dialectical philosophy of social science, along with a conception of praxis within which the agent is not so much a producer as a *"being of communication* who needs the other to enter into a dialogue" (p. 86).

In the English-speaking world in the 1980s, attention was on occasion brought to the kinship between Freire and Habermas, especially in the context of Australian critical action research (Carr & Kemmis, 1986; Grundy, 1987). In Canada, it was noted that "Paulo Freire's *Pedagogy of the Oppressed* is an enterprise akin to Habermas's" (Misgeld, 1985, p. 105); more specifically it was suggested that "in effect Habermas's linguistic turn . . . invokes a civil community of truth, equality, sincerity, and freedom. This ethical matrix bears a striking resemblance to the moral foundations of the pedagogy of the oppressed developed by Freire" (O'Neill, 1985, p. 58). More recently, two well-known Freirean educators suggested that "although the details of his metaphysic, ontology, and epistemology differ in significant ways from that of Habermas, his emancipatory project has a remarkably similar intent" (Lankshear & McLaren, 1993b, p. 41). To our knowledge, however, the only sustained comparative treatment including Habermas's later work has been a provocative M.A. thesis (Plumb, 1989).

PROBLEMS OF COMPARISON

The relationships among education, power, and personal biography in the development of educational theories are complex (Torres, 1998b). Not surprisingly, the remarkable differences between the respective careers of Freire and Habermas provide little overt indication of the kind of convergence proposed here.

Freire's work first gained national and international attention in his earlier experiences with literacy training in Angicos, North-East Brazil.

As the first director (1961–1964) of the Cultural Extension Service of the University of Recife, Freire was associated with the Catholic Left and helped inspire the theology of liberation movement in Latin America (Kadt, 1970; Mainwaring, 1986; Moreira Alves, 1969; Torres, 1992). His pedagogical work has been associated with the *Movimento de Educação de Base* or Movement for Grass-roots Education, the Centers for Popular Culture, and the Ecclessial Base Communities in Brazil (Beisiegel, 1982; Gadotti, 1986; Mainwaring, 1986). Appointed by the populist government of João Goulard as president of the National Commission of Popular Culture in 1963, and as coordinator of the National Plan of Literacy Training (1963), he had a profound impact on literacy training for citizenship building and the mobilization of the popular sectors. Given that before 1983 literacy was a prerequisite for voting, and in the early 1960s 15 of 25 million Brazilians were illiterate, the results are impressive: "In 1964, the year of the coup d'état, in the state of Sergipe alone, literacy training added 80,000 new voters to the 90,000 already existing. In Pernambuco, the total of voters went from 800,000 to 1 million" (Torres, 1990b, p. 40).

Arrested twice and spending some 75 days in jail (Freire, 1985, p. 180), Freire was eventually forced into exile for 16 years (1964–1980) by a military regime that labeled him an "international subversive, a traitor to Christ and the people of Brazil besides being an absolute ignoramus and illiterate" (cited in Horton & Freire, 1990, p. xxviii). At this point he was known primarily for his *Education: The Practice of Freedom*, which appeared in Brazil in 1967 (and included in Freire, 1973). Beyond introducing the practice of conscientization as a method of literacy training, this book proposed a diagnosis of Brazilian society from the perspective of a theory of mass society and economic dependency. Traveling first to Bolivia, where there were no opportunities for work, he and his family moved to Chile in 1964 where he became involved in agrarian reform projects that radicalized his approach in a more Marxist direction (Austin, 1997). He then departed to teach as a visiting professor at Harvard in 1969, a connection that facilitated the early appearance of some of his work in English. It was during this initial exile period that his more radical and famous educational writings appeared. Ironically, due to censorship in Brazil, his most important book—*Pedagogy of the Oppressed*—first appeared in Spanish and English in 1970 and did not appear in a Brazilian Portuguese edition until 1975 (Freire, 1970b, 1970c). But by the early 1990s it had sold over half a million copies worldwide.

In 1970 Freire accepted a permanent position as educational adviser in the World Congress of Churches headquarters in Geneva. A decade later he was allowed to return to Brazil, where he taught in several

Brazilian universities. In this period his pedagogical approach became widely known in Europe and throughout the world. In the mid-1970s he collaborated with the government of Guinea-Bissau in an attempt to extend his concept of literacy training to Africa (Freire, 1983). When the *Partido dos Trabalhadores* (Worker's Party) won the municipal elections of São Paulo in 1988, Freire—a member of the party since it was founded in 1979 and president of the Worker's University sponsored by the party— was a natural choice for Secretary of Education of the City of São Paulo (O'Cadiz, Wong, & Torres, 1998).

In the 1980s and early 1990s, a number of collections in English brought together scattered essays, as well as refinements in the form of dialogues (Freire, 1985, 1993, 1994; Freire & Faundez, 1989; Freire & Macedo, 1987). Despite lecturing worldwide, he tried to complete several long-postponed books, particularly *Letters to Cristina, A Pedagogy of Hope, Pedagogy of the Heart*, and *Teachers as Cultural Workers* (Freire, 1994, 1996, 1997b, 1998b). His last book, released in Portuguese just a month before his death, was entitled *The Pedagogy of Freedom* (Freire, 1997a, 1998a) and constitutes an important contribution to the ethics of teaching.

Overtly the career of Jürgen Habermas has been dramatically different. Born in Düsseldorf in 1929, he spent his early years in the shadow of German fascism, including being drafted into the German army at 15. During the years 1949–1954 he studied a wide range of subjects at the universities of Göttingen, Bonn, and Zürich, including philosophy, history, economics, psychology, and German literature. He spent a 2-year period as a freelance journalist, and an article of his came to the attention of Theodor Adorno, who invited him to become his assistant (1956–1959) at the newly revived Frankfurt Institute for Social Research. Ironically, however, the reestablished institute had largely abandoned the research program of the 1930s, which Habermas discovered only when he came upon the old institute journal *Zeitschrift für Sozialforschung* (1932–1941) hidden away in the basement. For this reason, the institute founder, Max Horkheimer—who had repudiated his earlier Marxist commitments, saw Habermas's revival of left-wing themes as a threat in the 1960s and opposed his association with the Frankfurt Institute on various occasions (Wiggershaus, 1994).

In 1961, he was awarded a professorship at Heidelberg, partly on the basis of the work that soon appeared in 1962 as the *Structural Transformation of the Public Sphere* (Habermas, 1989c). Whereas this book outlined a critique of modern democracy that underlies all of his writings, the first edition of a collection of essays, *Theory and Practice* (Habermas, 1973), initiated the critique of the Marxian tradition that anticipated his sharp break with the older Frankfurt School tradition. In 1964 he returned to a philosophy chair at the University of Frankfurt, as well as becoming actively involved in the emerging German student movement. The highlights of this period were his epistemological writings, *Knowledge and Human Interests* (Habermas, 1971), and a resulting critique of science and technology as ideology sketched in *Toward a Rational Society* (Habermas, 1970a). But he quickly became isolated from the student movement, charging it with "left-wing fascist" tendencies. This split long prejudiced the reception of Habermas on the German Left (Wiggershaus, 1994, p. 544). From 1971 to 1983 he worked as a director in the Max Planck Institute of Starnberg near Munich and coordinated a number of interdisciplinary research projects concerned with the welfare state and the reconstruction of historical materialism. His own work in this context included *Legitimation Crisis* (Habermas, 1975) and *Communication and the Evolution of Society* (Habermas, 1979). But it was also in this period that he synthesized his overall approach in the two-volume *Theory of Communicative Action* (Habermas, 1984, 1987b). On returning to a professorship in Frankfurt in 1983 (from which he recently retired), he began to elaborate a theory of discourse ethics and law that culminated in *Between Facts and Norms* (Habermas, 1996). Prior to completing that project, however, he published a highly controversial critique of French poststructuralism as *The Philosophical Discourse of Modernity* (Habermas, 1987a). Most recently, the collection of papers *The Inclusion of the Other* (Habermas, 1998a) brings together essays on deliberative democracy and the nation-state.

But Habermas has not been merely an ivory-tower professor of philosophy and sociology. Beyond his numerous interviews, speaking engagements, and visits around the world, he has often become involved in public debates through journalistic interventions on topics such as educational reform, student movements, conservative German historians, German reunification, the Gulf War, and so forth (Habermas, 1994, 1997a; Pensky, 1995). "Accordingly, he has played a role in German intellectual life that his American readers by and large have not fully appreciated" (Hohendahl, 1994, p. viii).

The absence of more sustained comparison stems in part from three apparent differences that make it difficult to mediate between the two authors: (1) geographic and cultural distance: their locations, respectively, in a Third World industrializing society (Brazil) and an advanced European one (Germany); (2) divergent personal intellectual trajectories stemming from a break between their early and later writings: Freire's shift from a liberal to a Marxist position, as opposed to Habermas's later rejection of the Marxism of his Frankfurt School predecessors; and (3) contrasting intellectual styles: Freire's *ad hoc*, practical philosophizing directed toward adult educational practice, as opposed to Habermas as a systematic (if postfoundationalist) philosopher and social theorist. The first contrast can be dealt with through a consideration of their work as a parallel response to the rise of fascism as a strategy for dealing with the crises of capitalist development, viewed respectively from the center and the periphery; the second will be resolved by suggesting that despite significant shifts of emphasis, both authors converge on a dialogical theory of knowledge; the third will be treated by viewing their approaches as complementary styles of inquiry that mutually inform and criticize each other.

From Center to Periphery

Despite their respective locations on the center and periphery, Habermas and Freire converged in viewing the failures of their societies of birth as the outcome of interweaving processes: the relationships among authoritarian educational institutions, one-sided strategies of technical modernization guided by the priorities of capital accumulation at the expense of human needs, and resulting failures of democratization culminating in authoritarian, fascist regimes.

For the Frankfurt School, the hierarchical and class-based system of education inherited in Germany by the Weimar Republic was a crucial aspect of the formation of the authoritarian social character that proved a crucial obstacle to working-class mobilization against fascism. These same educational institutions became a target of later de-Nazification policies developed by the allied occupation forces after 1945. Similarly, Freire was convinced early in his career that authoritarian educational traditions provided a crucial obstacle to democratization in Brazil, culminating in a right-wing coup in 1964.

Despite their contrasting metropolitan (Europe) and peripheral (Latin America) locations, Freire and Habermas also shared a concern with the problematic of societal modernization, though in quite different contexts of national development. In a manner analogous to that of the early Habermas's concern with the integration of post-fascist West Germany into the European community, the origins of Freire's thought can be traced to a concern with the "modernization" of Brazil (Paiva, 1982; Torres, 1978a, 1978b). To be sure, important differences derive from the contexts of an advanced as opposed to a relatively underdeveloped society. In the case of Freire the focus was literacy training, whereas for Habermas in West Germany it was the critique of remnants of National Socialist ideology, democratization of the university, and the enhancement of educational access (Habermas, 1969).

Career Trajectories

A comparative analysis of Habermas and Freire cannot avoid a basic question: Can their respective writings be compared as relatively unified wholes, or is it necessary to take into account fundamental theoretical shifts that preclude any general comparison?

Freire had the more discontinuous academic career, having lived in exile and engaged in diverse practical and academic activities. Yet beneath such career change lies conceptual continuity culminating in his most important book, *Pedagogy of the Oppressed* (Freire, 1970c): the notion of dialogue, along with related themes about democracy, liberatory education, domination, critical epistemology, and so forth. Yet there are significant discontinuities in the style of presentation. Whereas the writings of the 1960s took a more conventional academic form, those of the late 1970s and 1980s were more conversational, based on dialogues.

But claims about major shifts in Freire's thinking have been made. One version traces his movement from a "liberal" to a "Marxist" position that emerges in *Pedagogy of the Oppressed* (Elias, 1994, p. 42); another points to a shift from modernist essentialism to a quasi-postmodernist position in his later writings where he moves away from a focus on social class to issues relating to gender and race (Giroux, 1993). Though such shifts of emphasis can be noted, it is problematic to assume that they represented some kind of fundamental break, as opposed to an unfolding and filling out of principles there from the beginning, at least from around 1959 when the concept of "dialogue" became central to his pedagogy. What is at stake here is understanding the unique mode of intellectual creation underlying Freire's career. In his own biographical reflections, Freire sees himself gradually unpacking—in response to new readings and experiences—the theoretical themes always present in his personal life and teaching practices. Though class and politics were neglected in the earlier writings in Brazil, they were very much part of his practical understanding of education. Yet it was only in exile in Chile that he was confronted with the experiences, texts, and time for writing that allowed him to complement his literacy training method with a more complex analysis of societal crisis. Similarly, in acknowledging the lack of attention to the specificities of racial and gender oppression, he cautions against reading *Pedagogy of the Oppressed* ahistorically, as if it were written yesterday, affirming that it is wrong to criticize an author using tools that history had not yet given him (in conversation with Carlos A. Torres, 1986). But his early work did not preclude—indeed it invited—diverse readings. As Afro-American feminist writer bell hooks (1993) notes:

Paulo was one of the thinkers whose words gave me a language. He made me think deeply about the construction of an identity in resistance. There was this one sentence of Freire's that became a revolutionary mantra for me: "We cannot enter the struggle as objects in order to later become subjects". . . . There is no need to apologize for the sexism. Freire's own model of critical pedagogy invites a critical interrogation of this flaw in his work. But critical interrogation is not the same as dismissal. (p. 148)

Another way of understanding this question of consistency is through the form of eclecticism that characterized Freire's intellectual life and the peculiar ways in which "influences" were reflected in his writings.[4] His account of the genesis of *Pedagogy of the Oppressed* captures this creative process:

I remember, for example, how much I was helped by reading Franz Fanon. . . . I was writing *Pedagogy of the Oppressed* . . . when I read Fanon. I had to rewrite the book in order to begin to quote Fanon. . . . I had different cases like this, which I felt conditioned, "influenced," without knowing. Fanon was one. Albert Memmi who wrote a fantastic book, *The Colonizer and the Colonized*, was the second. The third who "influenced" me without knowing it was the famous Russian psychologist Lev Vygotsky . . . when I read him the first time, I became frightened and happy because of the things I was reading. The other influence is Gramsci. . . . When I meet some books, I remake my practice theoretically. I become better able to understand the theory inside of my action. (Horton & Freire, 1990, p. 36)

In contrast, Habermas's thought emerged through a very self-conscious process of dialogue with the Marxist tradition. The central question about continuity in his work stems from his break with the Frankfurt School. For example, it could be argued that the earliest work (late 1950s) of Habermas's critical theory is not fully compatible with Freire's social theory because of its reliance on a dogmatic conception of ideology critique associated with the older Frankfurt School. The convergence with Freire must be located in the 1960s when the theory of communicative action emerged and "he charted a course for himself which, in its spirit and deepest moral commitments, has not changed in any fundamental sense" (White, 1995b, p. 5). As Habermas (1992a) says of himself:

Everyone changes during the cycle of his or her life-history; however, I am, if anything, one of those stubborn types, to whom a rigid bourgeois identity is attributed. For this reason I do not believe that I have changed any more in my fundamental orientations than was necessary to hold true to them in altered historical circumstances. (pp. 183–184)

To summarize, both Freire and Habermas exhibit fundamental continuity in their perspectives once they reach the crystallization point of their respective syntheses at the end of the 1960s. In neither case did this require completely disowning their prior contributions, as opposed to suggesting certain weaknesses that could be overcome by reinterpreting the previous contributions in terms of the more or less finalized perspective that converges in a dialogical theory of knowing.

Divergent Styles

Third, we are confronted with a series of issues related to the contrasting academic styles of the two theorists. Both have been unfairly maligned by critics who fail to appreciate the specific characteristics of their mode of inquiry and writing. Habermas is often characterized as just another "grand theorist" who writes in a forbidding, inaccessible style about topics of no practical consequence. These charges are, however, very misleading. By the standards of French poststructuralist writing, Habermas's work stands as a model of clarity and a desire to communicate, a point most evident in his exemplary dialogical responses to critics. Moreover, Habermas's work has had a practical impact in a number of disciplines and professional fields and he has been a leading public intellectual in his native Germany. As the anthologist of some of these popular essays concludes, "in the last decade or so, Habermas has rather unobtrusively emerged as Germany's most prominent *intellectual*, as well as its most influential social theorist" (Pensky, 1995, p. 67).

In contrast, Freire's work has been charged with a lack of theoretical and methodological rigor. His slim body of nontechnical, overly "applied" theoretical work has been largely ignored outside educational circles. His work is indeed incompletely elaborated, a limitation deriving from his popular mode of presentation and preoccupation with practice. But these writings cannot be separated from the educational and other participatory experiments that have been conducted in the name of Freirean pedagogy, including Freire's own activity as the democratic socialist secretary of education in the city of São Paulo (O'Cadiz et al., 1998). As we will attempt to demonstrate, this body of written work and historical practice combines a theoretical richness and practical relevance—as critical theory in action—that becomes fully evident only through a dialogue with Habermas.

A FRAMEWORK FOR COMPARISON

Sympathetic commentators have dealt with the incompleteness of Freire's work in three basic ways: (1) assimilating it into a form of critical Marxism grounded in a theory of praxis and a general dialectical philosophy (Gadotti, 1996); (2) grounding his critical pedagogy in terms of a theologically based liberation ethics (Dussel, 1997); and (3) interpreting it as a contribution to critical social theory, whether in the form of a "resistance postmodernism" (McLaren, 1994) or his affinities with Habermas's critical theory—our strategy here. Though our systematic strategy is somewhat un-Freirean in spirit given his own colloquial style, it is quite consistent with his concern to justify his work in terms of both its practical *and* its scientific credibility. For us what is most remarkable about Freire is that he had remarkable intuitions about *the kind of social theory* that was necessary to ground his pedagogical vision.

The key to our comparative strategy is to locate Freire's work in the larger context of contemporary critical social theory and to identify the pedagogical implications of Habermas through Freire. The outcome is to read Freire *through Habermas* and Habermas *through Freire*. In short, *it allows us to see more concretely the theoretical depth of Freire, as well as the practical implications of Habermas* in relation to education and issues relating to developing societies. In the process we gain insight into a paradoxical criticism of Habermas: "Either he has erred on the side of science or on the side of passion" (Rasmussen, 1990, p. 7). Whereas Habermas may serve as a "scientific" corrective to Freire, Freire does the same for Habermas's underdeveloped passionate side. In the process Freire facilitates fleshing out the more abstract notion of a theory of communicative action in relation to a theory of dialogue and practical pedagogy. And by locating Freire's contribution as primarily a critical social psychology of educational practice, we avoid falling into the trap of evaluating his work in isolation as a comprehensive theory of society or the human sciences.

Our comparison of the approaches of Freire and Habermas to education and critical social theory is based on the identification of four shared themes: (1) a metatheoretical framework or philosophy of social science that justifies the specific tasks of a critical social science oriented toward emancipatory possibilities; (2) a theory of society as a system of social and cultural reproduction that identifies contradictions that create possibilities for transformation; (3) a critical social psychological understanding of the social subject as constructed in relation to universal developmental possibilities that are thwarted by historical forms of domination but potentially challenged through critique and practice; and (4) a conception of individual and collective learning that is suggestive of strategies for rethinking the relations between education and transformative change. Though each of these themes will be extensively discussed in the chapters that follow, introducing each theme is appropriate at this point.

Metatheory and Critical Social Theory

Both of the projects of a critical theory of society are embedded in a philosophy of social science, or a conception of metatheory, that attempts to mediate between the polarization of subjectivism and positivism (or idealism and materialism) that has long plagued the Marxist tradition, as well as social theory generally (Morrow, 1994a). As we will argue, both authors work within the broader metatheoretical tradition of a *critical hermeneutics* that attempts to ground social inquiry in the understandings of agents (hence its hermeneutic or interpretive dimension), as well as taking into account the social structural contexts of action.

Theory of Society: Social and Cultural Reproduction

Both authors also presuppose a critical theory of society that links education, social domination, and cultural reproduction. This does not presume that cultural reproduction is a static and deterministic process through which a society replicates itself from generation to generation. As we have argued elsewhere, integral theories of cultural reproduction guided by an understanding of historical specificity effectively deal with the dialectic of agency and structure (Morrow & Torres, 1995). Though Freire has made only occasional comments on such issues, they are obviously central to his whole project. Habermas has given much more explicit attention to a theory of society as part of his reconstruction of historical materialism.

Critical Social Psychology: Domination and the Developmental Subject

The third theme of comparison involves a focus on Freire and Habermas's shared theory of the dialogical and developmental subject—what we describe as a critical social psychology. This problematic is anticipated in Marx's theories of alienation and praxis, as well as the Frankfurt School's use of Freud to analyze authoritarian personalities. But Freire and Habermas radicalize these issues by confronting directly the (*social*) *psychological deficits* of classical Marxism. Only with the more recent appropriation of symbolic interactionist and phenomenological microsociology, along with cognitive developmental psychology, have critical theories of society finally incorporated a comprehensive framework for the analysis of agency, development, and resistance in social action. We will use the notion of *theories of a dialogical and developmental subject* to refer to the problematic shared by Freire's critical pedagogy and Habermas's theory of communicative action (Morrow, 1989). Such theories posit developmental models that are suggestive of universal human possibilities whose realization is impeded by relations of social domination.

Praxis as Collective Learning

The fourth shared concern of Freire and Habermas is with a dialogical and reflexive understanding of learning that has profound implications for formal and informal educational activities. The central thesis is that various forms of *critical literacy* are necessary for the development of individual autonomy and collective practice. This notion of reflexive learning not only underlies their respective conception of individual development, but also extends to processes of democratization and their relation to social movements. As a consequence, both conceive the tasks of intellectuals as "interpreters" rather than totalizing "legislators" of knowledge (Bauman, 1987); for both, transformative action can be carried out only by participants who construct their own collective learning process as part of changing their relationship to the social world.

OUTLINE OF THE BOOK AND STRATEGIES OF READING

Three features of our strategy of exposition should be singled out for comment. First, we begin our comparative discussions with a discussion of Freire and conclude with Habermas. We have generally avoided simultaneous comparison (except in our conclusions) to ensure that readers get a good grasp of each author *before* we address comparative issues. We begin with Freire because he is both more immediately accessible and more familiar to our potential readers in education. This strategy also allows a consistent focus on the problematic of critical pedagogy, yet facilitates working up gradually to the broader theoretical problematics of critical social theory as identified by Habermas.

Second, we have attempted to rather meticulously reconstruct their positions in their own terminology with direct quotes, rather than relying primarily on our interpretation of what they mean. The primary reason is that both have suffered from simplistic, selective interpretations—whether by critics or friends. Our task has been to allow them to speak for themselves in the context of a dialogue.

Finally, space constraints have precluded extending discussion to broader issues implicated by, but not developed in, their work. In particular, the anthropocentric focus of their concerns has to be complemented by the ecological context of "transformative learning" (O'Sullivan, 1999).

The four themes introduced above—metatheory, theory of society, theory of the developmental subject, conception of transformative pedagogical practices—provide the framework for the chapters that follow. *Chapter 2* prefaces this discussion with a consideration of the intellectual origins of Freire and Habermas's theory of the subject in German idealism, especially as part of a critique of Hegel's master-slave dialectic and Marx's theory of praxis.

We then proceed in *Chapter 3* with a comparison of the metatheoretical perspectives of Freire and Habermas with respect to ontology, epistemology, and methodology. In this context we can introduce the basic issues of the foundations of the human sciences and consider the way in which they both attempt to reconstruct the subject-object dialectic of social theory.

Chapter 4 considers the theories of history and society that underlie their conceptions of a social theory of knowledge. In the case of Freire the context is defined by the form of colonization associated with poverty and dependency; for Habermas, by the crises of rationalization experienced by the selective modernization of advanced capitalist societies. Despite these overt differences, however, their crisis theories converge on a shared understanding of the irrational consequences of instrumental rationalization without fundamental democratization.

Chapter 5 mediates between the earlier discussions of metatheory and the theory of society. In addressing the question of Freire and Habermas's critical social psychology of a developmental and dialogical subject, we will be developing key themes introduced in Chapters 2 and 3 regarding dialogue and mutual recognition.

Chapter 6 traces the implications of the resulting theory of society and social psychology for pedagogical practice understood in terms of individual and collective learning. This problematic can be understood more concretely with the term "organization for enlightenment." The primary differences here stem from Freire's concern with the immediate dialogic situation of learning, whereas Habermas's typical focus is on democratization as a collective learning process culminating in a more democratic public sphere.

On these foundations, we will then turn to a more evaluative, comparative discussion in *Chapter 7*, which focuses on reviewing complementarities of their work. Following a brief consideration of the foundational character of Habermas's project for Freire, we highlight the overall Freirean contribution to critical theory. In the concluding *Chapter 8* we respond to some of the criticisms of critical theory in education, especially in the context of postmodernist critiques of universalism and critical theory's neglect of postcolonial issues.

2

Modernity and German Idealism

Domination, Mutual Recognition, and Dialogue

I believe that without Hegel and Marx in our toolbox we are doomed to flounder in a world marked by the split between postmodern indifference and premodern passion. Inasmuch as postmodernism pronounces itself to be post-Hegelian and post-Marxian—if not post-Freudian—I think we are called to account for this remarkable shedding of intellectual weight as something akin to cultural anorexia. . . . We cannot afford to trash our Hegelian-Marxist culture because it contains the very engine of cultural renewal that has always been the mark of any great cultural apparatus.

—O'Neill, 1996b, p. 1

The best way to understand is to do. That which we learn most thoroughly, and remember the best, is what we have in a way taught ourselves. . . . In the culture of *reason* we must proceed according to the Socratic method.

—Kant, 1992, pp. 80–81

In the chapters that follow we will focus on the basic structure of the thinking of Freire and Habermas rather than its intellectual origins. In this introductory context, however, we would like to situate their approach to social theory in terms of the discovery of the social subject in the 18th century and its appropriation as part of a theory of the subject in German idealism, culminating in Marx. As we will attempt to show, the convergence of Freire and Habermas's social theory is rooted in their reconstruction of Hegel's master-slave dialectic and Marx's theory of praxis as an intersubjective model of mutual recognition and dialogue. In Habermas's terminology this is characterized as a paradigmatic shift from the monological "philosophy of consciousness" to an intersubjective communicative paradigm.

STRATEGIES OF CRITICAL APPROPRIATION:
RECONSTRUCTING THE DIALOGICAL SUBJECT

The origins of the concept of the social subject—the understanding of the individual person as something constructed by society—coincides with the origins of sociology. More specifically, it can be traced back to Montesquieu in 18th-century France and the appropriation of his work by the Scottish Enlightenment. But these traditions failed to adequately account for the social psychological mediations between the division of labor and the formation of the moral individual. The next major step in understanding the origins of the self can be traced to Jean-Jacques Rousseau (1712–1778). He was the paradoxical voice of a counter-enlightenment precisely because he challenged the facile assumption that the acquisition of the powers of reason and the formation of the self were simple processes reducible to either rationalist autonomy or materialist determinism. Rousseau, of course, was motivated by his anguish with respect to what he perceived to be the failures of education, a process he associated with the alienating and corrupting consequences of existing forms of civil society. The educational philosophy set out in *Emile* sought to isolate the social psychological processes involved in subject formation, whether in alienated or ideal forms, as the basis for creating more "natural" personalities not afflicted by the neuroses of modern "civilization." Though Rousseau could not provide an adequate theory of the mediating processes between the subject and society, he can be credited as the founder of the modern dialectical and critical theory of the subject, setting the stage for the discussions of Kant and Hegel (Geyer, 1997; Kelly, 1969).

As a response to Rousseau, the great achievement of the German tradition was to provide resources for potentially resolving the Enlightenment dilemma of identifying with "reason," but not being able to account adequately for its origins, diversity, and deformations. In the German context, such questions were defined in relation to human autonomy or freedom. Though the concept of "modernity" can be traced back to the Renaissance, as a *philosophical* problem the question of modernity emerged within German idealism as "the problem of 'autonomy,' or of genuine self-determination or self-rule" (Pippin, 1991, p. 3). For our purposes, it is the treatment of such issues in Kant, Hegel, and Marx that sets up the problematic inherited by Freire and Habermas.

KANT: WHAT IS ENLIGHTENMENT?

Kant (1724–1804) is the founder of modern philosophy because of the way in which he reformulated the question of the relationship between human reason and experience (the empirical world). Though it is rarely acknowledged by contemporary critics of Kant's ahistorical universalism, it was Kant's transcendental method that opened the way for a *constructivist* understanding of knowledge. A major difficulty of Kant's "critique" of knowledge, however, was that he tended to analyze epistemology ahistorically, as independent of history. However, beginning with Hegel (1770–1831), post-Kantian philosophy and social theory became concerned with identifying the contextual factors (e.g., history, class, nation, gender, etc.) that mediate the formation of epistemic subjects.

Yet the enduring significance of Kant's initial insight should not be underestimated: However problematic the details of his account of the constructed aspects of human cognition, it provided the point of departure for modern (and postmodern) thought. One of the most problematic ploys of general postmodernist critiques of Enlightenment thought is to conflate Cartesian and Kantian epistemologies as "foundationalist." Kant's epistemological program is much more radical and humble given its focus on the limits and appropriate uses of reason: "The Kantian principle of modernity is not Cartesian certainty, but 'the autonomy of reason'" (Pippin, 1997, p. 162).

As critics have noted from Hegel onward, a fundamental difficulty with Kant's account of autonomy and moral agency is that it is not anchored adequately in an understanding of historical and social contexts of subject formation. Yet Kant is hardly the completely ahistorical philosopher of the universalistic subject of transcendental knowledge as caricatured in postmodernist critiques. From the perspective of his political and historical writings, he acknowledges that the deployment of reason has a history and admits that the degree to which individuals may participate in its optimal use has been historically contingent. Kant's classic formulation of the question of "What is enlightenment" written in 1784 provides an instructive point of departure:

> Enlightenment is man's emergence from his self-imposed immaturity. Immaturity is the inability to use one's understanding without guidance from another. This immaturity is *self-imposed* when its cause lies not in lack of understanding, but in lack of resolve and courage to use it without guidance from another. *Sapere Aude!* "Have courage to use your own understanding!"—that is the motto of enlightenment. (Kant, 1983, p. 41)

Of crucial importance here is that Kant is not legitimating the imperial claims of experts in science or extravagant claims of an absolute Enlightenment "reason"; his primary concern is the condition of possibility of human history as an open-ended "universal" process that is linked to the unfolding of human capacities for autonomy. A limitation of this perspective, however, is the ambiguity of his account of the persistence of "immaturity," which at times he attributes to "laziness" and "cowardice" (Kant, 1784/1983, p. 41). Hence, on closer examination Kant anticipates a broader sociohistorical account of this immaturity of the species. He also identifies the anxiety and fear elicited by the prospect of autonomy—what later became called the "fear of freedom" (Fromm, 1965). Beyond such internal, depth-psychological forms of resistance, he also acknowledges the external context of socialization: "Man can only become man by education. He is merely what education makes of him" (Kant, 1992, p. 6). As a task of "the whole human race," this educational project nevertheless encounters two fundamental difficulties:

> (a) parents only care that their children *make their way* in the world, and (b) Sovereigns look upon their subjects merely as *tools* for their own purposes. . . . Neither have made their aim the universal good and the perfection for which man is destined and for which he has also a natural disposition. But the basis of a scheme of education must be cosmopolitan. (Kant, 1992, p. 15)

To be sure, Kant's suggestive formulations require expansion in several directions, above all a "fourth" critique—that is, *a critique of historical reason* of the type initiated by Hegel and Marx. Only on this basis does it become possible to develop the social sciences and a theory of the *social self* and of *domination* to account for the social psychological and social structural origins of "immaturity." As well, it becomes possible to address the implications of his cryptic acknowledgment that "there are two human inventions which may be considered more difficult than any other—the art of government, and the art of education" (Kant, 1992, p. 12). Despite an inadequately developed account of the historicity of knowledge, his universalistic conception of justice and of human autonomy incorporates initial insights that are the point of departure of all critical pedagogies. But to continue this story we need to turn to Hegel and Marx to trace the further developments of the problematic of emancipatory education.

HEGEL: HISTORICIZING THE SUBJECT

The aspect of Hegel's philosophy that is most important for our comparison is his account of *the origins of self-consciousness in mutual recognition*, a theme central to both Freire (Torres, 1994) and Habermas (1973, pp.

142–169). What is at stake here is how to deal with the *subject-object dialectic* that is a central epistemological theme of post-Kantian philosophy. In other words, in the social production of knowledge, what is the relationship between the knower (subject) and the external world (object)? For French rationalists such as Descartes the foundation of knowledge was the reasoning subject; for British empiricists such as David Hume it was the sense data of the empirical world. Kant took the first step in synthesizing these two perspectives by interpreting them as complementary: Knowledge requires both a priori categories *and* empirical evidence. Hegel took the further step seeing acts of cognition as part of historical relationships originating in self-other interactions.

This question of mutual recognition was addressed in Hegel's *Phenomenology of the Spirit* (Hegel, 1977), but must be read in light of some of Hegel's youthful theological writings and the 1806 Jena Lectures (Hegel, 1971, 1979). Within social philosophy, the primary reference point in discussions of Hegel's theory of mutual recognition has been his analysis of the dialectic of "lord" and "bondsman" in the *Phenomenology*. For Hegel, consciousness is not a quality of isolated individuals, but arises only through mutual recognition: "Self-consciousness exists in and for itself when, and by the fact that, it so exists for another; that is, it exists only in being acknowledged" (Hegel, 1977, p. 111). But self-consciousness also requires struggle, a point conveyed by the metaphor of the death struggle of the lord and the bondsman. In other words, humans come to understand freedom through the courageous acts of resistance required for self-reflection, a process illuminated by the extreme case of risking one's life:

> They must engage in this struggle, for they must raise their certainty of being *for themselves* to truth. . . . And it is only through staking one's life that freedom is won. . . . The individual who has not risked his life may well be recognized as a *person*, but he has not attained to the truth of this recognition as an independent self-consciousness. (Hegel, 1977, p. 114)

But the advantage of the lord in negating the bondsman as a mere unessential thing as the basis for his own sense of truth and certainty is paradoxical. For it is only the servile other who can understand the truth of freedom: "The *truth* of the independent consciousness is accordingly the servile consciousness of the bondsman" (Hegel, 1977, p. 117). The master has an illusory and narcissistic particular power that contrasts with the *universality* of the dependent other who has a more profound understanding of the dynamics of freedom. In short, the master is totally dependent on his subordination of the bondsman, whereas the latter at least has a utopian vision of freedom without exploitation.

Hegel's commentary on the meaning of this so-called master-slave dialectic has been highly contested (O'Neill, 1996a). But what many of these discussions ignore is that there is a second and more fundamental conception of mutual recognition in Hegel found in his early writings, though it was later abandoned. Though "being recognized" is the basic category of Hegel's social ontology, the master-slave dialectic is only part of the story and cannot serve as a self-sufficient basis for a theory of society and the social subject (Rauch, 1987, p. 50).

In contrast, in the earlier, fragmentary 1806 Jena Lectures, mutual recognition is not tied exclusively to struggle, but presupposed in the very fabric of ongoing social interaction. Most important, in this second version,

> the interrelation of selves is not struggle but love . . . in the fact that each part knows itself immediately in the other. . . . Thus, one negates one's being-for-oneself in one's being-for-another—and this is where recognition occurs: in implicit mutuality, not in conflict. (Rauch, 1987, p. 51)

We will see the importance of this second conception of mutual recognition as dialogue later on, especially in contrast to Marx's effort to use the master-slave metaphor as the basis of his social theory.

MARX: PRAXIS AND THE ALIENATED SUBJECT

The power of Karl Marx's (1818–1883) critique of Hegel is that it attempts to more strongly ground a theory of the social subject and mutual recognition in a theory of domination, that is, in the oppressive historical contingencies and structures of economic and social life. From this perspective, the master-slave confrontation is read as a metaphor that can be used to analyze social interaction in any class-divided society based on exploitation. The particular focus of Marx, however, is on capitalist societies where the commodification of labor results in "alienated" labor. According to this model, only the worker as "slave" is in a position to understand true freedom as equality; the resulting revolutionary consciousness then becomes the basis of a new form of society that abolishes class division.

But there are fatal problems with this strategy. How is the working class to become self-conscious and create a revolution? Marx's answer is revolutionary praxis, an activity that implies a *theory of learning*: the processes through which dominated consciousness might be transformed into emancipatory consciousness. But Marx's conception of historical materialism does not explicitly develop a *social psychological* conception of education or learning as transformation beyond metaphorical discussion of "dialectical" reversals.

Marx's writings on education, women, and children amount to just a few dozen pages, though various other texts are of educational interest (Lê, 1991). Nevertheless, these discussions are embedded in a very general premise about the intimate relationship between knowledge and social practice that is sketched in Marx's "Theses on Feuerbach," where it is charged that previous forms of materialism understood human activity as a form "of *contemplation*, but not as *human sensuous activity, practice,* not subjectively" (Marx & Engels, 1978, p. 143). But how can this general premise be translated into understanding the kind of learning that produces the collective consciousness of being "for-itself" presupposed by Marx's theory of revolution? As the contemporary German critical theorist Honneth (1996) charges, this model "represents a highly problematic confluence of elements from Romanticism's expressionist conception of human nature, Feuerbach's concept of love, and British political economy . . . that Marx, for lack of distance was never really able to recognize" (p. 147). The tragic consequence was that the door was left open for Leninists to claim that propaganda and terror might serve as "learning" processes that might facilitate revolutionary praxis.

Marx was more successful in developing a *negative* social psychology, that is, accounting for the factors that inhibit the self-realization of potential autonomy (i.e., the theory of alienation, class domination, and ideology). Though the theory of alienation presupposed an ontology of human nature that provided vague guidelines about universal human potentials (Archibald, 1989; Geras, 1981; Honneth & Joas, 1988), these potentials were speculatively grounded and little attention was given to the learning process required for such transformations of the subject. How does the culturally deprived, alienated worker became an active learner when these very conditions inhibit the formation of reflective consciousness?

To deal with the social psychological deficits of Marx, vulgar Marxism found a motivational explanation based on the utilitarian model of economic gain, but reformist outcomes proved more probable than revolutionary ones. But the ultimate expression of these weaknesses in Marx's conception of the revolutionary subject was its radical revision in an antidemocratic, elitist direction. Leninism resolved the dilemma of the formation of the revolutionary subject by declaring revolutionary intellectuals to be those possessing the objective knowledge necessary for creating "true" class consciousness from the "top down" in a "dictatorship of the proletariat" following a revolutionary seizure of power. Lenin thus solved the problem of how a class becomes "for-itself": "We" (the party) will construct "true" consciousness through a revolutionary education to be engineered by a party elite guided by the "laws of history."

THE PARADIGM SHIFT: FROM THE PHILOSOPHY OF CONSCIOUSNESS TO COMMUNICATIVE ACTION

The social theory of Freire and Habermas is grounded in responding to the dilemmas of Hegel's master-slave dialectic and Marx's theory of praxis. Our thesis is that *the fundamental convergence of the social theories of Freire and Habermas turns on subordinating the master-slave dialectic of struggle within a more encompassing theory of praxis as mutual recognition in communicative dialogue.* For Habermas, Hegel's early position had to be complemented with George Herbert Mead's naturalistic pragmatist reading through which identity formation can be seen to take place in the mutual recognition conveyed through reciprocal interaction. In the case of Freire, Hegel's master-slave dialectic is supplemented by Christian existentialist notions of mutuality and love, as well as dialogical hermeneutics, for similar purposes to reframe the struggle for mutual recognition: "True solidarity is found only in the plenitude of this act of love, in its existentiality, in its praxis" (Freire, 1970c, p. 35). The importance of this shift from mutual recognition as part of a subject-object paradigm of death struggle to mutual recognition as an intersubjective process involving both conflict and reconciliation becomes apparent in Freire and Habermas's respective interpretations of Hegel and Marx.

Interpretations of Freire have struggled to make sense of the complex origins of his thought by pointing to influences such as leftist Catholic thought in Brazil, liberation theology, existentialism, Buber's theory of dialogue, the early Marx and Hegel's master-slave dialectic, French structuralism, and thinkers associated with the earlier Frankfurt School tradition. But the meaning of those selective appropriations becomes fully apparent *only* from the overall perspective of Freire's account of praxis based on the richly textured synthetic vision of the "pedagogy of the oppressed." We would suggest that three key critical appropriations paved the way for his distinctive account of praxis and his convergence with Habermas.

First, Freire's point of departure for his critical social psychology of domination is an "archaeology of consciousness" based on a critical appreciation of Hegel, even if inflected through existentialism, phenomenology, Marx's concept of praxis, and Gramsci's theory of hegemony.[5] Key themes derived from Hegel include the subject-object relationship, the relationship between theoretical and practical consciousness, self-consciousness as a product of mutual recognition, the dynamics of dependency and autonomy in oppressor-oppressed relationships, the role of domination and fear in cultural formation, and so forth. (Torres, 1994, p. 431).[6] This appropriation of Hegel represented the key initial step that brought Freire's thought into the trajectory of the Frankfurt School.

Second, the dialectical hermeneutics of Eduardo Nicol (a philosopher who fled to Mexico after the Spanish Civil War) provided a rigorous (nontheological) basis for reconstructing the subject-object dialectic without lapsing into idealism. Freire had been sensitized to the need for overcoming the overemphasis on work and production in Marx's theory and praxis by the French Catholic Left's concern with *subject-subject dialogue*, a theme that emerged from the confluence of Christian concepts of mutual love, the existentialist preoccupation with everyday life, and the Marxist theory of exploitation. The idealism of this approach—the assumption that social transformation could take place through a Christian reform movement—contradicted Freire's growing radicalization and concern with a scientifically credible critique of society. Moreover, its theological foundations inhibited the construction of a more general hermeneutics that could encompass the natural sciences.

The significance of Nicol for Freire has thus far gone unnoticed, mainly because the accidents of intellectual history have left his remarkable corpus largely unknown (González, 1981). But the significance for Freire (based on a book—*Los principios de la ciencia*—published in Mexico in 1965) was that Nicol developed a secular, dialogical hermeneutics that replaced the subject-object dialectic with a communicative subject-subject account of knowledge—both natural scientific and social. This position converged with the kind of critical hermeneutics developed by Habermas in response to the German philosopher Hans-Georg Gadamer. Though the concept of dialogue (indebted to Buber and Jaspers in particular) was already central to Freire's thinking about the educational situation, Nicol gave this theme a broader grounding as a way of understanding historical change and as the basic of an ontology and epistemology of social life.

The third strategic influence was the publication in Spanish in 1967 of Czech philosopher Karel Kosík's *Dialectics of the Concrete* (1976), which influenced the construction of *Pedagogy of the Oppressed*. Though Freire had already worked out the basic principles of his own conception, his numerous references to this book suggest that it elaborated at a more rigorously philosophical level the interpretation of Marx he found most congenial. Though the experience of exile in Chile pushed him toward a more Marxist position, it could also be argued that through Kosík he found a version of Marx's theory of praxis that was compatible with his previous intuitions regarding a critical pedagogy, above all his focus on everyday life. But this conception of praxis was implicitly read through the lens of the subject-subject dialectic of Nicol's dialectical hermeneutics.

Similarly, Habermas made a parallel but more explicit critique of Hegel and Marx by suggesting that their social theory presupposes a monological "philosophy of consciousness" that culminates in a problematic "production paradigm." The philosophy of consciousness refers to the tendency beginning with Descartes and Kant of conceptualizing the individual epistemological "subject" as confronting the external "object." This cognitive relation is *monological* in the sense that it begins with an isolated ego that initiates the process of knowing, as opposed to a subject that has already been constituted within a world of interaction.

Though the philosophy of consciousness virtually defines modern Western philosophy, Habermas's most important target is its influence on Marx's theory of praxis, which is also grounded in a philosophy of consciousness. Hence Marx's theory of action takes the form of a "production paradigm" that views praxis as a form of productive activity (work) understood in terms of a subject-object relation. This philosophy of consciousness is rooted in a standard version of Hegel's analysis in the phenomenology of the subject (Habermas, 1987a, pp. 75–82). According to Habermas, the model of praxis as production tends to equate action with work (instrumental action), thus downplaying the linguistic and communicative aspects of social life.

Habermas thus differentiates between two contending paradigmatic frameworks for social theory: the individualistic *philosophy of consciousness* that has dominated post-Kantian philosophy (including Hegel and Marx's theory of praxis) and the intersubjective *theory of communicative action* that he reconstructed from the early Hegel, Gadamer's dialogical hermeneutics, George Herbert Mead's pragmatic interactionism, and Wittgenstein's theory of language games. He also links this paradigm shift to the notion of a "linguistic turn" that rejects any strong "foundation" of knowledge outside of language. As part of his critique of Marx, Habermas proposes a reinterpretation of Hegel's early Jena writings, arguing that Hegel there schematically developed a superior interactionist and communicative model of mutual recognition that he had abandoned by the time of *Phenomenology of the Spirit*. As we shall see, though Freire retains the language of praxis theory, he interprets it in a manner that also moves in the direction of an intersubjective account of the type proposed by Habermas. When the full consequences of this subtle revision of Hegel and Marx by Freire is recognized, then the details of our thesis on the complementarity of Freire and Habermas fall quickly into place.

Though Habermas's rejection of the "production paradigm" appears completely at odds with Freire's continuing reliance on praxis philosophy, there are two grounds for suggesting that the differences are not all that fundamental. On the one hand, it can be argued that Habermas casts his criticism rather too widely, ignoring forms of praxis philosophy that do not essentialize the concept of production. On the other hand, there are good reasons for concluding that Freire's concept of praxis has largely escaped the problems of a conception of praxis based on labor and a monological philosophy of consciousness. If this is the case, the primary tension between Freire and Habermas is that Freire still works within the paradigm of praxis as a *rhetorical* device. As a consequence, we will argue, even though he uses the praxis model of reappropriating essential powers, this process is defined in *dialogical* rather than individualistic terms, and is not coupled with an ontology of labor as the basis of the self-realization of the species. As a consequence, Freire's account of praxis is inconsistent with classic Marxian formulations. First, the point of departure of Freire's ontology is a subject-subject relation, not a subject-object relation built around individuals' reappropriating their essential powers. Second, primacy is given neither to conflict nor to instrumental action in this model of praxis. Tellingly, Freire gives priority to communicative relations and "love" rather than conflict in pedagogical and social relations, as in Hegel's early account of mutual recognition:

> If what characterizes the oppressed is their subordination to the conscious-ness of the master, as Hegel affirms, true solidarity with the oppressed means fighting at their side to transform the objective reality which has made them these "beings for another." The oppressor is solidary with the oppressed only when he stops regarding the oppressed as an abstract cate-gory and sees them as persons who have been unjustly dealt with, de-prived of their voice, cheated in the sale of their labor—when he stops making pious, sentimental, and individualistic gestures and risks an act of love. True solidarity is found only in the plenitude of this act of love, in its existentiality, in its praxis. (Freire, 1970c, pp. 34–35)

Though many intellectual influences could be cited for this position (including liberation theology), it should be stressed that it ultimately presupposes the two models of self-recognition in Hegel: a death struggle between individuals locked in a subject-object opposition, and a more fundamental account of intersubjective processes of communication and potential reconciliation. Though Freire does not develop a systematic theoretical rationale for his general position, we should not ultimately judge it in terms of its philosophical rigor. Instead, there is an "empirical" reference point for Freire's experientially grounded stance that requires taking him at his word:

> Thought and study alone did not produce *Pedagogy of the Oppressed*; it is rooted in concrete situations and describes the reactions of laborers (peasant or urban) and of middle-class persons whom I have observed directly or indirectly in the course of my educative work. (Freire, 1970c, p. 21)

On the other hand, Habermas's position is rigorously developed directly from his critique of Marx's reliance on the category of labor as production as the ontological foundation of social theory. Yet it would be erroneous to assume that Habermas's insights here merely reflect abstract thinking: They are also grounded in his own experience in the student movement and the crisis of the Marxist tradition. As Habermas argues with reference to the concept of mutual recognition in Hegel's early writings, emancipatory practice must be conceived of in communicative terms, a form of practice in which moral relations and love—not antagonism—are the ultimate grounds of constructive transformations of identity:

> Unlike synthesis through social labor, the dialectic of class antagonism is a movement of reflection. . . . This can be seen in the dialectic of the moral relation developed by Hegel under the name of the *struggle for recognition*. Here the suppression and renewal of the dialogue situation are constructed as a moral relation. The grammatical relations of communication, once distorted by force, exert force themselves. Only the result of dialectical movement eradicates this force and brings about the freedom from constraint contained in dialogic self-recognition-in-the-other: in the language of the young Hegel, love as reconciliation. (Habermas, 1971, pp. 58–59)

With Habermas's critique in mind, it becomes possible to reframe Freire's theory of praxis in terms of a "theory of communicative action." In the process, it will be argued that whereas Habermas's communicative paradigm has the advantage of formulating a postfoundationalist yet universalistic framework for a theory of society and the justification of the possibility of a "moral point of view," Freire's complementary humanistic strategy retains value in the context of concrete, local struggles and social movements where agents must articulate particular utopian visions from within their own unique life-histories.

For Freire and Habermas, therefore, the key to reconstructing the theory of praxis is found in the *dialogical learning processes* that might mediate between the realities of human need and the capacity to reflect and act in liberating ways. Paradoxically, emancipation does not proceed automatically from the extension of technical rationality, nor from the mere satisfaction of basic needs. The failure of classical Marxism rests in part on its tendency to associate liberation with the technical rationality involved in the expansion of productive forces, hence without sufficient clarification of the nature of the substantial moral "rationality" required for the realization of the autonomous, human subject. As Habermas concludes his assessment of Hegel and Marx in this context:

> *Liberation from hunger and misery* does not necessarily converge with *liberation from servitude and degradation,* for there is no automatic developmental relation between the two dimensions. Neither the Jena *Realphilosophie* nor *The German Ideology* has clarified it adequately, but in any case they can persuade us of its relevance: the self-formative process of spirit as well as of our species essentially depends on that relation between labor and interaction. (Habermas, 1973, p. 169)

As has been cogently suggested of Habermas—though we would include Freire here as well—he "places learning processes at the center of his critical project. This signifies a major shift within Western critical theory—shall we call this the 'learning turn' and think of this development as a revolution in social theory?" (Welton, 1995a, pp. 25–26) In short, though Freire and Habermas draw inspiration from aspects of the German idealist and Marxian traditions, *the result is a distinctive, post-Marxist dialogical theory of the social subject that grounds a reformulation of a critical theory of society.* The next chapter will consider in more detail the metatheoretical shift from a philosophy of consciousness to an intersubjective communicative paradigm that follows from this reconstruction of the subject-object dialectic.

3

Metatheoretical Foundations

Reconstructing the Subject-Object Dialectic

Communication between Subjects about the object is established by
means of intersubjectivity.

—Freire, 1973, p. 136

The vindicating superiority of those who do the enlightening over those
who are to be enlightened is theoretically unavoidable, but at the same
time it is fictive and requires self-correction: *in a process of enlightenment there can only be participants.*

—Habermas, 1973, p. 40; emphasis added

Both Freire and Habermas approach the issues of theory and practice
from a systematic, philosophically grounded position, that is, a *metatheory*
or philosophy of the social sciences. A metatheory is distinctive in that
it is in effect a "theory about theory," hence theorizing about the grounds
for justifying approaches to knowledge and inquiry. For example, positivism is the metatheory that argues that the social sciences should emulate
the natural sciences. In contrast, the metatheory of phenomenology suggests that social relations are unique and should not be analyzed in terms
of causality. Against both of the strategies, Freire and Habermas presuppose a radically reconstructed historical materialism—based on a critical
hermeneutics—to mediate the opposition between positivism and phenomenology. This chapter will approach these issues by considering their
respective positions with respect to some of the basic questions of metatheory: ontology, epistemology, and methodology of social inquiry.

PARADIGMS OF METATHEORY

Though Freire and Habermas are antipositivist in the sense that they
reject the traditional model of the natural sciences for the human sciences,

they do not abandon a concern with scientific adequacy. In this respect they differ fundamentally from those postmodernists who declare that understanding the constructed nature of all knowledge undermines all claims that aspire to be "scientific." They share the metatheoretical perspective of a distinctive form of *critical social science*. On the one hand, they break with the positivism and determinism that characterize classical Marxist theory. On the other hand, they also reject dogmatically grounding the moral perspective of their critical theory. The distinctive features of their approach can most readily be conveyed through a comparison with related paradigms of inquiry.

Metatheoretical concepts facilitate the analysis of strategies of inquiry as "paradigms" or "research programs" (Guba, 1990; Morrow, 1994a). From this perspective inquiry is not constituted by "theory" as some kind of homogenous type of concept formation that can be reconstructed in terms of a single (scientific) logic. Rather, social inquiry is best understood in terms of three basic types of theorizing: *metatheory, empirical theory, and normative theory*. Whereas metatheory involves theorizing about the presuppositions of constructing knowledge (and is best known as methodology), empirical theory is concerned with claims about explaining social relations and interpreting the meanings of social actions. In contrast, normative theory is concerned with justifying claims about values, about how social reality should or ought to be organized. The primary focus in this chapter will be on metatheory: assumptions about the nature of and justifiable ways of constructing knowledge about social reality.

To further develop an analysis of their respective metatheoretical positions, it is necessary to introduce some more distinctions with respect to types of metatheory, especially ontology, epistemology, and methodology. For example, it is useful to differentiate paradigms of inquiry in terms of their respective response to three metatheoretical questions:

1. *Ontological*: What is the nature of the "knowable"? Or, what is the nature of "reality"?
2. *Epistemological*: What is the nature of the relationship between the knower (the inquirer) and the known (or knowable)?
3. *Methodological*: How should the inquirer go about finding out knowledge? (Guba, 1990, p. 18)

On the basis of these criteria, it is possible to differentiate four basic paradigms of inquiry that have been influential in educational research: positivist, postpositivist, critical theory, and constructivist. "Critical theory and related ideological positions" are characterized at the level of ontology as "historical realist"; with respect to epistemology as "transactional and subjectivist"; and as methodology as "dialogic and dialectical"

(Guba & Lincoln, 1994, p. 110). We will see the full implications of these characteristics in the course of this chapter.

What we do need to consider at this point, however, is the relation of Freire and Habermas to the varieties of critical theory and related approaches. Their overtly "political" character contributes to describing critical theory approaches as a form of activist-driven ideological critique: "A more appropriate label would be 'ideologically oriented inquiry,' including neo-Marxism, materialism, feminism, Freireism, participatory inquiry, and other similar movements as well as critical theory itself" (Guba, 1990, p. 23).

The trouble with this conflation of positions as a "critical theory" paradigm is that the shared identity is *negative*, primarily that of sharing an opposition to "value-free" social science, *as if* there were some kind of consensus with respect to the alternative. As we will argue, *the positions of Freire and Habermas resist simplistic reduction to "ideologically oriented inquiry" based on a fixed or specific standpoint* such as class or gender. Nor do they reduce the methodology of critical theory to forms of investigation where researchers are "interactively linked" with their subject or claim that there must always be a transformative outcome of research. Though it is acknowledged that all research has political dimensions, it is not reduced to mere "politics." To be sure, these remain *regulative ideals* for critical knowledge, but do not exclude other forms of postempiricist inquiry. Much important research is necessarily highly objectivistic (e.g., demography, political economy) and only in the special case of participatory action research is there an immediate potential relation between investigation and social transformation.

As we argue, the distinctive form of critical theory in question here ultimately presupposes a *critical realist ontology* that rejects essentialism; *a constructivist and pragmatist conception of epistemology* that is antipositivist but not antiscientific or purely subjectivist; and a *pluralist conception of methodology* within which participatory dialogue provides a regulative ideal, but is not an exclusive model of social inquiry. The meaning of these characterizations and necessary qualifications will be elucidated in the course of this chapter and reiterated in the concluding comparative section.

ONTOLOGY: WORK AND LANGUAGE

Introduction: Critical Realism

In characterizing the ontological positions of Freire and Habermas as a form of *critical realism*, we wish to emphasize that they reject naive realism and the essentializing assumption that reality can be directly understood "in itself" (e.g., as in a reflection or correspondence theory of truth). In this respect their position is "postmetaphysical" and "postfoundationalist" in spirit. But they also reject the postmodernist tendency to stress the arbitrariness of all ontological starting points.

In discussing the ontological perspectives of Freire and Habermas, we will be focusing on their understanding of the subject-object relation as the foundation for the human sciences. Three interpretive themes will organize our discussion: (1) that both theorists begin with an ontology of praxis, reconstructing it in the direction of a theory of communication; (2) that both see that communicative activities are challenged by their opposite, that is, relations of domination that distort and inhibit communication; and (3) that both argue that dialogue presupposes certain possibilities of communication that open the way for processes of emancipatory individual development.

Freire: The Subject-Object Paradigm and Dialogue

Praxis: Action-Reflection. The point of departure of Freire's pedagogy is an ontology of praxis as a distinctive human quality. Whereas animals are "submerged in reality" and hence "creatures of mere *contacts*," humans are defined by a "separateness from and openness to the world" that distinguishes them as beings of "relationships," hence "not only *in* the world but *with* the world" (Freire, 1973, p. 3). Furthermore, animals relate to the world by means of "adaptation" instead of "humanizing it by transforming it. For animals there is no historical sense, no options or values," no "project" or "vocation" (Freire, 1970a, p. 6). Without projects, human action "is not praxis. . . . And not being of praxis, it is action ignorant both of its own process and its own aim" (Freire, 1970a, p. 6). Such action may be "adaptive" or "adjusted" in the biological sense, but such a person is a mere "object," not a "subject" capable of making choices and transforming reality (Freire, 1973, p. 4).

Freire's social ontology overtly operates within the framework of a humanist and existentialist Marxian framework based on the subject-object distinction. As a consequence, Freire's humanism potentially runs the risk of an essentialist conception of the subject (he does refer to "man") and a theory of praxis that suffers from the limitations of an individualistic philosophy of consciousness and the model of praxis as "work." As we argue, however, Freire's actual use of the praxis model moves in a communicative direction that avoids most of the problems associated with essentialist forms of humanism (and related gender bias); hence, it is not based on a deterministic, teleological model of a human essence to be realized, as opposed to diverse possibilities to be created within the limits of "humanization." This interpretation can be sustained by considering his characterization of the subject-object paradigm.

Freire's revision of the subject-object paradigm is most simply and explicitly stated in his critique of traditional efforts by agronomists in rural extension work to "persuade" peasants to adopt new techniques. In effect, the ontological basis of his formulation is a distinction between three types of relations: *a subject-object relation, a subject-subject relation,* and *a subject-subject relation with an external object.* A subject-object relation in social inquiry takes the form of a deterministic, control-oriented behavioral social science (or the Marxist equivalent). In his example, there is the oppressive Subject-Object relation between technocratic rural-development educators who treat the peasant as "objects" to be manipulated strategically through propaganda:

> To persuade implies, fundamentally, a Subject who persuades, in some form or other, and an object on which the act of persuading is exercised. In this case the Subject is the extension agent—the object the peasants. They are the objects of a persuasion which will render them all the more susceptible to propaganda. Neither peasants nor any one else can be persuaded or forced to submit to the propaganda myth, if they have the alternative option of liberation. . . . In their role as educators, they must refuse to "domesticate" people. Their task is *communication,* not *extension.* (Freire, 1973, p. 97)

What is implied by this ideal relation of communication is subject-subject relation between educators and peasants that allows them to mediate together in relation to nature as an object, a third term. What he calls the "gnosiological relationship" or act of knowing is grounded in a subject-subject relation that opens the way to the object:

> Intersubjectivity, or intercommunication, is the primordial characteristic of this cultural and historical world. The gnosiological function cannot be reduced to a simple relationship between a Subject that knows and a knowable object. Without relations of communication between Subjects that know, with reference to a knowable object, the act of knowing would disappear. The gnosiological relationship does not therefore find its terms in the object known. Communication between Subjects about the object is established by means of intersubjectivity. (Freire, 1973, p. 136)

Given this communicative focus, Freire also refrains from reducing the peasant subject to the categories of "labor" or "production" in the classic Marxist sense. Though work is a dimension of praxis, it is subordinated to "action-reflection" as a communicative process of naming. As he puts it in *Pedagogy of the Oppressed*:

> To exist, humanly, is to *name* the world, to change it. Once named, the world in its turn reappears to the *namers* as a problem and requires of them a new *naming*. Men are not built in silence, but in word, in work, in action-reflection. (Freire, 1970c, p. 76)[7]

Moreover, this action-reflection is intersubjective and dialogical, hence Freire's critique of the monological subject:

> The thinking Subject cannot think alone. In the act of thinking about the object s/he cannot think without the co-participation of another Subject. There is no longer an "I think" but "we think." *It is the "we think" which establishes the "I think" and not the contrary.* This co-participation of the Subjects in the act of thinking is communication. Thus the object is not the end of the act of communicating, but the mediator of communication. (Freire, 1973, p. 137; emphasis added)

Though Freire works with the vocabulary of a labor-based praxis philosophy, he subordinates the instrumental aspect of labor to its symbolic grounds, hence his ontology is not based on a conception of "homo faber." Citing Pierre Teilhard de Chardin, he refers to humans as "reflective animals" (Freire, 1970a, p. 29, n. 4). Marx's *Capital* is cited as defining humans as "beings who pro-ject": "But what distinguishes the worst architect from the best of the bees is that, that the architect raises his structure in the imagination before he erects it in reality" (Marx, cited in Freire, 1970a, p. 30).

For this reason as well, he cites Gramsci in criticizing the distinction between "manual" and "intellectual" work: "All work engages the whole man as an indivisible unity. A factory hand's work can no more be divided into manual or intellectual than our in writing this essay" (Freire, 1970a, p. 32). As Freire concludes:

> Action without this dimension is not work. . . . Action is work not because of the greater or lesser physical effort expended in it by the acting organism, but because of the consciousness the subject has of his own effort, his possibility of programming action, of creating tools and using them to mediate between himself and the object of his action, of having purposes, of anticipating results. (Freire, 1970a, p. 31)

As a consequence, he argues that the dialogical is an ontological feature of social life, a necessary condition of its historicity:

> We should understand liberating dialogue not as a technique, a *mere* technique, which we can use to help us get some results. . . . On the contrary, dialogue must be understood as something taking part in the very historical nature of human beings. It is part of our historical progress in becoming human beings. That is, dialogue is a kind of necessary posture to the extent that humans have become more and more critically communicative beings. (Shor & Freire, 1987, p. 98)

Freire's developmental ontology follows European structuralism in placing language at the origins of human experience. The theory of dialogical action clearly illustrates the distance of Freire from more traditional accounts in praxis philosophy given his stress on understanding the pragmatic origins of language as the basis for creative social action. Hence, language should not be viewed simply as an instrument, but should be analyzed with respect to how the ontological properties of the "word" reveal the origins of truth:

> As we attempt to analyze dialogue as a human phenomenon, we discover something which is the essence of dialogue itself: *the word*. But the word is more than just an instrument that makes dialogue possible; accordingly, we must seek its constitutive elements. Within the word we find two dimensions, reflection and action, in such radical interaction that if one is sacrificed—even in part—the other immediately suffers. There is no true word that is not at the same time a praxis. Thus, to speak a true word is to transform the world. (Freire, 1970c, p. 75)

Dialogue is thus grounded in several fundamental forms of relationship that are ontologically the conditions of possibility of human society:

> Founding itself upon love, humanity, and faith, dialogue becomes a horizontal relationship of which mutual trust between the dialoguers is the logical consequence. It would be a contradiction in terms if dialogue—loving, humble, and full of faith—did not produce this climate of mutual trust, which leads the dialoguers into ever closer partnership in the naming of the world. . . . Nor yet can dialogue exist without hope. (Freire, 1970c, pp. 79–80)

In short, dialogue presumes a matrix of interaction grounded in relations of "empathy" that are "loving, humble, hopeful, trusting, critical" (Freire, 1973, p. 45). Further, there must be linguistic media of communication through which these relationships can be made comprehensible: "There can be no communication, if the comprehension of the meaning (signification) of the sign is not established among the Subjects-in-dialogue" (Freire, 1973, p. 141).

Anti-dialogical Action and Domination. The theme of the word in dialogue is elaborated in somewhat different ways by contrasting dialogue with its opposite, or what Freire refers to more concretely as *dialogical* versus *antidialogical actions.* The antidialogical matrix of interaction breaks the relation of empathy because it is based on vertical (hierarchical) relations that are "loveless, arrogant, hopeless, mistrustful, acritical. . . . Thus, anti-dialogue does not communicate, but rather issues communiqués" (Freire, 1973, p. 46). As a consequence, antidialogical action constitutes the linguistic mediation of the reproduction of relations of domination, hence of dehumanization. Dehumanization is identified with the possibilities of "alienation" and "marginality." Since the marginal do not choose their condition, "marginal man has been expelled from and kept outside of the social system and is therefore the object of violence" (Freire, 1970a, p. 10). But in reality the marginalized are very much integral to a social structure of domination, and "in a dependent relationship to those whom we call falsely autonomous beings, inauthentic beings-for-themselves. . . . There is no other road to humanization—theirs as well as everyone else's—but authentic transformation of the dehumanizing structure" (Freire, 1970a, p. 11).

The Ontological Structure of Humanization. Finally, the transformative potential of words is linked to postulating hope as an "ontological need" and a necessary condition of struggle. On the one hand, hope is related to how struggle not merely expresses the interests of this or that group, but is implicated in a "truth" that justifies the ethical claims of participants. On the other hand, describing hope as a need does not mean that it is always available to the consciousness of participants. Educational practices must seek to elicit hope: "To attempt to do without hope . . . is tantamount to denying that struggle one of its mainstays. . . . Hope, as an ontological need, demands an anchoring in practice" (Freire, 1994, p. 9).

Though Freire's use of the term *hope* has theological origins, he refrains from anchoring it in an essentialist or teleological metaphysics. He very consistently avoids referring to this vocation as a "destiny," especially one that can be grounded in the teleology of realizing "God's" purposes for the human species. Freire's emphasis is twofold. First, he always stresses the open-ended character of the process of humanization. The means of expressing this are the paired terms *humanization-dehumanization,* where humanization is identified as "incompletion": "Within history, in concrete, objective contexts, both humanization and dehumanization are possibilities for man as an uncompleted being conscious of his incompletion" and "only the first is man's vocation" (Freire, 1970c, pp. 27–28). Moreover, "in this incompletion and this awareness lie the very roots of education as an exclusively human manifestation" (Freire, 1970c, p. 72). Second, this process of humanization is known not primarily by some necessary and fixed endpoint, but more importantly from its opposite, dehumanization, defined as the denial of "freedom." For the oppressed this condition is expressed negatively as the "fear of freedom": "Freedom would require them to reject this image and replace it with autonomy and responsibility. Freedom is acquired by conquest, not by gift. . . . Freedom is not an ideal located outside of man. . . . It is rather the indispensable condition for the quest for human completion" (Freire, 1970c, p. 31). Nor can humanization be realized individualistically or at the expense of others: It "cannot be carried out in isolation or individualism, but only in fellowship and solidarity; therefore it cannot unfold in the antagonistic relations between oppressors and oppressed" (Freire, 1970c, p. 73). In short, Freire proposes a nonteleological model of contingent humanization:

> In a dialectic, nonmechanistic conception of history, the future evolves from the transformation of the present as it occurs. Thus, the future takes on a problematic and underdetermined character. The future is not what it needs to be, but whatever we make of it in the present. (Freire, 1996, p. 111).

Despite his existentialist vocabulary, Freire aspires to legitimate his historicized humanism in "scientific" terms, even if the "scientific" basis for this contention is not clearly established (though Habermas will take up this challenge). Such a humanism is "concrete" and "rigorously scientific," hence it does not project an "ideal human being, separated from the world" or "a timeless model" (Freire, 1973, p. 44).

In short, Freire's ontological approach (1) suggests a theory of praxis that stresses the reflective and dialogical dimensions of action; (2) points to the origins of domination in dehumanizing antidialogical action; and (3) postulates that the incompletion of human nature creates the basis for species-specific possibilities of humanization to be contingently realized.

Habermas: Critique of the Production Paradigm

Reconstructing Praxis: Work Versus Interaction. Habermas is much more self-conscious than Freire of the radical implications of his reconstruction of the Marxian ontology of praxis, which is charged with implying a reductionist ontology of labor. In essentializing work as productive activity—as a form of instrumental or technical action—Marx leaves himself open to subsequent economistic interpretations. Instead, Habermas argues for the necessity of a categorical distinction between labor and symbolic interaction to ground the concept of praxis. As he concludes, "Marx does not actually explicate the interrelation of interaction and labor, but instead, under the unspecific title of social praxis, reduces the one to the other, namely: communicative action to instrumental action" (Habermas, 1973, pp. 168–169). As a consequence, Marx's "brilliant insight into the dialectical relationship between the forces of production and the relations of production could very quickly be misinterpreted in a mechanistic manner" (p. 169). Habermas characterizes the consequence as a reflection of Marx's "latent positivism," which reduces reflection to instrumental action. Relying on an ontology of labor, "*Marx conceives of reflection according to the model of production*" (Habermas, 1971, p. 44). This production paradigm is based on a monological "philosophy of consciousness" that does not fully grasp the intersubjective and linguistic foundations of practice.

As an alternative, Habermas develops a categorical distinction between "work" and "interaction" as the ontological basis for an epistemology in which "knowledge-constitutive interests take form in the medium of work, language and power" (Habermas, 1971, p. 313). Though he would today perhaps shy away from the transcendentalist language of the a priori, this early formulation of the relationship between language and freedom captures one of the most fundamental intuitions of Habermas's social theory:

> The human interest in autonomy and responsibility is not mere fancy, for it can be apprehended *a priori*. What raises us out of nature is the only thing whose nature we can know: *language*. Through its structure, autonomy and responsibility are posited for us. Our first sentence expresses unequivocally the intention of the universal and unconstrained consensus. (Habermas, 1971, p. 314)

This view of language as implicitly presupposing moral imperatives is elaborated under the heading of the later *theory of communicative action*. Drawing on linguistic and speech act theory, Habermas argues for a "universal pragmatics," that is, that all human communication reveals fundamental structural properties that transcend cultural and historical differences.[8]

Strategic Action and Domination. For Habermas there is a key onto-logical distinction between two polarized forms of human action: *strategic action* oriented toward control and success (as in technology or administration) and *communicative action* oriented toward consensus and mutual understanding. Though communicative action serves as a condition of possibility of social life and its democratization, it is continuously threatened by its opposite: strategic action that takes on a life of its own, suppressing communicative action. The origins of domination can be traced to the concealed forms of strategic action communication that emerge in the context of either manipulative, strategic actions that curtail dialogue or *systematically distorted communication* that undermines it altogether (Habermas, 1984, pp. 332–333). The communicative logic of strategic action can be understood in terms of critiques of technology and bureaucracy, whereas distorted communication can be understood in terms of analogies drawn from pathological communication in the psychiatric literature (Habermas, 1970b).

Validity Claims and Developmental Competence. In the context of elucidating the concept of communicative action, Habermas introduces the notion of implicit *validity claims* as the ontological foundation for a discourse theory of truth. The key premise is that the act of dialogical communication is embedded in a shared desire for mutual understanding and recognition that is the foundation of all truth claims, whether empirical or normative:

> The goal of coming to an understanding (*Verständigung*) is to bring about an agreement (*Einverständnis*) that culminates in the intersubjective mutuality of reciprocal understanding, shared knowledge, mutual trust, and accord with one another. Agreement is based on recognition of the corresponding validity claims of comprehensibility, truth, truthfulness, and rightness." (Habermas, 1979, p. 3)

Paraphrasing Habermas, these four validity claims can be described in more detail as follows (Habermas, 1979, pp. 2–3):

1. *Comprehensibility*: That communication is possible because we use grammatically equivalent forms and mutually understandable modes of representation.
2. *Truth*: That we use empirical propositions about the world that we believe to be factually valid.

3. *Sincerity* (Truthfulness): That we share intentions that give us the mutual trust necessary for openness and self-disclosure.
4. *Rightness*: That we evaluate social worlds in terms of mutually recognized normative principles (i.e., practical reason).

Beyond these fundamental validity claims, Habermas also argues that individuals are born incomplete but have innate potential for the development of competence in various domains, that is, cognitive, moral, ego, and interactional. He does not ground these claims in the traditional ontological terms of a philosophical anthropology; rather, he suggests that they can be made plausible, as in the case of the universal pragmatics for the four validity claims, by reference to "reconstructive sciences" that reveal the deep structures of social action. Whereas the claims of a universalistic pragmatics are grounded in the reconstructive science of linguistics, those of competence development are linked to developmental psychology (Habermas, 1983). We will turn to the specifics of this argument in Chapter 5, which takes up the social psychological themes of his conception of the developmental subject.

To summarize, Habermas's ontological perspective is based on the following arguments: (1) that against Marx's theory of praxis, work and symbolic interaction must be sharply differentiated; (2) that a communicative paradigm based on the universal pragmatic structure of language makes possible a categorical distinction between communicative and strategic action; and (3) that the validity claims implicit in communicative action, as well as human potentials for development, can be made plausible through recourse to the findings of the reconstructive sciences.

The basic ontological positions of Freire and Habermas are compared in Table 3.1.

TABLE 3.1. ONTOLOGY: FREIRE AND HABERMAS

ONTOLOGY	FREIRE	HABERMAS
Nature of praxis	Action-reflection	Symbolic interaction
Origins of domination	Antidialogical action	Strategic action
Structures of possibility	Humanization as an ontological vocation	Validity claims and developmental competencies

EPISTEMOLOGY: KNOWLEDGE AND PRACTICE

Introduction: Beyond Subjectivism and Objectivism

Epistemological disputes in the social sciences have been typically characterized by the polarization between "positivist" and "antipositivist" perspectives. Positivism in the 19th century emerged as a position that stressed the *unity* of the logic of science; consequently, there was no basis for a methodological differentiation between the natural and the social sciences. Classic positivists defended the natural scientific model of causality and invariant laws as the logical basis of all inquiry, whereas antipositivists held that the role of meaning and consciousness in social life required a fundamentally different model of inquiry based on interpretative methods. The outcome was two contrasting models: the nomothetic or generalizing explanations of the natural sciences (*Naturwissenschaften*) and the ideographic or individualizing, descriptive accounts of the human sciences based the methods of classical hermeneutics (*Geisteswissenschaften*). Freire and Habermas work within a tradition that rejects this epistemological polarization as inadequate to grasp the nature of the human sciences: "The opposition between the universal and the unique, between nomothetic analysis and ideographic description, is a false antinomy" (Bourdieu & Wacquant, 1992, p. 75). They seek to preserve a distinctive status for the human sciences, but without rejecting the importance of causal relations in the genesis of social structures. We will discuss this alternative in terms of a "critical hermeneutics" that seeks to transcend the polarization between interpretive and explanatory approaches.

This epistemological rejection of both positivist naturalism and classical hermeneutics is based on the ontological assumptions just reviewed. In challenging the latent dualism evident in the classic subject-object paradigm, Freire and Habermas stress the priority of knowledge as a communicative process in which there are no absolutely privileged knowers, and where knowledge claims are ultimately grounded in the competition—the dialogue—of perspectives.

The metatheoretical framework for their shared approaches to the human sciences can be described as a form of *critical hermeneutics*. The term *hermeneutics* refers to the tradition of textual interpretation that originated in methodological questions regarding the Bible, a problematic that also becomes central for the study of cultural documents. Critical hermeneutics is differentiated by its orientation toward a "hermeneutics of suspicion" or what in social theory has often been called the ideology critique of cultural criticism (Ricoeur, 1974). Though this characterization has only more recently been applied to Freire (Gallagher, 1992; Peters &

Lankshear, 1994), it has long been recognized as a distinctive aspect of Habermas's methodology (Thompson, 1981).

A distinctive feature of a critical hermeneutic perspective is that it rejects complete reliance on agents' self-reports or native interpretations of texts in terms of a given tradition. A critical hermeneutic perspective argues that social agents and the documents of a culture must be confronted with cognitions and experiences that allow a form of "distanciation" from everyday reality based on explanatory accounts that elucidate the constraining and enabling effects of social structures. Such distanciation produces dialogical situations that become the potential basis for new forms of emancipatory reflection. For example, for a given traditional community, having as many children as possible may be interwoven in a web of meanings that are completely taken for granted. However, when presented with the demographic facts of the consequences of overpopulation, some members may gain a defamiliarizing or reflective distance from existing traditions, thus initiating a process of "critique"—and intracommunity debate—that leads to a revision of traditional meanings.

In our discussion of Freire and Habermas in the context of their shared critical hermeneutic epistemology, four themes will be taken up: (1) their understanding of the human sciences; (2) their analysis of the logic of critique as a transformative process; (3) their theory of truth grounded in dialogue and consensus; and (4) their contrast between communicative and technical rationality.

Freire: A Dialogical Theory of Knowledge

Dialectics of Consciousness: Subjectivism Versus Objectivism. Freire, of course, is not concerned with epistemology in the strict sense of a philosophical specialty or of systematically developing a theory of knowledge. Nevertheless, he does make a number of assumptions that refer to "gnosiology" (a term used more often in Spanish to describe epistemology) from a perspective that he and others characterize as "dialectical." Though this characterization is strictly speaking correct, the more difficult question is *how* he deploys dialectical principles as the basis of a historical and relational account of social reality. At one level, he posits a basic dialectical ontology of social life as a set of historical relation in which parts must be understood in relation to social wholes. Though this perspective is broadly indebted to the Hegelian Marxist tradition, it merely serves to provide a background for his more focused investigations. At no point does he make any particular claims for an "objective dialectics" of history or dialectical methods in any terms beyond those of guiding principles of inquiry. For example, he sometimes comments about leader-mass relations in revolutionary theory in terms of a dialectical relationship. As well, he views developmental stages as discussed by Piaget as involving dialectical transitions.

But for the most part he is concerned with differentiating subject-subject and subject-object relations with respect to their implications for knowledge and learning. Above all, he characterizes his approach as dialectical in the sense that it refuses to privilege or give absolute primacy to any two terms of opposing relationships (e.g., subject-object, consciousness-reality, thought-being, theory-practice). Otherwise thought falls into the fallacy of a dualism that does not understand the "dialectical unity" of such relations:

> The dualist vision implies the negation either of objectivity (submitting it to the powers of a consciousness created at will) or of the reality of the consciousness—a transformed one. In the first hypothesis we have the subjectivist error, the expression of an antidialectical and pre-Hegelian idealism. In the second, we are dealing with the mechanical objectivist one, equally antidialectical. (Freire, 1985, p. 153)

As we have already seen, subject-object relations are considered by Freire to involve an absence of communicating, hence treating the "object" as if it were a mute "thing." But this does not involve an epistemological claim that such objectivist knowledge is impossible or, under the right conditions, of practical value. In general, he rejects such positivist forms of inquiry because their deployment is associated with dominant groups concerned with manipulative social control, even in ostensibly revolutionary regimes. As a consequence, the *ideal form* of social knowledge for Freire draws on the possibilities of a subject-subject dialectic within which investigators and their subjects are involved in a communicative relationship of the type envisioned in participatory action research. But even in a subject-subject relation it is necessary to make reference to objective conditions as analyzed by the natural and social sciences (as, for example, in demography or political economy).

Critique: Conscientization and Distantiation. Though concerned about the abuse of objectivist social knowledge, Freire necessarily links the social awareness of agents to the possibility for empirical social knowledge. His crucial point, however, is that such "scientific" knowledge cannot be divorced from an understanding of the "commonsense" realities of social agents: "Science is super-posing critical thought on what we observe in reality, after the starting point of common sense" (Shor & Freire, 1987, p. 106)

How then does this transition from naive to critical consciousness occur? The technical term he uses is the concept of *conscientization* (sometimes misleadingly translated as "consciousness raising"). Though he does not employ the specific term *hermeneutics*, the epistemological basis of his analysis is rooted in a particular approach to the interpretive processes involved in consciousness formation. Freire employs several terms to describe the way in which conscientization derives from a capacity to view reality from new vantage points: gaining distance, re-recognition, "ad-miration": "The critical position holds that by gaining a certain epistemological distance from the concrete world, I can know it better and make the dream of a better world a reality" (Freire, 1996, p. 187). The details of this process in its educational context will be taken up in Chapter 6.

The process of conscientization makes use of two different forms of knowledge that produce distantiation. On the one hand, there is the possibility of bringing to the learning situation empirical knowledge with respect to how society works, for example, to produce poverty or create the conditions of hunger. This type of critical insight corresponds to the Enlightenment model of critical consciousness. Though this possibility may be important in some contexts, the primary interest of Freire lies elsewhere. The second type of distantiation is more characteristic of problem-posing education, which starts by discovering the theory hidden in the practices of human agents and social movements. In the development of new theoretical insights discovered in that practice, Freire's epistemological perspective seeks, in turn, to produce new knowledge based on the experience of learners in revising their own self-understanding: "The question for me is that inside of practice, we have a hidden theory. The point for me is how to unveil the practice at its moments in order to take into the hands the unknown theory" (C. Torres, personal communication, May 15, 1991). In other words, Freire's understanding of conscientization as enlightenment is based on the tension between two modes of distantiation: that produced by the "knowledge" contributed by "outsiders" (experts, intellectuals) and that latent in the experience of "insiders" (participants).

Truth: Subject-Subject Dialectics. The epistemological ideal for Freire—whether in everyday life or in scientific activity—involves a movement toward subject-subject dialogue. What this constructivist theme suggests is that knowledge is continuously changing, hence has a "historicity" that makes it "humble" in ways that are obscured by the arrogance of most scientists (Shor & Freire, 1987, p. 102). The dialogical foundation of social knowledge implies a distinctive philosophy of science based on dialogue. Beginning in 1968 with his essay on "extension or communication" (Freire, 1973) and as late as *Pedagogy of Hope* (1994, p. 117), Freire cites the work of Eduardo Nicol on the communicative or dialogical foundations of science (Freire, 1973, p. 136).

Rationality: Extension Versus Communication. The existence of two different types of knowledge—one oriented toward communication, the other toward control—gives rise to two notions of rationality or rationalization. Though they are formally parallel to Freire's well-known distinction between "banking" and "critical" approaches to learning, viewing these as two forms of *rationality* provides the basis for seeing Freire's position in more specifically epistemological terms that converge with that of Habermas. Concretely he expresses this distinction in terms of the technical approach used by "extension" agents in agricultural reform, as opposed to the communicative relation found in subject-subject communication (Freire, 1973, p. 95). More generally, he sees the unconstrained expansion of such technical rationality (whether in industry, dependent modernization, or the mass media) as a major source of alienation in the modern world (Freire, 1973, pp. 34–35).

To summarize, Freire's epistemological assumptions involve the following: (1) grounding knowledge in a subject-object unity ultimately legitimated in subject-subject relations; (2) a critical hermeneutics based on the eliciting of conscientization through distantiation, whether via objective knowledge or commonsense experience; (3) a conception of scientific truth based on the dialogue generated within subject-subject relations; and (4) a differentiation between the rationalities of communication (as in subject-subject dialogue) and technical control (as in "banking" education or agricultural "extension").

Habermas: A Discourse Theory of Knowledge

Subjectivism Versus Objectivism: Communicative Action. The basis of Habermas's conception of knowledge is a constructivist (i.e., historical and social) theory of truth based on the notion of knowledge as a kind of discourse involving a provisional "consensus" within a scientific community. From this perspective knowledge is created by particular types of discursive communities whose mode of argumentation is based on the principle of *fallibilism*, that is, the notion stressed by the philosopher Karl Popper that science is an unending process of "conjectures and refutations" rather than of absolute proofs and confirmations. In the radicalized fallibilism proposed by Habermas, the basis of all knowledge is *procedural*, that is, the result of procedures of argumentation. In this respect

his metatheoretical approach is *postfoundationalist* because truth is ultimately the product of a particular kind of "discourse" rather a correspondence between theories and facts:

> Post-empiricist philosophy of science has provided good reasons for hold-
> ing that the unsettled ground of rationally motivated agreement among
> participants in argumentation is our only foundation—in questions of
> physics no less than in those of morality. (Habermas, 1982, p. 238)

Nevertheless, this pragmatist form of postfoundationalism differs
from most postmodernist epistemologies because it does not conclude
that the constructed character of knowing necessarily makes knowledge
arbitrary or unreliable. Rather, its constructed and historical character is
taken as an expression of the fallibilistic character of all knowledge claims,
which are subject to continuous revision in the light not only of new
evidence, but also of metatheoretical debates (Habermas, 1970a, pp. 6–7).
Knowledge, in short, is grounded in processes of intersubjectively tested
communicative action.

Knowledge Interests: Emancipatory Knowledge. The basic argument
of Habermas's early epistemological contributions is that the construction
of knowledge is guided by three different kinds of universal human
interests in knowing. What he terms a *knowledge constitutive interest* is
similar in some respects to what Kant called "a priori" knowledge. For
Habermas, however, such capacities are not just given; they are also the
outcome of the evolutionary adaptive process through which humans
became "humanized." The crucial point of this argument is a rejection of
technological determinism. The fact that human civilizations have become
more able to exploit nature for human purposes cannot be attributed
exclusively to the advance of scientific and technical knowledge: These
are necessary but not sufficient conditions. For Habermas three interests
in knowledge are presupposed by the achievements of the human species:
the empirical-analytical knowledge characteristic of the natural and generalizing sciences; *the historical-hermeneutic interest* corresponding to disciplines
oriented to the interpretation of meanings; and the *critical-emancipatory*
cognitive interest that does not remain content with either empirical science or given traditions of meaning. The critical-emancipatory interest
provides insight into relations of domination that may appear to express
"natural" laws, but can potentially be changed:

> It is concerned with going beyond this goal to determine when theoretical
> statements grasp invariant regularities of social action as such and when

they express ideologically frozen relations of dependence that can in principle be transformed. To the extent that this is the case, the *critique of ideology* . . . [takes] into account that information about lawlike connections sets off a process of reflection in the consciousness of those whom the laws are about. (Habermas, 1971, p. 310)

But what is the nature of the processes of *reflection* that underlie critique? It is essentially the same as what we referred to as the "distanciation" involved in Freire's notion of conscientization. By revealing the socially constructed origins of contemporary "realities" with inhuman effects, it becomes possible to imagine their transformation.

In his earlier work, Habermas introduced an analogy with psychoanalysis to illustrate his argument about the relationship between distanciation and reflection. The resulting psychoanalytic analogy is thus a methodological heuristic, not a claim about the identity of the processes involved in the critique of ideology and psychoanalytic practice. The thesis is that like the neurotic's rationalizations, the oppressed person suffers from internalized distorted communication (ideology) that can be potentially overcome through therapeutic dialogue:

The analyst instructs the patient in reading his own texts, which he himself has mutilated and distorted, and in translating symbols from a mode of expression deformed as a private language into the mode of expression of public communication. This translation reveals the genetically important phases of life history to a memory that was previously blocked, and brings to consciousness the person's own self-formative process. (Habermas, 1971, p. 228)

As Habermas later acknowledged in response to critiques, there are a number of problems with the analogy between the neurotic and the oppressed. Most important, the therapeutic model implies a relation between expert and client that is already problematic in the case of the dubious scientific claims of therapy, let alone "experts" in the critique of false consciousness. As a consequence of these difficulties, in his more recent work Habermas has shifted away from a therapeutic model of critique toward an open-ended communicative model that is more postfoundationalist because it no longer relies directly on a knowledge claim of ideology critique as a "higher" kind of truth that is distinct from the social sciences generally.[9] Instead, critical social science is merely another voice that contributes to, but is not sufficient for, the construction of undistorted communication.

Discourse Theory of Truth: Consensus and Ideal Speech. Instead of pursuing the psychoanalytic analogy, Habermas turns away in the late 1960s from distorted communication toward its opposite, the construction of a model of consensus as communicative action. The gain of this alternative strategy was to bring into clearer focus the dialogical character of knowledge, a theme initially developed in his critical appropriation of American pragmatist Charles Sanders Peirce's theory of science and scientific communities. For Peirce the primary task of epistemology was not to clarify the logical structure of theories, but to understand their social origins in discursive communities oriented toward "uncompelled and permanent consensus": "This consensus does not have to be definitive, but has to have a definite agreement as its goal" (Habermas, 1971, p. 113). For Habermas, consensus formation within scientific communities is ultimately grounded in *intersubjective* processes, not the monological formalisms associated with logical procedures such as deduction and induction. Ultimately, knowledge cannot be reduced to formal procedures because it "arises from the symbolic interaction between societal subjects who reciprocally know and recognize each other as unmistakable individuals" (Habermas, 1971, p. 137).

A key aspect of Habermas's argument about knowledge is a technical distinction between *action* and theoretical *discourse*. In part this contrast is familiar in Western thought in the form of the distinction between the "commonsense" attitude of everyday life and the "theoretical" attitudes associated with activities related to science, phenomenological reflection, critique, and so forth. He recasts this distinction in terms of two different types of communication: "In actions, the factually raised claims to validity, which form the underlying consensus, are assumed naively. Discourse, on the other hand, serves the justifications of problematic claims to validity of opinions and norms" (Habermas, 1973, p. 18). In Habermas's terms "discourse" is thus a form of communication in which the participants subject themselves to the "unforced force of the better argument," in order to produce a tentative consensus about problematic claims:

> The supposition that attaches to such an agreement is that it represents a "rational consensus," that is, that it is the result not of the peculiarities of the participants or of their situations but simply of their subjecting themselves to the weight of evidence and the force of argument. The agreement is regarded as valid not merely "for us" (the actual participants) but as "objectively" valid, valid for all rational subjects (as potential participants). (McCarthy, 1978, pp. 291–292)

As a consequence, the possibility of science is grounded in an implicit model of "ideal speech," despite the fact that scientists may have psychological reasons for resisting better arguments and that every "consensus" is always contested.

The problematic of the "ideal speech situation" brings us to the most frequently misunderstood aspect of Habermas's overall theoretical strategy. Endless amounts of ill-informed and confusing commentary have been directed toward Habermas's ostensible naiveté with respect to the possibility of authentic "consensus," since all real communicative situations are rife with conflicts, interests, misunderstandings, and so forth. In particular, the very term *ideal speech situation* has been read to imply that the concrete goal of social practice would be to literally turn the social world into a seminar where asymmetrical relations of power would be mysteriously suspended and "equals" would dialogue in pursuit of truth. As Habermas has acknowledged, his use of the term has been guilty of "the fallacy of misplaced concreteness":

> These images are concretist, because they suggest a final condition that might be achieved in time, which cannot be what they are intended to suggest. But I continue to insist on the idealizing content of the inescapable pragmatic presuppositions of a praxis from which only the better argument is supposed to emerge. (Habermas, 1997a, p. 148)

The crucial point is that for Habermas (as well as Freire) the status of idealized consensus and dialogue is an *empirical counterfactual*: That people act *as if* this were a real possibility is the necessary (though not sufficient) condition for whatever forms of collective learning might transcend the mutually destructive and tragic struggles of the type metaphorically described in Hegel's master-and-slave dialectic. Rather than being an expression of their presumed ignorance about the obstacles that get in the way of dialogue, this position reflects the most consistent attempt to place awareness of this problem at the heart of questions of ontology, epistemology, and social practice. For it was here that both classical metaphysical theories of truth and positivism failed; both presumed that the ideal of Socratic dialogue (implicit in language) could be realized within existing structures of distorted communication:

> The ontological illusion of pure theory behind which knowledge-constitutive interests become invisible promotes the fiction that Socratic dialogue is possible everywhere and at any time. From the beginning philosophy has presumed that the autonomy and responsibility posited with the structure of language are not only anticipated but real. (Habermas, 1971, p. 314)

Pure theory—theory that is not reflective about the social contexts of its production—cannot take into account "the traces of violence that deform repeated attempts at dialogue and recurrently close off the path to unconstrained communication" (1971, p. 315). Hence, it is only through thematizing "the historical traces of suppressed dialogue" that critical theory can imagine the conditions of possibility of an "emancipated society" whose responsible and autonomous members might begin to transcend the traces of violence that circumscribe the human condition as we have known it. Accordingly, "one should not imagine the ideal speech situation as a utopian model for an emancipated society" (Habermas, 1992a, p. 93) as opposed to a strategy for reconstructing the concept of reason.

Further, the creation of such theoretical discourses is a unique human achievement that has been historically contingent on the institutionalization of such discourses, a process closely bound up with the European project of modernity. Following Max Weber's understanding of the historical process of the rationalization of world views here, Habermas suggests that the notion of "rationality" implied by theoretical discourses presupposes preunderstandings that historically emerged in modern conditions: "We are implicitly connecting a claim to *universality* with our *Occidental understanding of the world*, a difference that is illustrated by the historical comparison with mythical understandings of the world" (Habermas, 1984, p. 44). Even if the colonial context of the origins of modern science may have often distorted evaluation of non-Western traditions, the latter can now only selectively validate and rehabilitate those excluded perspectives through universalistic procedures.

Rationality: Instrumental Versus Communicative Reason. A central theme of the theory of communicative action is a distinction between two fundamental forms of discourse—communicative and strategic. Habermas thus seeks to redefine the opposition—inherited from the German sociologist Max Weber—regarding the interplay between the "instrumental" rationality of technical means and the "substantial" rationality of ultimate ends or values. The first form of rationality corresponds to the "cognitive-instrumental rationality" as defined by empiricism in the sciences and is oriented toward rationality as technical mastery. The second is associated with the notion of communicative rationality:

> If we start from the communicative employment of propositional knowledge in assertions, we make a prior decision for a wider concept of rationality connected with the ancient conceptions of *logos*. This concept of *communicative rationality* carries with it connotations based ultimately on the

central experience of the unconstrained, unifying, consensus bringing
force of argumentative speech, in which different participants overcome
their merely subjective views and, owing to the mutuality of rationally
motivated conviction, assure themselves of both the unity of the objective
world and the intersubjectivity of their lifeworld. (Habermas, 1984, p. 10)

The crucial importance of this distinction between two kinds of
knowledge (which has an ontological correlate based on differentiating
work and symbolic interaction) is that it allows understanding the quite
different implications of technical control over external nature as opposed
to human nature. The realization of normative reason cannot be achieved
instrumentally: It can only be constructed dialogically, at least if it is to
avoid the negative effects of domination.

To summarize, Habermas's epistemological perspective can be reconstructed in terms of the following: (1) a grounding of knowledge in a
theory of argumentation based on subject-subject dialogue of communicative action; (2) a conception of critical hermeneutics based on a distinction
between three knowledge interests, one of which—the critical-emancipatory interest—functions as a critique of domination; (3) a consensus theory
of truth based on discursive communities guided by an implicit model
of ideal speech as fallibilistic discourse; and (4) a differentiation between
instrumental and communicative forms of rationality as the basis for
understanding the distinctive features of normative reasoning.

The epistemological positions of Freire and Habermas are compared
in Table 3.2.

METHODOLOGY: CONSTRUCTING AND APPLYING KNOWLEDGE

Introduction: Critical Methodology

Reference to the methodology of critical theory (here including Freire) is
closely connected to slogans invoking the "unity of theory and practice."
What is at stake here, to speak more concretely, is the forms of research and
knowledge that facilitate transformations of consciousness and society.
Though we would agree that the thesis of the unity of theory and practice is
broadly valid as the *regulative ideal* of Freire and Habermas, it is misleading
when it becomes overgeneralized as a prescriptive basis for invalidating
other types of research. A simplistic focus on the unity of theory and
practice as a universal and exclusive criterion of methodological adequacy
pushes critical theory into a dogmatic antipositivist position and contributes to the common identification of critical theory with ideologically

TABLE 3.2. EPISTEMOLOGY: FREIRE AND HABERMAS

EPISTEMOLOGY	FREIRE	HABERMAS
Grounds of knowledge	Subject/object unity and subject-subject dialogue	Theory of argumentation and communicative action
Logic of critique (critical hermeneutics)	Conscientization as distantiation and a reflective reappropriation of reality	Critical-emancipatory knowledge interest and ideal of undistorted communication
Theory of truth	Subject-subject dialogue as means of appropriating the external object	Intersubjective consensus within discursive communities
Conception of rationality	Communicative vs. technical (banking education)	Communicative vs. instrumental rationality

driven research strategies. The danger here is that the excessive politicization of knowledge distorts a realistic appraisal of social realities and prematurely undermines dialogue among conflicting standpoints.

The construction of a tradition of critical research knowledge inevitably requires the deployment of the full range of methodological techniques. A critical theory of methodology, we would argue, is *reflexively pluralist but not relativist* because there are both situated (pragmatic) and universalizing criteria for assessing and evaluating research traditions and specific research practices (Morrow, 1994a).

We will consider several basic issues here in relation to Freire and Habermas: (1) an approach to the human sciences based on the agency-structure dialectic; (2) the relationship between a critical social science and other methodologies, especially in relation to participatory knowledge; and (3) the relationships between facts and values in inquiry and practice.

Freire: Scientific Humanism and Participatory Knowledge

Critical Social Science Versus Practice. Freire's general conception of the social sciences must be understood in relation to his impact on a methodology that is distinct from literacy training: *participatory action research.* The goal of such research is to involve members of communities in the actual process of research, ideally enabling them to undergo a process of conscientization by appropriating simple social scientific techniques for analyzing their local realties (Torres, 1995b). Not unjustifiably, many suggest that the source of inspiration for this approach is the notion of the unity of theory and practice found in the works of the early Marx. We argue, however, that reducing Freire's methodology to participatory action research fails to differentiate between the unity of theory and practice as a regulative ideal and the multiplicity of forms of knowledge that are necessary preconditions for practice-oriented research to become successful and enduring in its consequences. Preference for the participatory practice model thus must be situated in relation to Freire's broader historical conception of the social sciences, a "scientific humanism" (Freire, 1970a, p. 20) based on the claim that "for those who undertake cultural action for freedom, science is the indispensable instrument for denouncing the myths created by the Right. . . . Science and philosophy together provide the principles of action for conscientization" (Freire, 1970a, p. 47). Though "the Right subordinates science and technology to its own ideology" because of technocratic imperatives of control, a participatory account of knowledge can be appropriated for "utopian" ends (Freire, 1970a, p. 47).

Though Freire does not explicitly develop a theory of a comprehensive philosophy of the human or social sciences, he does consistently cite the French structuralist sociologist Lucien Goldmann, especially *The Human Sciences and Philosophy* (1969). In particular, Freire draws on Goldmann's concept of "maximal possible consciousness" as part of his own conception of conscientization and critical consciousness (Freire, 1985, pp. 32, 87). In the 1950s Goldmann's historical structuralist approach reflected two of the primary sources of Habermas's thought: the German Frankfurt School and Piaget. In drawing on the Hegelian Marxist Georg Lukács and the Weberian sociologist Karl Mannheim, as well as incorporating methodological aspects of Jean Piaget's genetic structuralism, Goldmann's antipositivist conception of methodology proposed a Marxist-influenced but independent historical sociology. His approach was oriented toward the problem of totality (i.e., society understood as a contradictory whole), but from the perspective of a subject-object dialectic that takes into account "the creative power of the individual as well as the relation between individual consciousness and objective reality" (Goldmann, 1969, p. 34). Freire draws primarily, however, on the more voluntaristic side of Goldmann, that is, how changes in social structures create objective conditions for new forms of consciousness, hence the possibility of "the maximum of potential consciousness" (Freire, 1970a, p. 46). Yet from this historical structuralist perspective Freire would also admit the necessity of addressing "objectively verifiable" questions such as those involving the contradictions between the oppressor and oppressed, the structure of inequality, the effects of poverty and hunger, and so forth.[10] Similarly, Freire borrows from Goldmann's structuralism by employing "codification" procedures in literacy training to reveal the "deep structures" of social relations: "To analyze the codification in its 'deep structure' is . . . to reconstruct the former praxis and to become capable of a new and different praxis" (Freire, 1970a, p. 17). It is crucial to understand the hegemonic codifications of the past in order to create the re-codifications required for cultural transformation.

It is in this broader context that Freire's criticisms of manipulative empirical social research must be understood. For example, he rejects the imposition of ostensibly value-neutral technocratic solutions on peasants that do not take into account either local knowledge or the impact on the community (Freire, 1973, p. 128). In such contexts social science becomes a tool of "cultural invasion": "To this end, the invaders are making increasing use of the social sciences and technology, and to some extent the physical sciences as well, to improve and refine their action" (Freire, 1970c, p. 151, n. 29). Such "behaviorism" simply fails to "comprehend the dialectic of men-world relationships" and cannot engage the possibility of conscientization: "Conscientization is viable only because men's consciousness, although conditioned, can recognize that it is conditioned" (Freire, 1970a, p. 30).

Similarly, in revolutionary contexts there is the danger that "scientific revolutionary humanism" might treat the oppressed as "objects" (Freire, 1970c, p. 128). Even a process of agrarian transformation involving land reform will not succeed unless the introduction of new technology is accompanied by "cultural transformation" and "action in the field of 'popular culture'" (Freire, 1973, p. 135). Such reform also required strategies of "evaluation" understood as a dialogical process of accountability, as opposed to processes of supervisory control. Underlying this conception is not only a critique of dogmatism and wishful-thinking, but a fallibilistic understanding of attempts to intervene to facilitate social change. No institution can dispense with rigorous evaluation procedures: "Without this it runs the risk of committing errors, responsibility for which always gets transferred to others by a natural defense mechanism" (Freire, 1968a, Chapter 8, p. 12).

Methodological Pluralism. Despite a preference for the type of critical social science advocated by Goldmann (1969) and his own focus on participatory action methods, Freire also acknowledges the need for methodological and political pluralism to generate the diverse forms of knowledge required for critical reflection on reality. Indeed, it is only on the basis of empirical claims on the social origins of dehumanization that normative calls for change can be persuasively made "that the concrete situation which begets oppression must be transformed" (Freire, 1970c, p. 35). Conscientization also depends in part on revealing the relations between hunger and economic structures, or between "hunger and violence and hunger as violence"(Freire, 1996, p. 183).

On the other hand, pluralism also has an intrinsic value as part of a dialogical understanding of tolerance. As Freire notes ironically, his defense of pluralism in knowledge is problematic from a traditional Marxist perspective: "Probably, upon making my ideas known, some revolutionists, not revolutionaries, are already sanctioning my bourgeois weakness. Nonetheless, I would claim that my 'bourgeois weakness' is fundamentally a democratic and radical dimension of my personality" (Escobar, Fernández, Guevara-Niebla, & Freire, 1994, p. 91).

Facts, Values, and the Autonomy of Inquiry. Finally, though Freire advocates an engaged conception of inquiry within which explicit values and politics play a decisive role, he respects the autonomy of inquiry and is not willing to reduce research to mere ideological struggle, concluding that "I cannot take advantage of the space that the university provides to proselytize for the party I belong to" (Escobar et al., 1994, p. 138). Nevertheless, his stance also rejects the dominant ideology of a value-free conception of science (Freire & Faundez, 1989, p. 31). Yet Freire's constructivist critique of value neutrality does not entail a postmodernist dismissal of "Western" science in the manner of the self-proclaimed "post-development" theorists (Rahnema, 1997). The fact that science is not neutral does not mean that scientific rigor is not important: "The critical investigator wants the truth of reality and not to adapt reality to one's own truth"; the more one is politically engaged, the more one needs "objective truth" (Freire, 1978, p. 70). In short, it is crucial that one "not confuse a concern with truth—which characterizes all serious scientific effort—with the myth of this neutrality" (Freire, 1985, p. 157). Even though knowledge has "historicity," this does not undermine "the fundamental certainty that I can know" or "the possibility of knowing with more methodological rigor that would enhance the level of the accuracy of the findings" (Freire, 1997b, p. 31). Where he does invoke postmodernist themes is in viewing scientific and value claims as more uncertain and fallibilistic than envisioned by the foundationalist "modernist" Marxist Left.

To summarize, Freire's methodological position with respect to social inquiry can be viewed in terms of the following orientations: (1) a conception of the human sciences based on "potential consciousness" within the agency-structure dialectic; (2) a focus on participatory methods within a pluralist conception of methodology in relation to practice; and (3) an understanding of the interplay of facts and values that respects the autonomy of inquiry.

Habermas: A Critical Social Science

Hermeneutic and Analytic Methodologies. As with other metatheoretical issues, Habermas's concerns range far beyond Freire's more practical ones (Habermas, 1988). Suffice it to recall that early in his career Habermas developed a critique of positivism that stressed the dangers of "technocratic consciousness," that is, how science and technology function as ideology in advanced capitalism by declaring that technical "imperatives" require ignoring democratic participation. At least traditional ideologies were relatively visible given their confusion of "private" with "public" interests. In contrast, the new technocratic ideology draws on the mystique of science by making exaggerated claims for scientific expertise, a problem that has more recently been brought to light by the counter-science of environmental movements:

> Technocratic consciousness is, on the one hand, "less ideological" than all previous ideologies. . . . Today's dominant, rather glassy background ideology, which makes a fetish of science, is more irresistible and farther-reaching than ideologies of the old type. For with the veiling of practical problems it not only justifies a *particular class's* interest in domination, but affects the human race's emancipatory interest as such. (Habermas, 1970a, p. 111)

Accordingly, Habermas defends the concept of a critical social science that is reflexive about its relation to social control, rejecting an engineering model of planning for one based on participation. Following from the epistemological perspective of critical hermeneutics, Habermas's philosophy of the social sciences is based on the interpretive structuralist premise that social knowledge must be both *hermeneutic* and *analytic* (Habermas, 1988, p. 3). It is analytic in its structuralist attempt to represent forms of causality and determination that shape and limit the forms of consciousness available to participants in social practice. But unlike those who approach analytic methodologies from a classic positivist or behavioral perspective, for Habermas critical theory must also engage in hermeneutic analysis relating to the consciousness of agents. In short, a critical social science presupposes a kind of "quasi-causal" structural analysis of "depth interpretation" that illuminates the constraining and enabling effects of material (institutional) realities (Thompson, 1981, pp. 173–181); but to be translated into practice this analytic knowledge must be "rooted in the *felt* needs and sufferings of a group of people" even though "a great deal of what people do to one another is not the result of conscious knowledge and choice" (Fay, 1975, pp. 93–94).

Methodologies and Contexts of Practice. If critical theory seeks to link theory with practice, then it is confronted with the question of priorities with respect to social scientific methods. For Habermas this does not imply that research should always be linked directly to practice. Rather, such unity can serve only a regulative ideal. Critical social science cannot dispense with a concern with explanatory knowledge that is not tied immediately to practice. Habermas's crucial thesis is that the theory-practice relation must be linked to specific contexts and defined in terms of different criteria. For example, three such contexts of practice are differentiated in relation to the question of political organization: the construction of scientifically credible theoretical claims; processes of enlightenment that initiate reflection; and strategies of struggle oriented toward the reorganization of relations of political power. "On the first level, the aim is true statements, on the second, authentic insights, and on the third, prudent decisions" (Habermas, 1973, p. 32). The first assumes a relatively autonomous scientific community. The second context of practice applies to activities that are in the broadest sense educational: "the organization of processes of enlightenment, in which such theorems are applied and can be tested in a unique manner by the initiation of the processes of reflection carried on within certain groups toward which these processes have been directed" (Habermas, 1973, p. 32). Though all such educational activities have a "political" dimension, the relationship between theory and practice here is quite distinct from that involved in the third context of actual struggle dominated by "the selection of appropriate strategies, the solution of tactical questions, and the conduct of the political struggle" (Habermas, 1973, p. 32).Consequently, *no single principle* can unite theory and practice in these three distinct contexts (Habermas, 1973, pp. 33–34).

In short, the thesis of the unity of theory and practice in critical theory is simultaneously directed toward the autonomy of inquiry, the dialogical basis of enlightening educational process, and the participatory basis of leadership in political mobilization. The result is the paradoxical, dialogical structure of the unity of theory and practice in political transformation, where

> the vindicating superiority of those who do the enlightening over those who are to be enlightened is theoretically unavoidable, but at the same

time it is fictive and requires self-correction: *in a process of enlightenment there can only be participants.* (Habermas, 1973, p. 40; emphasis added)

Though Habermas is closely identified with a critique of positivist social science, this should not be confused with a blanket rejection of empirical social research. In fact, his antipositivist position implies a methodological pluralism with respect to the use of social scientific techniques to uncover the causal and functional relations that operate behind the backs of social agents. If critical social science has a particular defining trait, it is not simply the regulative ideal of the unity of theory and practice; it is also that the idealized goal of participation presupposes a prior capacity to analyze scientifically the historically specific relations between agency and structure that can inform—though not determine—the practices of participants. Political organization cannot be reduced to general theory, revolutionary slogans, or pseudo-science; these must be replaced by "an empirical analysis that is sensitive to contemporary history and is social-scientifically well informed . . . according to national traditions, regions, subcultures and according to contingent historical constellations" (Habermas, 1982, p. 222).

Facts, Values, and Practice. Finally, with respect to the question of facts and values, Habermas's approach has diverse implications, but two are central in the present context. First, he rejects positivism's tendency to deny the ideological functions of science, technology, and other claims to expertise. Yet he is critical of tendencies that would reduce scientific or social inquiry to nothing but ideology. Second, he argues that though value questions are logically distinct from empirical ones, some types of normative questions can be addressed in terms of rational justifications. The consequence of the first point is that the constructed character of knowledge cannot be taken to imply that scientific discourse is a rhetorical illusion. Despite his critique of positivist social science, he still regards the relative autonomy of scientific communities as a necessary condition of complex, democratic societies.

In response to the second question, Habermas accepts the logical force of Hume's fact-value distinction, the conclusion that normative statements cannot be derived from empirical ones: "Hence it seems advisable not to confuse decisions about the choice of norms, that is, about moral or political problems, with problems of the empirical sciences" (Habermas, 1970a, p. 6). At the same time, he rejects the conclusion of Max Weber that value questions are inherently nonrational or irrational. Rather, for Habermas value questions follow *different* principles of rationality. Indeed, the central objective of his whole project is to develop a theory of discourse (or communicative) ethics as a rationally justifiable normative foundation for a critical theory of society, though not one that would replace situated ethical decisions. Again, he is here responding not only to Weber's value relativism, but also to one of the key deficits of classical Marxism—its tendency to reject ethical discourse as "bourgeois idealism."

To summarize, Habermas's critical methodology is based on (1) an explanatory strategy that requires the use of both hermeneutic and structural-causal analysis as part of elucidating the agency-structure dialectic; (2) a conception of the unity of theory and practice where participatory research serves as an ideal, but assumes a methodological pluralism that differentiates scientific, educational, and political contexts of practice; and (3) an understanding of facts and values that stresses their logical differences and respects the necessary autonomy of inquiry, yet also points to the possibilities for rationally justifying certain types of value orientations.

The relation between the general methodological approaches of Freire and Habermas is comparatively summarized in Table 3.3.

COMPARATIVE COMMENTARY: FROM STRUGGLE TO RECONCILIATION

In concluding, we would like to reiterate the basic argument of this chapter regarding the broad metatheoretical convergence between Freire and Habermas in the context of ontological, epistemological, and methodological assumptions. Their broadly shared orientations can be summarized as follows:

TABLE 3.3. METHODOLOGY: FREIRE AND HABERMAS

METHODOLOGY	FREIRE	HABERMAS
Nature of the human sciences	Dialectic of structure and potential consciousness	Interplay of structural and hermeneutic analysis
Relations among methods	Priority of participatory methods within a pluralist context	Contextually defined, but regulated by the ideal of participation
Relations between facts and values	Engaged research, but respecting the autonomy of inquiry	Logically distinct, but related in practice

- *A communicative, critical realist ontological perspective* based on a revision of the theory of praxis (subject-object dialectic) away from a paradigm of production to one of intersubjective communication in which mutual recognition is achieved through both struggle and reconciliation.
- *A dialogical epistemological strategy* based on a historical conception of knowledge constructed in communicative subject-subject relations in scientific communities and in which the unity of theory and practice serves as a regulative ideal.
- *An interpretive structuralist methodology* of the human sciences that is pluralistic, but gives particular importance to approaches that can elucidate agency-structure relations involved in social and cultural reproduction and change, as well as rationally justifying value priorities.

Ontology: Critical Realism

Freire's and Habermas's ontological positions are broadly critical realist in the sense of presupposing the existence of structural realities, but acknowledging that they can be known only indirectly through linguistically and historically mediated processes.[11] The key difference lies in the tensions between Habermas's communicative paradigm and Freire's continuing reliance on the language of praxis with its problematic links to an individualistic philosophy of consciousness. Our preceding discussion, however, has attempted to show that Freire's position can be readily reframed in Habermas's communicative terms along the following lines, recognizing: that despite using potentially "productivist" praxis terminology, Freire's position is based on an intersubjective subject-subject dialectic; that his notion of a humanistic ontological vocation is not metaphysical because it implicitly presumes communicative validity claims embedded in the structure of language; and that his justification of normative rationality is grounded in the regulative ideal of domination-free (undistorted) communication.

Freire's critique of the subject-object dialectic moves away from the classic theory of praxis in giving primacy to the intersubjective and linguistic basis of action, as well as locating the master-slave dialectic within the larger framework of a model of love and reconciliation. In the case of Habermas, parallel shifts are made more theoretically explicit in a categorical distinction between work and interaction that culminated in the shift from a philosophy of consciousness (production paradigm in the case of Marx) to a communications paradigm.

Further, Freire's humanistic notion of an ontological vocation of humanization implies a universal pragmatics of language: It suggests what Habermas calls a conception of the validity claims implicit in the very act of communication. For Freire, dialogue presumes media for making communication comprehensible, as well as requiring humility, faith in man, mutual trust, hope, and critical thinking (Freire, 1970c, pp. 78–81). From the perspective of speech act theory, Habermas similarly argues that linguistic communication as such implies claims to truth, rightness, authenticity, sincerity, and appropriateness. Where Freire's position is distinctive is the stress he gives to love as a component of dialogue: "Love is at the same time the foundation of dialogue and dialogue itself. It is thus necessarily the task of responsible Subjects and cannot exist in a relation of domination" (Freire, 1970c, pp. 77–78). As one feminist theorist has argued without reference to Freire, this theme needs to be incorporated into the theory of communicative action (Bertilsson, 1991). We will return to some of these questions in Chapter 6, which covers educational strategies for organizing processes of enlightenment.

Finally, both Freire and Habermas ground normative rationality in a theory of communication. Much as Freire's ethics is grounded in the link among language, "hope," and "practice," for Habermas the deeper structure of human communication contains an implicit ideal grounded in the "hope" of reaching authentic, unconstrained mutual understanding.

Epistemology: Theory and Practice

In relation to epistemology, Freire's approach converges with that of Habermas in two key respects but diverges in a third: Freire's dialogical conception of learning presupposes the three knowledge interests elucidated by Habermas; his distinction between "banking" and "critical" learning implies a distinction between instrumental and communicative rationality. But Habermas's stress on the differences between contexts of theory and praxis calls into question the direct application of the principles of dialogical learning to the politial sphere.

Freire's pedagogical theory and practice presuppose something like Habermas's account of knowledge interests: that technology, as a form of empirical-analytical knowledge, is indispensable for the purpose of fulfilling basic human needs; that hermeneutic-historical interpretation is the basis of discovering the cultural themes necessary for establishing subject-subject communication; and that critical-emancipatory insight is required for the movement toward critical consciousness—conscientization—that transforms reality.

Freire's epistemology is, like that of Habermas, also based on a distinction between two rationalities of action: first, manipulative strategies (such as agricultural extension models) that treat people as objects to be technically controlled; and second, dialogical relations in which there is subject-subject co-participation and mutual learning. In Habermas's work this distinction is elaborated in terms of differentiating two forms of rationality: strategic rationality (whether as instrumental rationality over nature or manipulative control of people) and communicative action defined by implicit validity claims oriented toward mutual understanding.

Freire and Habermas do differ with respect to the question of the relationship between two contexts of practice: the organization of enlightenment as opposed to direct political struggle. Habermas more sharply differentiates between the two, arguing that whereas educational activities are driven by the goal of insight and reflection, political action is necessarily governed by strategic considerations. From this perspective, it is argued that organizational questions are of such an uncertain, situated, and future-oriented character that the model of reflection cannot be directly applied, though it is conceded that "the objective application of a reflexive theory under the conditions of strategic action is not illegitimate in every respect" (Habermas, 1973, p. 39). In contrast, Freire attempts to extend the principles of dialogical learning directly to the political sphere under the heading of a conception of revolutionary leadership that will be discussed in the next chapter.

Methodology: Interpretive Structuralism

We can summarize the shared stances of Freire and Habermas in the context of social scientific methodology as follows: a defense of a critical social science as a form of "interpretive structuralism" (Morrow, 1994a), coupled with a methodological pluralism that nevertheless gives priority to knowledge that potentially can be appropriated by subordinated agents to enhance their critical consciousness; an emphasis on the ideal of linking theory and practice that also recognizes the strategic importance of other forms of knowledge; and a recognition of the importance of the interrelation of facts and values in social practice, but a defense of the autonomy of inquiry in order to avoid distorting research outcomes through dogmatism and wish-fulfillment.

Taken together, these convergent methodological themes point to the weaknesses of Guba's general characterization of critical theory as "ideologically oriented inquiry." Neither Freire nor Habermas anchors inquiry in a fixed social standpoint that defines critique, arbitrarily limits research to particular methods, or irrationally mixes facts and values in ways that undermine the autonomy of knowledge. Though in his earlier writings Freire tended to speak in terms of the "oppressed" as the working class, his methodology was in fact comprehensive, reflexive, and open to difference—to the chagrin of some of his Marxist critics. Similarly, though Habermas makes frequent reference to class issues, one of the distinctive features of his social theory—as distinct from classical Marxism—is that it is not grounded in the perspective of the proletariat as a universal class. Again, the openness of the resulting theory of communicative action leaves room for diverse subject positions whose perspectives have been taken up in forms of critical theory concerned with race and gender.

What is missing in our preceding characterization of Freire's and Habermas's accounts of metatheory, methodology, and practice is an analysis of the specific conditions and contexts under which such transformative practices can be organized. Three further steps are required for explicating these issues. In the next chapter we will consider the theory of society and history that follows from these metatheoretical presuppositions. On that basis we can turn in subsequent chapters to the implications for a critical social psychology of the subject and the specific problems posed for a theory of educational practice.

4

Theories of History and Society

Crisis, Reproduction, and Transformation

A society beginning to move from one epoch to another requires the development of an especially flexible, critical spirit. . . . *Conscientização* represents the *development* of the awakening of critical awareness. It will not appear as a natural byproduct of even major economic changes, but must grow out of a critical educational effort based on favorable historical conditions.

—Freire, 1973, pp. 7, 19

It is my conjecture that the fundamental mechanism for social evolution in general is to be found in an automatic inability not to learn. Not *learning*, but *not-learning* is the phenomenon that calls for explanation at the socio-cultural stage of development. Therein lies, if you will, the rationality of man. Only against this background does the overpowering irrationality of the history of the species become visible.

—Habermas, 1975, pp. 14–15

Though our focus in this study is on the theory of the developmental subject shared by Freire and Habermas, this question cannot be separated from their theories of society and history, hence of development at the societal level. In this chapter we will consider their respective crisis theories of social development, with particular emphasis on how they conceptualize the links between domination, rationalization, and democratization.

RECONSTRUCTING HISTORICAL MATERIALISM

Theories of society necessarily fall back on some kind of metaphor as a model of society. The most influential have been biological models based on the organic analogy. In the case of sociological functionalism, the organic metaphor involves the assumption that society is a kind of system (composed of parts that make up a whole) organized around principles of differentiation and evolution. In contrast, the work of Freire and Habermas can be situated in relation to conflict-oriented theories of social and cultural reproduction from Marx to Gramsci and Pierre Bourdieu (Morrow & Torres, 1995). Such models share some characteristics with functionalist organic models because of analyzing society as a whole and postulating that societies tend to sustain a kind of equilibrium that maintains the given type of social order. But *historicist* social reproduction models differ in fundamental respects.

A foundational assumption of theories of social and cultural reproduction is that class-divided societies sustain their identities through processes of *domination* that facilitate the reproduction of power relations from one generation to another. In complex, highly differentiated societies this involves a process of *complex reproduction* where sustaining the identity of a particular form of society requires extensive adjustments and reforms that may give the appearance of change, but serve the more fundamental function of preserving the given social order. For example, though the modern "welfare" state has changed significantly in providing basic safety nets to protect its members, it still remains a "capitalist" state because it depends for its survival on the revenues derived from capital accumulation.

Central to such reproduction models is that any given social formation is characterized by both conflictual and integrative processes. In modern nation-states conflict is traced in part to class divisions rooted in the production process, but also to divisions stemming from various other historical sources (race, ethnicity, gender, etc.). For cultural reproduction theories the symbolic means of legitimation—hegemonic relations—have become increasingly important in modern societies. More recently, the *interdependence* of societies has been stressed in the theories of the world-system, globalization, and the network society. For Habermas, this suggests the need for a transnational, cosmopolitan conception of democracy (Habermas, 2001a, pp. 38–129).

Given their interpretive structuralist metatheoretical orientations, Freire and Habermas approach the questions of cultural reproduction with distinctive assumptions in mind. They reject classical Marxist models based on an evolutionary "dialectic" of inexorable laws of development. Accordingly, they are concerned about the interplay between action and structure, or agents and systemic processes. The ends of development are not predetermined, but they are also not arbitrary. For Freire and Habermas human history reveals a consistent struggle for democratization and the realization of individual autonomy that is linked to the dialogical and developmental nature of the human subject. For both, however, there is a problematic relationship between *instrumental rationalization* (under-stood as one-sided economic modernization) and *social rationalization* as manifest in authentic democratization and individuation. More specifi-cally, their concerns with a theory of society are shaped by a respective focus on underdeveloped, dependent capitalism (Freire), on the one hand, and advanced democratic capitalism on the other (Habermas). Yet there is a suggestive continuity of language of strategic importance: a focus on processes of *colonization*—as a manifestation of antidialogical action (Freire) or strategic rationality (Habermas)—and their implications for irrationality.

Though the crisis theories of Freire and Habermas address very differ-ent contexts, they should not be seen as mutually exclusive or fundamen-tally incompatible. On the one hand, as globalization theories emphasize, pockets of the "Third World" now exist in the first. On the other hand, the middle and upper classes of less-developed countries increasingly resemble their counterparts in more advanced ones. Further, the emer-gence of fledgling democratic states in previously authoritarian contexts—the problem of "democratic transition"—recapitulates many of the prob-lems faced by democratic reconstruction in postfascist Germany, though now in the context of globalization. To use Habermas's terminology, both dependent and dominant societies are afflicted by *selective modernization* and the *colonization of the lifeworld*. Modernization is one-sided and selec-tive because of the often irrational—even if profit-motivated—use of some forms of technical and social rationality and not others. This abuse of strategic rationality increasingly takes the form of colonizing or invading the taken-for-granted experiences of everyday life—the lifeworld—through markets and administrative systems. A central task of critical social re-search is thus to empirically analyze these novel forms of social domina-tion and suggest constructive strategies of resistance within civil society (e.g., new social movements).

An aspect of Habermas's project necessarily frames this chapter as a whole: his call for a *reconstructed historical materialism*. His claim is that the foundations of the Marxist tradition need to be completely re-thought by critical theory, even if the result is no longer recognizably "Marxist." There is no equivalent ambition in Freire's occasional comments relating to a theory of society, though we will be arguing that his overall perspec-tive—which cannot readily be assimilated into given Marxist para-digms—calls for something like Habermas's approach. A key aspect of this reconstructive strategy is often misunderstood by critics who reject his use of neo-evolutionary concepts as outmoded rationalism, a kind of deterministic "metanarrative" of history. Habermas's neo-evolutionary conception of the "advance" of social formations is not based on the automatic succession of modes of production and technologies. Instead, his approach focuses on the highly contingent, successive emergence of cultural capacities linked to social rationalization, that is, *collective learning processes*. Institutionally, such collective learning is embodied in formal discourses based on rational deliberation in discursive communities, for example, theology, the natural and human sciences, education, and the dialogue of democracy. In short, the cumulative development (and colonizing use) of science and technology is the outcome of more fundamental advances (or regressions) in capacities for collective learning, which becomes the procedural reference point for defining "progress."

Though we can touch only cursorily on the question of Habermas's reconstruction of historical materialism, this chapter takes up three comparative themes that are broadly shared by Freire and Habermas in this context: (1) a theory of societal crisis based on a critique of economistic theories of societal development characterized by a one-sided conception of rationality; (2) a questioning of the contemporary model of "advanced" liberal democratic societies as a full realization of the theory of democracy; and (3) a concern with the alternative "rationalities" of modernity as the basis for a critique of the selective modernization initiated by European capitalism, as well as strategies for the revitalization of the democratic public sphere.

CRISIS THEORIES OF SOCIETY AND DEVELOPMENT

Freire: Mass Society and Dependency as a Rationality Crisis

Freire was never preoccupied with the problematic of a theory of society or a general sociology as a specialized academic pursuit. Such issues were far removed from his engagement with the Brazilian social and political crisis, and later with other parts of Latin America. Nevertheless, his approach to education and pedagogy *presumes a conflict theory of society* and at times refers to and takes positions with respect such issues. Freire's general approach can be summarized in terms of the following themes: (1) how traditionalism and later processes of massification have impeded the formation of the critical consciousness necessary to ensure that technological modernization realizes its full potential for meeting human needs; (2) how national dependency deepens these problems, involving a neocolonial relation that undermines self-determination and creates new forms of inequality; and (3) how democratization—understood from the perspective of conscientization—offered the only plausible strategy for dealing with the dilemmas of massification and dependency.

Freire's early writings are based on a theory of *mass society* strongly indebted to Erich Fromm and C. Wright Mills. Though mass society theory has subsequently been subjected to considerable criticism because of its often elitist disdain for popular culture, the themes stressed by Mills and Freire focus on the effects of the industrialization of popular culture and the manipulative uses of new technologies. Due to the effects of specialization, which cuts off a view of the whole and contributes to the manipulative uses of technology by elites,

> the rationality basic to science and technology disappears under the extraordinary effects of technology itself, and its place is taken by myth-making irrationalism. . . . Technology thus ceases to be perceived by men as one of the greatest expressions of their creative power and becomes instead a species of new divinity to which they create a cult of worship. (Freire, 1970a, p. 50).

Freire thus rejected from the outset any slavish imitation of given forms of "modernization" driven by the unregulated capitalist exploitation of technologies. Citing C. W. Mills' analysis of power elites, he concludes:

> Certainly we could not rely on the mere process of technological modernization to lead us from a naive to a critical consciousness. Indeed, an analysis of highly technological societies reveals the "domestication" of man's critical faculties by a situation in which he is massified and has only the illusion of choice. Excluded from the sphere of decisions made by fewer and fewer people, man is maneuvered by the mass media to the point where he believes nothing he has not heard on the radio, seen on television, or read in the newspapers. (Freire, 1973, p. 34)

Massification refers here to those technically mediated processes—in production, the media, bureaucracies—that may undermine individual autonomy, local traditions, and the formation of critical consciousness. But Freire is no Luddite enemy of technology or a dogmatic defender of traditions. Despite accepting the general thesis that "mass production as an organization of human labor is possibly one of the most potent instruments of man's massification," making him into a "passive, fearful, naive being," Freire concludes (citing the Left Catholic philosopher Emmanuel Mounier) that "the answer does not lie in rejection of the machine, but rather in the humanization of man" (Freire, 1973, p. 35).

A second aspect of Freire's analysis of social development concerns national *dependency*, a theme popularized as economic "dependency theory" in the 1960s but today also analyzed in cultural terms in postcolonial theory. Despite the limitations of traditional dependency theory, *the political, social, and cultural effects of dependency* remain central to critical theory despite the apparent absence—in the context of the current form of transnational capitalist globalization—of the economic alternative envisioned by protectionist, import-substitution models of economic growth. Hence, the *victims* of neoliberal government policies and transnational development strategies remain the focus of resistance and critique for critical theory, despite the absence of a credible economic model for "abolishing" the capitalist mode of production.

Writing in the 1960s, Freire found Brazilian democracy confronted by a contradictory situation. On the one hand, internal paternalistic cultural traditions were an obstacle to democratization. On the other, the external pressures for modernizing change were "mechanical" and "manipulative," undermining national autonomy: "The society in transformation is not the subject of its own transformation. . . . Hence, while all development is modernization, not all modernization is development (Freire, 1973, pp. 129–130).

The development of Brazilian democracy created acute cultural obstacles to a political culture capable of dialogue: "Our colonization, strongly predatory, was based on economic exploitation of the large landholding and on slave labor—at first, native, then African" (Freire, 1973, p. 21). The social distance created by great estates did not allow dialogue and "even the most humane relationships between masters and slave which prevailed on some estates produced not dialogue but paternalism, the patronizing attitude of an adult towards a child" (Freire, 1973, p. 24).

The problematic of postcolonial theory thus lies at the center of his theory of society. As he puts it, "What I defend and recommend is a radical breach with colonialism and an equally radical rejection of neo-colonialism" (Freire, 1994, p. 179). Citing Alberto Memmi, he notes that no individual or nation conquers without appropriating the other's language and discourse, resulting in the "neocolonial." Accordingly, "the fundamental theme of the Third World—implying a difficult but not impossible task for its people—is the conquest of its right to a voice, of the right to pronounce its word" (Freire, 1970a, p. 4). As a consequence, "the 'salvation' of the Third World by the director societies can only mean its domination, whereas in its legitimate aspiration to independence lies its utopian vision: to save the director societies in the very act of freeing itself" (Freire, 1970a, p. 20). Freire deploys his interpersonal, Hegelian-inflected dependency model, in short, at the level of North-South dialogue:

We must aim for an interdependence in which the one cannot be if the
other is not. . . . In reality, the imbalances between North and South—from
which results the domination of the latter and violence of the former, the
exaggerated power of the North and the exaggerated weakness of the
South—ends up affecting the North's interests and jeopardizing the advancement of global democracy. The master-slave relationship, regardless
of how colorful its disguise, dehumanizes the slave and the master. From
an ethical point of view, and as the radical importance of ethics only
grows, both the dominator and dominated are dehumanized. (Freire, 1996,
p. 180)

Habermas: Selective Modernization and a Bi-level Model of Society

In the present context, we can refer only in a sketchy way to the complex
set of arguments that Habermas has developed under the headings of
the analysis of the logic of crisis potentials in advanced capitalism. Central
to this approach is a bi-level model of society based on the distinction
between *system* and *lifeworld*, which requires systemic analysis of objective
structures such as markets and capital, along with understanding the
subjective world of everyday experience (Habermas, 1975, 1979, 1987b).
Our primary focus will be on the general theory of collective learning
that underlies his theory of social change, a conception that depends
strategically on the careful use of evolutionary models. Three themes will
organize our discussion: (1) how the distinction between two modes of
societal rationalization provides an evolutionary framework based on two
forms of learning; (2) how this approach allows extending the problematic
of crisis theory from the sphere of production to those of political administration and individual motivation; and (3) the broader implications of
this model for an account of the incompleteness of modernity and the
one-sided character of capitalist "modernization."

The point of departure for Habermas's theory of society is the distinction between two forms of rationalization: the rational-purposive or *instrumental rationality* associated with production and technology, as opposed
to the *substantial rationality* of social institutions and relations. Whereas
technical rationality is based on the efficiency of means to realize ends,
social rationality is concerned with the adequacy of ends, with values.
For Habermas the most fundamental value that should define social rationality is the reduction of domination through undistorted communication. The crucial thesis is that increases in technical rationality do not
necessarily enhance social rationality:

The development of the productive forces can be a potential for liberation
if and only if it does not replace rationalization at another level. *Rational-*

ization at the level of the institutional framework can occur only in the medium of symbolic interaction itself, that is, through removing *restrictions on communication*. . . . The growth of productive forces is not the same as the intention of the "good life." It can at best serve it. (Habermas, 1970a, pp. 118–119)

The distinction between the developmental logics of "instrumental" and "social" rationalization is crucial for understanding the three basic dimensions of evolutionary development: the economic, the political, and the sociocultural. The units of analysis for studying change are *social formations*, which are defined by the organizational principles—the social rationality—that underlie their use of technology. In contrast, classic evolutionism (whether Marxist or functionalist) forgets that technical advance is no guarantee of adequate cultural development (Habermas, 1975, pp. 12–13).

Habermas argues that instrumental rationalization and normative rationalization have followed evolutionary paths that can be understood as *collective learning processes* that have distinctive logics. Whereas the growth of productive forces is linked with "theoretical" insight, the growth of normative structures involves a "practical" logic. But these developments are not determined in advance: They "explain only the logically necessary sequence of *possible* developments. The *actual* developments, innovations and stagnations, occurrence of crises, productive or unproductive working out of crises, and so on can be explained only with the aid of empirical mechanisms" (Habermas, 1975, pp. 14–15).

The paradox of social evolution is that there is no direct link between learning related to the forces of production and normative learning. Though humans have an inherent capacity to learn in both dimensions, the tragedy of human history is that all past and present social formations have distorted the conditions of learning. As a consequence, for Habermas a theory of social domination is the key to explaining historical failures of "not-learning."

Second, applied to the diagnosis of contemporary societies, this approach entails a critique of classical Marxist economic crisis theory based on the contradiction between the working class and capital. Though class struggles have not disappeared, they have assumed a multidimensional form in advanced societies that requires, according to Habermas, a reconstructed model of society. From his perspective the key axis of the logic of struggle can be found in the opposition between the "system" (e.g., markets, bureaucracies) and the "lifeworld" (e.g., family and personal relations) as two levels of society.[12] On the one hand, the systemic rationalities of administrative power (as understood by Weber's theory of instrumental rationality) and money (as understood in terms of Marx's theory of commodification) have become increasingly autonomous and "uncoupled" from the lifeworld, thus invading or "colonizing" the lifeworlds of everyday experience. For example, the stress of the modern family stems in part from how the systemic requirements of economic survival (e.g., both parents working, commuting) tend to undermine the everyday social relations required for quality parenting and the formation of local communities. This account of domination takes into account both the effects of market relations (Marx) and those of technical rationalization (Weber). Furthermore, it points to how these systemic forms of rationalization (i.e., power, money) are characterized by "delinguistified media of communication" that "steer a social intercourse that has been largely disconnected from the norms of values" (Habermas, 1987b, p. 154). On the other hand, the concept of the lifeworld locates the everyday contexts within which the institutions of *civil society* (as opposed to governments) seek to defend diverse social groups from the incursions of systemic power and mobilize political alternatives (Cohen & Arato, 1992; Keane, 1988). Rather than locate the site of resistance in some abstract notion of a "universal" working class, this formulation points to the diversity of shared interests and bases of social rationality that have to be represented in order to challenge the autonomy of systemic power.

A strategic implication for the Left is a critique of welfare state "paternalism," a theme otherwise monopolized by right-wing ideologies. However well intended, attempts to use processes of "juridification"—the writing of laws—may result in a kind of "internal colonization" of the lifeworld: "The expression 'juridification' . . . refers quite generally to the tendency toward an increase in formal (or positive, written) law that can be observed in modern society" (Habermas, 1987b, p. 357). Drawing up the example of "four global waves" of juridification in the history of German education, he argues that the translation of social policy into legal measures may have ambiguous—even colonizing—effects related to the contradictions of administrative power. The dilemma stems from the way such measures (drawing on both administrative power and monetary coercion) have the effect of "guaranteeing freedom and taking it away," thus exacting "a noteworthy price in the form of restructuring interventions in the lifeworlds of those who are so entitled" by social legislation (Habermas, 1987b, p. 362). In this respect Habermas's critique of the disciplining effects of state intervention broadly parallels that of Michel Foucault.

But in his later work on law, Habermas softens this criticism by suggesting, "I no longer believe that juridification is an *inevitable* consequence of the welfare state" (Habermas, 1997a, p. 154). Nevertheless, he still maintains that the paternalistic extension of rights is problematic from the perspective of a proceduralist model of justice: "Private legal subjects cannot enjoy equal subjective freedoms if they fail, in their political role as co-legislators, to make use of their communicative freedoms by participating in public debates about how needs are to be interpreted" (Habermas, 1997a, pp. 154–155).

Third, this framework points to the "incompleteness" of modernity: Its "one-sided" conception of rationalization cannot take advantage of the full range of cultural possibilities opened up in the post-Enlightenment period. The resulting technical rationalization is one-sided or selective because technologies could have been introduced in ways different from those that happened to be chosen. Many of the negative results stem from inadequate democratic regulation of the colonizing effects of administrative power and commodification. A good example of these processes can be found in the chaotic history of urban development in the United States, resulting in inner-city ghettos and sprawling suburbs with little public transportation (Gottdiener, 1985). There are few grounds for describing this rather idiosyncratic historical outcome as a "model" (hence optimal) with respect to any universalizing notion of the "modern" as a value or the "rational" as the efficient deployment of technology for human purposes.

In short, Habermas's theory of rationality does not entail any uncritical defense of universalistic "reason" in the abstract. Instead, he proposes to differentiate various types of reason: how dominant forms of rationality have suppressed "alternative" modernities whose potential has been blocked by an "incomplete" process of rationalization. However much Habermas may be a defender of certain aspects of modernity, he is also an acute critic of Enlightenment and scientistic conceptions of rationality: "This discursive rationality, the 'unfulfilled potential' of modernity, is both the epistemological grounding for Critical Theory and, most important, the impetus behind the formation of emancipatory social movements" (Ray, 1993, p. xvi). Moreover, this diagnostic strategy can potentially be extended to contexts of dependency, underdevelopment, and globalization, where the one-sided character of technical modernization is further burdened by relations of intersocietal domination that further distort the application of technical rationality (Ray, 1993).

THE DOMINATED SUBJECT AND THE PUBLIC SPHERE

A key aspect of Freire's and Habermas's diagnoses of the present is how to conceive the consciousness and motivational character of the social subjects that are to advance the process of democratization. For Freire this issue is closely linked to a process of consciousness transformation required for overcoming "naive" consciousness in traditional societies. For Habermas, domination is linked in modernized societies to the "fragmentary" forms of consciousness that are unable to resist encroachments on the lifeworld.

Freire: Popular Culture and Naive Transitivity

Freire's approach to politics takes its point of departure from an analysis of the cultural implications of domination (hegemony). In particular he is concerned with the study of consciousness within the "culture of silence" of marginalized groups, which is seen as the outcome of "historical conditioning imposed by social relations of power (Freire, 1970a, p. 32).

Though Freire has been accused of neglecting politics and class in his earlier writings, it should not be forgotten that as early as 1965 he names the "violence" underlying relations of domination, a theme later popularized by Pierre Bourdieu as "symbolic violence" in education. In Freire's vocabulary, however, the term embraces both the "coercive" dimension of domination and its "symbolic" aspects:

> Every relationship of domination, of exploitation, of oppression, is by definition violent, whether or not the violence is expressed by drastic means. In such a relationship, a dominator and dominated alike are reduced to things—the former dehumanized by an excess of power, the latter by lack of it. And things cannot love. (Freire, 1973, pp. 10–11, n. 9)

The foundation of Freire's account of the relationship between social formations and social subjects is an analysis of dominated forms of consciousness based on a distinction among *semi-intransitive, natively transitive, and critical consciousness.* He begins with a characterization of a "naive" or "semi-intransitive" consciousness of the type associated with illiteracy and traditionalism. Only as people "amplify their power to perceive . . . and increase their capacity to enter into dialogue not only with other men but with their world" do they become "transitive" (Freire, 1973, p. 17). Given its "quasi-immersion" in everyday life and its "fatalism," semi-intransitive consciousness is incapable of objectifying reality "in order to know it in a critical way" (Freire, 1970a, p. 36). Instead, "lacking structural perspective," people "attribute the sources of such facts and situations in their lives either to some super-reality or to something within themselves; in either case to something outside objective reality" (Freire, 1970a, p. 36). Such consciousness is characteristic of "closed societies" with a rigid hierarchical social structure (Freire, 1970a, p. 35; 1973, pp. 21–31). With the appearance of "cracks" in this type of social order, and signs of a process of "transition," populist movements emerge but are characterized by a "naive transitive" consciousness that can be readily manipulated by authoritarian regimes, even though it marks a new form of democratic mobilization. In these circumstances, however, the persistence of semi-intransitive thinking means that a traditionalist magical form of thought is replaced by a populist one: "Modernization will proceed to mythologize technology. The myth of technology will replace the magical entities which formerly explained problematical situations" (Freire, 1970a, p. 37, n. 20).

Habermas: From the Decline of the Public Sphere to the Colonization of the Lifeworld

The problematic of democratic theory was at the heart of Habermas's early writings, which were concerned with erosion of democratic citizenship through the decline of the *public sphere* (Habermas, 1989c).[13] The significance of the public sphere problematic lies in its ability to suggest criteria for assessing the quality as well as the quantity of democratic participation. Nancy Fraser (1994) summarizes clearly this notion of the public sphere, a term that

> designates a theater in modern societies in which political participation is enacted through the medium of talk. It is the space in which citizens deliberate about their common affairs, hence, an institutionalized arena of discursive interaction. This arena is conceptually distinct from the state; it is a site for the production and circulation of discourses that can in principle be critical of the state. The public sphere in Habermas' sense is also conceptually distinct from the official economy; it is not an arena of market relations but rather one of discursive relations, a theater for debating and deliberating rather than for buying and selling. This concept of the public sphere permits us to keep in view the distinction between state apparatuses, economic markets, and democratic associations, distinctions that are essential to democratic theory. (pp. 82–83)

Habermas's argument is that despite the anticipations found in the ancient Greek polis, only from the mid-17th century onward did there emerge the notion of rational deliberation about public issues. Though the principles of democratic deliberation were institutionalized in the idea of parliamentary debate, the reality of 19th- and 20th-century social life prevented the full realization of democracy despite the gradual extension of universal suffrage. Whereas the emergence of mass politics in the 19th century succeeded in diverting new democratic participants from fully articulating their interests, the emergence of the culture industries of the mass media in the 20th century led to a spectacularization of political communication, where the advertising campaign became the primary means for political success. At the same time, political parties became increasingly enmeshed in existing relations of power, thus relating to "the public sphere as invaders from outside rather than operating from its center" (Habermas, 1997a, p. 137). Only a revitalization of civil society outside the formal institutions of the state and party politics holds any possibility for new forms of effective public participation.

Later work considered the sociocultural conditions under which the public sphere might be reactivated. In the early 1970s, Habermas (along with Claus Offe) developed a theory of *legitimation crisis* that hypothetically held out the possibility for new bases of radical democratization (Habermas, 1975; Offe, 1984). According to this formulation, the classic Marxist account of economic crisis had been displaced to the legitimating functions of the welfare state. Given the fiscal crisis of the welfare state, however, it faced a crisis of administrative rationality that created objective conditions under which new movements of resistance might emerge to demand radical economic reorganization. Furthermore, within the sphere of socialization, as evident in the student movements of the late 1960s, there had also emerged a crisis of "motivation" that created the social-psychological basis of resistance quite distinct from the older forms of economic class interest.

But the subsequent success of neoliberal efforts to challenge and downsize the welfare state falsified any optimistic reading of the legitimation crisis thesis. Instead of providing an impetus for radical democratic change, legitimation crises had instead precipitated a process of post-Fordist restructuring and resulted in neoliberal movements that have scaled down welfare state capitalism and delegitimated alternative strategies of change (Castells, 1996; Lash & Urry, 1987). These circumstances have pushed Habermas toward a significant reconceptualization of the new ways in which ideology—increasingly taking advantage of the fragmentary character of consciousness—works under the conditions of advanced capitalism. The concept of the colonization of the lifeworld by administrative power and money becomes the basis for understanding the specific processes of change under the conditions of advanced capitalism, culminating in an increasing "fragmentation of consciousness":

> Everyday consciousness sees itself thrown back on traditions whose claims to validity have already been suspended; where it does not escape the spell of traditionalism, it is hopelessly splintered. In place of "false consciousness" we today have a "fragmented consciousness" that blocks

enlightenment by the mechanism of reification. It is only with this that the conditions for a *colonization of the lifeworld* are met. When stripped of their ideological veils, the imperatives of autonomous subsystems make their way into the lifeworld from outside—like colonial masters coming into a tribal society—and force a process of assimilation upon it. The diffused perspective of the local culture cannot be sufficiently coordinated to permit the play of the metropolis and the world market to be grasped from the periphery. (Habermas, 1987b, p. 355)

DEMOCRATIZATION AND THE REVITALIZATION OF THE PUBLIC SPHERE

Beyond their general diagnosis of the tensions between capitalist, one-sided technical modernization and the forms of learning required for social rationalization, Freire and Habermas are also concerned with strategies for renewing the process of democratization. Whereas Freire develops his account primarily in terms of a model of cultural action and political struggle directed toward the Brazilian case of underdevelopment and dependency, Habermas's discussion is oriented toward a conception of democracy's relationship to the public sphere in advanced democratic, pluralistic societies.

Freire: Democracy, Domination, and Everyday Life

Freire's more specifically political writings are characterized by a distinctive combination of realism and optimism, an attitude that could best be described as a radically democratic "Gramscianism." Though Freire's pedagogy has been used over the years in diverse and contradictory ways in Latin America (Puiggrós, 1994), the most consistent version is that of a Gramsci adapted to the politics of democratic transition (Morrow & Torres, 2001). Three central themes guide his discussion: (1) the affirmation of democratization as the most fundamental basis of resistance to domination; (2) a very general account of the ideals of "revolutionary" leadership from the perspective of a dialogical theory of education; and (3) a critique of models of socialist leadership that are not based on understanding the politics of everyday life, the primacy of democracy, and the complex dynamics of social movements. Unlike Habermas, he does not make a sharp distinction between questions of organizing enlightenment as an educational activity and political struggle as strategic organization; yet he does acknowledge some of the difficulties of applying his pedagogical principles at the collective level of political struggle.

Throughout Freire's career, the problematic of democratization served as the primary frame of reference for political struggles against domination. This point is spelled out in his distinction between "dialogical" and "antidialogical" action. An important manifestation of antidialogical action was its use of paternalistic "humanitarianism" to sustain processes of social reproduction. In particular the strategy of "assistentialism"—a Latin American term for paternalistic welfare schemes—is employed as a strategy of social control and domination (Freire, 1970c, pp. 60–61). Further, the transformation of economic relations and administrative structures must be complemented by cultural action: "Revolution is always cultural, whether it be in the phase of denouncing an oppressive society and proclaiming the advent of a just society, or in the phase of the new society inaugurated by the revolution" (Freire, 1970a, p. 51).

In the context of the revolutionary movements of the early 1970s, Freire develops a second theme: an idealized model of "revolutionary" leadership based on dialogical principles. "What distinguishes revolutionary leaders from the dominant elite is not only their objectives, but their procedures"; they must "seek out true avenues of communion with them, ways of helping the people to help themselves critically perceive the reality which oppresses them" (Freire, 1970c, p. 166). These possibilities are discussed under the headings "cooperation," "unity for liberation," "organization," and "cultural synthesis."

The topic of cooperation suggests that the focus of leadership and the people should be on the "reality" that mediates their own relationship. Though there is a role for revolutionary leadership, it should be based on the I-thou principle identified by Buber in the form of "co-Subjects": "Dialogue does not impose, does not manipulate, does not domesticate, does not 'sloganize'" (Freire, 1970c). Yet he warns leaders that the required mutual trust and confidence should not be naive: "As long as the oppressor 'within' the oppressed is stronger than they themselves are, their natural fear of freedom may lead them to denounce the revolutionary leaders instead" (Freire, 1970c, p. 169). Guevara is taken as a model of such revolutionary leadership based on dialogical theory: "*Communion* in men elicits *cooperation*, which brings leaders and people in the *fusion* described by Guevara. This fusion can exist only if revolutionary action is really *human*, empathetic, loving, communicative, and humble, in order to be liberating" (Freire, 1970c, p. 171).

Under the heading "unity for liberation," Freire resists the suggestion that the goal of dialogical action is to simply shift "the oppressed from a mythological reality in order to 'bind' them to another reality" because the "consciousness of being an oppressed class must be preceded (or at least accompanied) by achieving consciousness of being oppressed individuals" (Freire, 1970c, p. 174). Sloganizing and propaganda cannot provide authentic class unity, something more than a mechanistic juxtaposition of individuals, because "the unity of the oppressed occurs at the human level, not at the level of things" (Freire, 1970c, p. 175). Only cultural action can achieve this objective.

At the level of organization it is argued that "in the dialogical theory of action the organization of the people presents the antagonistic opposite of this manipulation" through exemplary actions involving "witness emerging from cooperation in a shared effort" (Freire, 1970c, p. 176). On the one hand, such witnessing needs to be both fully contextual and to express general "essential elements of witness," "leading both the witnesses and the ones receiving that witness to increasing action; *courage to love* . . . and *faith* in the people, since it is to them that witness is made" (Freire, 1970c, p. 177).

Finally, cultural action as a "cultural synthesis" is viewed as Janusfaced: It "either serves domination (consciously or unconsciously) or it serves the liberation of men" when it is oriented toward a cultural synthesis that facilies a structure to "become" that which is possible through surmounting its contradictions (Freire, 1970c, pp. 180–181). At the same time, however, such synthesis cannot be limited by revolutionary leadership to these local aspirations: "Neither invasion by the leaders of the people's world view nor mere adaptation by the leaders to the (often naive) aspirations of the people is acceptable" (Freire, 1970c, p. 184).

A third theme reflects the shift of the focus in Freire's later work to the more pragmatic concerns of democratic organization in political parties and social movements. Without making any reference to his problematic use in the late 1960s and early 1970s of "exemplary" revolutionary leaders such as Guevara and Castro, Freire has confronted indirectly an implicit disillusionment with the outcomes of that epoch: "The mistake of the Left, or a sector of the Left, today and yesterday, has been the desire for authoritarianism, a by-product of the Left's dislike for democracy," a problem resulting from its antihistorical, inflexible, fatalistic conception of history (Freire, 1996, p. 84).

As part of the general shift of the Latin American left, but grounded in his theory of cultural action, Freire has shifted his discussion away from "revolution" toward the theme of democratic organization (Castañeda, 1993). When democracy is not merely a strategic weapon, "leftist parties must become truly pedagogical instruments" (Freire, 1997b, p. 52), thus drawing on a sense of humility to offset the older pretensions of certainty "as the final word, one who defines and enlightens" (Freire, 1997b, p. 78).

In this spirit, following his return from exile in 1980, Freire for the first time accepted an explicit party affiliation by working for the *Partido dos Trabalhadores*, or Workers Party. For this new democratic practice it was necessary, beyond theory, to pay attention and listen to the popular culture that inhabits the favelas, that walks in the streets: "To be wet by reality" was necessary to understand the different rationalities at play. Nevertheless, the challenge of "forging the unity between democracy and socialism" is merely "hope of utopia and not fate. The future is a problem, a possibility, and not inexorable" (Freire, 1996, p. 137)

Habermas: Deliberative Democracy

Whereas Freire has been preoccupied with the process of democratic transition in Latin America, Habermas's concerns have focused on the less dynamic situation of advanced societies. Above all, his analysis provides a fundamental challenge to the models of class struggle that have defined the tradition of Western Marxism and related socialist projects. Four concerns of Habermas can be used to illustrate the basis of his diagnosis: (1) the suggestion that the changed role of work in society has facilitated the exhaustion of traditional forms of utopian energies in advanced societies; (2) how the integration of the state and the economy under capitalism has assumed a form that calls into question the classic socialist project of abolishing capitalism by seizing control of the state; (3) a theory of law that might envision and faciliate the conditions under which radical democratization might advance under the conditions of complex, plural societies; and (4) the resulting need to rethink the democratic public sphere, which—by way of an internal, immanent critique—confronts the reality of liberal democracy with its initial promise.

Habermas's point of departure for the reconstruction of socialist theory is that there has been a decline of "utopian energies" related to the traditional working class. At the same time this has called into question two of the "illusions" of leftist thought and the self-understanding of modernity. On the one hand, it was assumed that work provided a smooth link among economic production, happiness, and emancipation. In the process, images of the good life become part of "a deceptive symbiosis with the rational domination of nature" (Habermas, 1989a, p. 299). On the other hand, it is no longer credible to imagine the future in terms of concrete ideological projections, a singular conception of the good life; all that can be anticipated normatively is the general communicative conditions necessary to "put participants *themselves* in a position to realize concrete possibilities for a better and less threatened life, on *their own initiative* and in accordance with *their own* needs and insights" (p. 199).

Second, Habermas has also become convinced that the complexity of the differentiation of modern societies makes the prospect of classical socialist planning problematic, that is, that such a transformation cannot take place "without damage to their proper system logic and therewith their ability to function. The abysmal collapse of state socialism has only confirmed this" (Habermas, 1992b, p. 444). Instead, "radical democratization" can now be conceived only *defensively* in order to "erect a democratic dam against the colonializing *encroachment* of system imperatives on areas of the lifeworld" (Habermas, 1992b, p. 444).

Third, the bi-level model of the opposition between system and life-world is used in two somewhat different ways to envision the conditions under which radical democratization might make headway. In the case of the defensive "siege" model developed in the context of the theory of communicative action, new social movements are viewed as forces that can challenge the colonization of the lifeworld by administrative power and money. But the possibilities here are viewed as involving primarily a defense of the lifeworld, rather than any intention of actually seizing power. From this perspective the tasks of an environmental movement or party would not be to govern society but to reform state power. As Habermas has noted, "My purpose in proposing the image of a 'siege' of the bureaucratic power of public administration by citizens making use of communicative power was to oppose the classic idea of revolution—the conquest and the destruction of state power" (Habermas, 1997a, p. 135). From this perspective, the public uses of reason "can become effective only if they affect administrative power—so as to program and control it—without intending to take it over" (p. 135).

On the other hand, from the later perspective of his theory of law (Habermas, 1996), the siege model appears "too defeatist" in that it did not take seriously enough the ways in which public administration is dependent on forms of law that also need to be challenged. The alternative "sluice" model is based on a center-and-periphery relation through which citizens can influence the center (i.e., legislatures, courts, public administration). Citizen participation must pass from periphery to center through the "sluices" of communicative processes organized according to the principles of deliberative democracy that affect the basic principles of law. In other words, not only the administrative "application" of law is at stake, but also its "grounding." For example, the task of environmental law would not be merely to regulate corporate actions, but to redefine the legal status of nature itself: "In this respect, the sluice model counts on a more far-reaching democratization than the siege model does" (Habermas, 1997a, p. 136).

Finally, the preceding and other considerations create a new context for rethinking Habermas's earlier account of the public sphere. In using the benchmark of the procedural rationality of political debate, he sought to ground criteria for evaluating the illusory aspects of contemporary psuedo-consensus built on the manipulative strategies of states. This overtly pessimistic critique also had a constructive side involving a "'proceduralization' of the Rousseauean conception of popular sovereignty in which the notion of a localized sovereign body is replaced with that of an anonymous network of communication processes comprised of autonomous associations, independent of the mass media, and other institutions of the public sphere" (Baynes, 1992, p. 180). Despite its weaknesses relating to gender and the inevitability of conflict, Habermas's early formulation of the public sphere problematic has stimulated a remarkable literature on deliberative democracy, which we can only allude to here (Benhabib, 1996b; Bohman, 1996b; McAfee, 2000).

COMPARATIVE DISCUSSION: THE CRITIQUE OF ONE-SIDED MODERNIZATION

This chapter has been organized around three comparative themes:

- A *crisis theory of society and development* based on a reconstruction of historical materialism that gives primacy to the rationalization of normative structures over those of technical rationalization (Habermas), as well as reiterating the specific effects of such one-sided technical "modernization" on dependent societies (Freire).
- A *theory of the dominated democratic subject*, understood in terms of the forms of populist irrationality that confront democratic transition in relatively underdeveloped contexts (Freire), as well as the more general decline of the democratic public sphere, a process further complicated by the forms of fragmented consciousness generated by the colonization of the lifeworld by administrative power and market relations (Habermas).
- A *model of fundamental, radical democratization* based on a critique of traditional socialist models of leadership that fail to give priority to democratization (Freire), as well as an analysis of the communicative preconditions of a radical democratization that might challenge both systemic rationalization and the grounds of law (Habermas).

Crisis Theory: Two Forms of Rationalization

With respect to a crisis theory of society, Freire's remarks are limited to a rudimentary account of a radical version of mass society theory coupled with a Latin American dependency model that serves as a critique of modernization. For Habermas, the point of departure is a reconstruction of historical materialism that analyzes collective sociocultural learning processes as the crucial basis of evolutionary transitions. Both of these basic strategies call into question economistic models of development and point to the potential cultural bases of forms of "modernization" that might avoid the pitfalls of one-sided or selective modernization. In both bases the resulting critiques of development depend on a *differentiated conception of rationality* that can be used to evaluate the distinctive problems of economic, political, and sociocultural rationalization.

Freire's concern with Brazil as a dependent society (in the sense of dependency theory) has its roots, of course, in the imperial *colonization* of the New World that represents a way of analyzing domination in macro-sociological terms that parallel the micro-sociological focus of domination in interpersonal relations. It is not by accident that Habermas eventually re-deployed the concept of colonization for the purpose of analyzing the *colonization of the lifeworld* through instrumental rationality and commodification to identify emergent features of advanced capitalism. In both cases a central concern is the problematic of an alternative understanding of *rationality*. For Freire this suggests the cultivation of forms of critical consciousness that avoid the negative effects of both traditionalism and massification; for Habermas, it implies forms of undistorted communication capable of providing resistance within the lifeworld. Once again, the logic of convergence between critical pedagogy and critical theory becomes apparent. Though Habermas does not directly discuss issues of underdevelopment, his analysis of one-sided modernization can be expanded to understand the specific forms of the colonization of the lifeworld that have emerged in peripheral and dependent societies. Though Habermas's thesis regarding the unfulfilled potential of the modern has been directed against the postmodernists, it is even more crucial for peripheral societies that have yet to benefit from the promise of "modernity": "questions of fundamental rights, access to control of resources, social justice, management of anonymous social interactions, inequalities of power and money, and above all the creation of conditions for social differentiation and political pluralization" (Ray, 1993, pp. 177–179).

In sum, our focus has been on ways in which each author is preoccupied with the diverse outcomes of modernity. For Freire the primary concern is with strategies of "modernization" uncoupled from democratization and fundamental social reform. For Habermas the central concern—from the perspective of an enlarged and more differentiated conception of rationality—is with the *selectivity* of processes of rationalization that are otherwise treated as natural and inevitable.

The Dominated Democratic Subject

The societal diagnoses of Freire and Habermas also involve an account of the forms of deformed consciousness that serve as the primary obstacle to the formation of new forms of thought and action. Freire's account of the semi-intransitive and naive transitive consciousness in dependent Latin American societies converges with Habermas's diagnosis of fragmented consciousness under conditions of advanced capitalism. In both cases one-sided modernization through capitalist expansion and technical rationalization have the effect of disturbing traditional orders without providing alternative ways to resist or redirect these processes. For both the colonization of the lifeworld blocks the possibilities of transformative change. For Freire such colonization in Brazil operates both at the level of international relations of dependency and internally in relation to processes of massification and internal colonization of regions and social classes. For Habermas, the general logic of colonization is elaborated through the differentiation of administrative power and money as distinctive bases of control that are uncoupled from normative reflection and democratic dialogue. Even in the apparently constructive case of social welfare legislation, processes of juridification may create paternal relations that immobilize those who are the supposed beneficiaries. Similarly, Freire has criticized Latin American bureaucratic "assistentialism," which undermines participation and dialogue (Freire, 1973, p. 15). Though Freire's criticism is directed to the more blatant case of using welfare as a palliative to avert confronting major social contradictions, Habermas points to how even the most sophisticated legal procedures may have similar antidialogical effects, reaffirming the Freirean principle that freedom cannot be granted as a "gift."

Radical Democratization: Global Perspectives

How is the relationship between technical and social rationalization to be redirected given the processes constraining the formation of democratic citizens? For Freire and Habermas, radical democratization provides the only conceivable medium of transformation as a form of educational experience. For Freire these circumstances define a kind of uncertainty: "A progressive, postmodernist requirement is that we not be too certain of our certainties, that we operate contrary to the exaggerated certainties of modernity" (Freire, 1996, p. 4). For Habermas, with the exhaustion of the classical revolutionary model, "both *revolutionary self-confidence* and *theoretical self-certainty* are gone, and not only because in the meantime bureaucratic socialism has turned out to be a worse variant of what was to be fought against" (Habermas, 1982, p. 222).

Though Freire was concerned in the late 1960s and early 1970s with the possibility of a revolutionary transition, the most fundamental theme of his thought is the question of *fundamental democratization* (a term he borrows from Mannheim). Even the question of leader/mass relations is interpreted primarily in terms of the necessity of a democratic relationship that fosters mutual learning between leaders and a revolutionary movement. In his later writings this theme is reiterated in the context of the democratization of Brazil, the need for an effective democratic socialist movement, and the complementary tasks of educational reform as part of fostering democratic citizenship.

In the case of Habermas, his concern with the exhaustion of utopian aspirations in advanced societies contrasts sharply with the conditions of Brazil and Latin America. Further, Habermas is more Weberian in his sense of the tensions between the organization of enlightenment as an educational process and political struggle as requiring the priority of strategic imperatives. Habermas's account provides a theoretical basis for understanding the failure of revolutionary leaders to live up to Freire's somewhat romantic vision of "communion with the people."

For both authors the decisive problematic for modern societies is the creation of forms of *democratization* that might reshape the relations among power, technology, and culture without necessarily abolishing capitalism. Freire refers to the example of Mannheim's concept of "fundamental democratization," which envisioned that "through collective deliberation, and in which re-evaluations should be based upon intellectual insight and consent, a completely new system of education would be necessary" (Mannheim, cited in Freire, 1973, p. 33).

Though rarely referring to Mannheim otherwise, Habermas has made a similar appeal to Mannheim's concept, though linking it to the student movement of the late 1960s and his own concept of the democratic "public sphere" (Habermas, 1992a, p. 234). Habermas has not devoted specific, detailed attention to the reorganization of relations between civil society and existing party politics that is presupposed by the revitalization of public spheres. Yet he does call for forms of "institutional imagination" that might create a "media charter" that could, for example, provide public resources for marginalized groups to express themselves publicly or to political strategies that might facilitate citizen initiatives outside of traditional party frameworks (Habermas, 1997a, pp. 76, 137). But as he stresses, any generation of public spheres can be only indirectly facilitated, not directly legislated as imagined by traditional socialism (Habermas, 1997a, p. 76). Moreover, at one point he has suggested that in advanced capitalism changing the educational system "might possibly be more important for the organization of enlightenment than the ineffectual training of cadres or the building of impotent parties. With this I only wish to state that these are empirical questions which must not be prejudged" (Habermas, 1973, pp. 31–32)

Despite his focus on issues in advanced societies, Habermas has more recently argued for a global perspective that can analyze both the "achievements and limits of the nation-state," especially in relation to the notion of a revival of the Kantian notion of "perpetual peace" in relation to a "cosmopolitan" democracy (Habermas, 1998a, pp. 105–236; Held, 1995). On the one hand, there is an increasing need to develop a capacity to act on a "supranational basis," a process that makes the world ever more "postnational" (Habermas, 2001a). Only on this basis is it possible to imagine dealing with the "problems of a long overdue reorganization of world economic relationships" (Habermas, 1997a, p. 141). At this global level, "a situation that existed at the beginning of the European worker's movement is repeating itself; then the masses rose up against the domination of the bourgeoisie, but now it is occurring on a worldwide basis and with a different portent. However, the masses from the impoverished regions of the world lack effective sanctions against the North: they cannot go on strike; at most, they can 'threaten' with waves of immigration" (Habermas, 1997a, p. 63). On the other hand, the social integrative achievements of nation-states in creating a multicultural sense of solidarity and mutual responsibility also serve as our primary model for a global community: "From the conflict-ridden and painful processes of making the transition to a multicultural society emerges a form of social integration that already points beyond the nation-state: The formation of nations is repeated on a more abstract level: the structures of political decision making acquire a new cultural substrate (Habermas, 1997a, p. 175). Above all, the creation of a global community requires social movements and nongovernmental organizations that transcend national frontiers in the hope that market globalization can be countered by a political counter-mobilization deriving from a "universal civil solidarity" (*Weltbürgerliche Solidarität*) (Habermas, 1998b, p. 10). Whereas citizenship claims are limited by state sovereignty, the universalizing discourse of human rights has "opened up a space for a cosmopolitan public sphere" (Yeatman, 2000, p. 1499).

In short, for both Habermas and Freire the institutionalization of critical discourses—public spheres—both within nation-states and globally is viewed as a necessary condition of progressive change, even though such strategies run the risk of co-optation and failure. But on this point Freire is adamant: "The choice is between doing nothing in order not to be co-opted, or doing something in order to be an object of co-optation. I prefer to be an object of co-optation" (Horton & Freire, 1990, p. 206). For Freire as well as Habermas, in short, democracy is "the real 'unfinished project of modernity'"(Bohman, 1996a, p. 211).

To deal with these societal issues in terms of their implications for theories of the subject, we turn in the next chapter to Freire and Habermas's efforts to ground the conditions of possibility of transformation in a developmental account of the human subject—a critical social psychology.

5

From Philosophical Anthropology to Critical Social Psychology

The Concrete and the Universal Other

Problem-posing education affirms men as beings in the process of *becoming*—as unfinished, uncompleted beings. . . . As we attempt to analyze dialogue as a human phenomenon, we discover something which is the essence of dialogue itself: *the word*.

—Freire, 1970c, pp. 72, 75

The decisive innovation . . . was made through a turn to the pragmatics of language, a turn that concedes primacy to world-disclosing language—as the medium for the possibility . . . for social cooperation, and for self-controlled learning processes. . . . This frees up the basic concepts needed to capture an intuition that has long been enunciated in religious speech. From the structure of language comes the explanation of why the human spirit is condemned to an odyssey.

—Habermas, 1992c, pp. 153

The preceding two chapters outlined the broadly convergent metatheory of the human sciences shared by Freire and Habermas, as well as the theory of society and historical crisis suggested by this conception of critical social theory. In this chapter we will turn to a crucial context for applying this framework of social knowledge: their respective conceptions of social action, or what we will be describing as a *critical social psychology*. The specific way in which they address these issues is closely linked with their preoccupation with the *normative foundations* of critical social theory. Our central theme will be that the outcome is *a critical social psychology of the developmental subject* that links empirical and normative claims in a manner anticipated in, but insufficiently developed by, the classic Marxian theory of praxis and alienation. Their general argument is that given the philosophically plausible and partly empirically demonstrable, innate developmental potentials of human beings, certain concrete (situated) and universal ethical-moral imperatives to overcome historical relations of domination become evident.

DEVELOPMENTAL ANTHROPOLOGY TO
CRITICAL SOCIAL PSYCHOLOGY

Some comment is required to explain the implications of the relationship between *critical pedagogy* and a *critical social psychology* based on a conception of the subject that is simultaneously *historical, dialogical, and developmental*. Though largely absent in introductory texts in psychology and social psychology, the interdisciplinary tradition of a "critical social psychology" or a "critical psychology" is now well developed, overlapping with but not identical to social constructionism (e.g., Boer, 1983; Fox & Prilleltensky, 1997; Ibáñez, 1994; Sullivan, 1990; Wexler, 1983). A related tradition is the "dialectical" and "critical psychology" that builds on Piaget's developmental psychology and genetic structuralism (Furth, 1996; Piaget, 1995), though criticizing aspects of its formalism, failure to analyze adult thinking, and the need to address more effectively interactionist and sociohistorical questions (Basseches, 1984; Broughton, 1987; Buck-Morss, 1980; Buss, 1979; Riegel, 1979). We prefer the more inclusive term *critical social psychology* because it clearly labels the concerns that have long been part of the Frankfurt Critical Theory tradition from the work of Fromm and Adorno to contemporary work (Langman & Kaplan, 1981; Strien, 1982; Wexler, 1983).

These concerns were originally addressed from the 18th century onward in terms of theories of human nature, or in the specific context of European philosophy, concerns with *philosophical anthropology* (Honneth & Joas, 1988). Whereas social and cultural anthropology as an empirical discipline was primarily concerned with the analysis and description of cultural differences, philosophical anthropology involved reflection on the constants and uniformities of the human species. Given their strong Eurocentric and masculine biases, such inquiries typically suffered from an *essentialist* conception of human nature.

Our *historical* conception of the subject takes its point of departure from the thesis of constructivism, but takes cognizance of the constraints of both the deep structures of communication and developmental potentials. On the one hand, the origin of selfhood in intersubjective communication implies a *dialogical subject* whose actions cannot be reduced to individualistic self-interest. Dialogical approaches build on the communicative, interactional models developed in diverse ways in Wittgenstein's theory of

language-games, the symbolic interactionist approach in American pragmatism, and dialogical reinterpretations of Kant, Hegel, and Marx (Bakhtin, 1981; Sampson, 1993). On the other hand, the theme of a *developmental
subject* relates back to the naturalistic metaphor of growth that has been
a part of Western thought from Aristotle through Hegel, Piaget, and
Dewey.

The dialogical and developmental character of self-formation and
identity broadly limits the relativistic implications of constructivism (Hoover, Marcia, & Parris, 1997). Relativist conceptions of the social constructionism and related postmodernist critiques of "humanism" stress how
"arbitrary" constructions of particular groups are imposed on "others"
as "natural." But this deconstruction of imposed identities (a concern
shared by critical theory's conception of domination) must be complemented by a critical developmental approach that provides ethical reference points for shared human possibilities. Such a critical developmental
theory, however, also must be sensitive to the Eurocentric and gender
bias within the developmental tradition (Buck-Morss, 1987; Burman,
1994), hence responsive to the more legitimate postmodernist critiques
(Chandler, 1997). Nonetheless, these problems have not precluded devis-
ing a "human development index" as a framework for comparative evalu-
ations of nation-states on a global scale (United Nations Development
Programme [UNDP], 2000).

BEYOND PIAGET AND FREUD

A distinctive feature of the critical social psychology shared by Freire
and Habermas is that the possibilities for individual development are
prefigured in the form of species-specific potentials and yet achieved only
through processes of moral struggle. These dual dimensions are reflected
respectively in Piaget and Freud as paradigmatic points of departure
(Honneth, 1991, pp. xxix–xxx). Whereas the Freudian model focuses on
the depth-psychological obstacles to self-reflection, Piaget's elucidates
how emancipation is propelled by socially conditioned stages of cognitive
and moral development. Following Piaget, both Freire and Habermas
postulate a positive developmental trajectory based on the unfolding of
human competencies. Though accepting the general cognitive developmental perspective of the Piagetian tradition, they also argue that the
model should be extended to adulthood, thus requiring a form of critical
consciousness based on the dialectical operations that lie beyond the
formal operations of natural scientific reasoning. Though Piaget touches
on such issues in his sociological writings influenced by the French sociolo-

gist Durkheim, they are never systematically incorporated into his theory of development (Piaget, 1995).

Following a historicized version of Freud, Freire and Habermas are also aware of the obstacles and negative (irrational, distorting, regressive) dimensions linked to both inherent intrapsychic conflicts and historically contingent relations of domination. Though psychic conflict is necessary for human development, the structure of society remains a crucial determinant in whether those conflicts have productive or destructive outcomes. Consequently they reject classic Freudian theory, which postulated a tragic relationship between "civilization" and "repression," suggesting that liberation from repression was an illusion; instead, they share the relatively (though not naively) optimistic assumption that social emancipation (from both oppression and the commodification of need and desire) might be reconciled with lower levels of psychological repression.

Freire's critical developmental psychology is elaborated informally by invoking the philosophical problematic of humanization as an ontological vocation, the empirical (and structuralist) theme of cognitive and moral development described by Piaget and Vygotsky, and the theory of praxis as critical consciousness developed by Hegel and Marx. Habermas follows a parallel but more systematic strategy based on the identification of "reconstructive sciences," that is, disciplines such as linguistics and development psychology that attempt to reconstruct universal, species-specific capacities.[14]

A key contribution of a critical developmental psychology is that it provides a universalistic framework for linking empirical and value questions—or what "is" and what "ought to be." In this respect the empirically derived concept of human competence is radicalized through its intimate relation to the justification of general moral principles. To use a simple example: If a feral child presumably "socialized" outside a human community cannot develop adequate linguistic competence (an empirical claim), then it follows that this child was in universally important respects "abused"' (a normative judgment). As we will see, the critical social psychologies of both Freire (implicitly) and Habermas (explicitly) assume this logical and methodological form. If human beings have certain innate potentials, and a given form of society systematically inhibits their realization, then this factual characteristic logically entails a negative value judgment.

THEORIZING A CRITICAL SOCIAL PSYCHOLOGY

The critical developmental perspectives of Freire and Habermas can be compared in terms of five themes, which are taken up in the next section:

1. *The dialogical presupposition*: A grounding of social life in terms of a phenomenology and pragmatics of intersubjectivity understood in dialogical terms.
2. *The reconstruction of developmental potentials*: An account of universal, species-specific processes of developmental potential.
3. *The analysis of the distorting effects of unequal power*: A theory of the domination that analyzes the social processes that inhibit or facilitate the realization of developmental possibilities.
4. *The possibility of emancipatory self-reflection*: Conceptions of thresholds of critical consciousness that define the emancipatory concerns with autonomy that define modernity.
5. *The necessity of a moral point of view*: The justification of a universal (discourse) and concrete ethics.

The first four themes will be considered in the following section, concerned with the critical social psychologies, respectively, of Freire and Habermas; the final will be taken up in a concluding section, which focuses more explicitly on the ethical implications.

Freire: Humanization Versus Dehumanization

One of the distinctive characteristics of Freire's critical pedagogy—and one most frustrating for his critics—is the peculiar mixture of empirical claims about the nature of learning and normative claims about human values to be realized through this pedagogy: "The pedagogical, the anthropological and the political is the conceptual nucleus of the point of departures of Freire's reflections" (Torres, 1978b, p. 61) and the result is "not a general pedagogy, rather the pedagogy of the oppressed" (1978b, p. 63). The most appropriate way to sort out these claims is to situate Freire's approach as a form of critical social psychology. In the process, his contributions are neither left exclusively to education nor overextended as a self-sufficient general philosophical system. In other words, the problematic of humanization as a vocation should be read not in essentializing metaphysical terms, but as a historical challenge made empirically plausible by developmental psychology.

The critical social psychology underlying Freire's project can be reconstructed in terms of: (1) a phenomenology of subject-subject communication as the basis of everyday life; (2) a general process of humanization grounded in a theory of human development; (3) a phenomenology of oppression as a process of domination based on violence and sustained through antidialogical action; (4) a three-phase developmental model of consciousness for overcoming domination; and (5) a critical pedagogy oriented toward conscientization as a process of liberation. The first four themes will be discussed now, and the final one in the second section of this chapter.

The Dialogical Subject. Selfhood is not an independent entity but the ongoing outcome of dialogue with others. As noted in the previous chapter, the ontological foundation of Freire's theory of action is the subject-subject dialogical situation. Consequently, his conception of praxis is not based on an individualistic philosophy of consciousness, as opposed to an interactive and intersubjective account of communication. As previously noted, the sources of this basic position are diverse (i.e., Hegel, Marx, phenomenology, existentialism), reflecting a synthesis that underlies his conception of praxis (Torres, 1995a, pp. 7–27).

Humanization as Incompletion. Humanization is not a teleological outcome, but an open-ended process. For reasons that are rooted in his processual methodology, Freire does not have much to say about the specific content of humanization. The notion of an "ontological vocation" is not rooted in a fixed, metaphysical essence as portrayed by the philosophical anthropologist; rather, humanization is envisioned as a creative struggle for freedom through which people may regain their humanity and take responsibility for it in specific contexts of dialogue because the "understanding of history as possibility defeats determinist understandings, overcoming the notion of the inexorable future and problematizing it" (Freire, 1996, p. 111).

Yet this struggle for freedom is not arbitrary, nor does it occur in a biological vacuum. Social theory must assume a conception of human nature, though "understood to be socially and historically constituted . . . taking place in history, rather than prior to history. I cannot think about the issue of liberation, and all that it implies, without thinking about human nature" (Freire, 1997b, p. 87). And it is structuralist developmental theory that provides a framework for linking history, learning, and liberation: "The present studies in sociolinguistics and psycholinguistics as well as the contributions of Piaget, Vygotsky, Luria, Emília Ferrero, Madalena Weffort, and Magda Soares, can, if well applied, rectify and improve some of my propositions" (Freire, 1996, p. 129). Though Freire's comments here are hypothetical, Habermas provides a more systematic strategy for linking developmental and critical theory.

Domination, Violence, and Anti-dialogical Action: The Culture of Silence. If dehumanization is the antithesis of freedom and humanization, then the *culture of silence* is the state of being within which dominated subjects attempt to act. Speaking of the culture of silence thus allows Freire to identify some of the key problems of learning under conditions of dependency and fear (Freire, 1970c, p. 133ff.). In the extreme form of abject oppression, "to exist is only to live. The body carries out orders from above. Thinking is difficult, speaking the word, forgotten" (Freire, 1970a, p. 22).

But these relations of domination exercise a power that goes beyond purely cognitive manipulation: They penetrate to the identity of the dependent subject, thus rendering liberation all the more difficult. Here influenced by the work of Erich Fromm, Freire draws selectively on Freudian depth-psychological assumptions about the relationship between aggression and repression, though in a historically contextualized manner. Paradoxically, the victims of aggression tend to become self-destructive (or mutually destructive), rather than reacting violently to their oppressors. This Freudian theme adds a depth-psychological dimension to alienation as understood in Marx and Hegel and greatly complicates any process of transformation. Oppression is not simply an external act of coercion, but is internalized in the form a servile consciousness.

This servile consciousness, which grows out of the effects of dependency as mediated by defense mechanisms, is expressed in self-destructive psychological tendencies: fatalism, horizontal violence, love of the oppressor, self-depreciation, lack of confidence, and emotional dependence (Freire, 1970c, pp. 47–51). In addition, this culture of silence is reinforced through the active use of *antidialogical actions* on the part of the dominant groups, which use various manipulative strategies to preserve their cultural hegemony and domination.

Freire's psychoanalytic argument with respect to the origins of the social character of oppressors (including revolutionary leadership) draws on Erich Fromm's approach to the question of the "authoritarian personality." The distinction between the "necrophilic" (death-oriented) and "biophilic" (life-oriented) forms of social character is used as an explanation for the psychological appeal of antidialogical strategies of control and manipulation. Though the Left is capable of necrophilic action in the form of revolutionary bureaucratization, the Right is the primary target of analysis (Freire, 1970a, p. 44). Freire attempts to explain the origins of antidialogical action within the structures of socialization—child-rearing practices and educational institutions: "The homes and schools . . . function largely as agencies which prepare the invaders of the future" (Freire, 1970c, p. 152).

Stages of Consciousness. Though he sketches it in rudimentary terms, Freire offers a basic sociohistorical three-stage model of individual development culminating in dialectical thought (Freire, 1970c, pp. 36ff.; 1973, pp. 17ff.). This schema is designed to characterize different possibilities for adults, though it also has implications for a model of development from childhood through adolescence. At one level, this could be read as a type of "false consciousness" theory, but this would be potentially misleading. Freire's claim is not directly epistemological (about what is true knowledge or consciousness), but rather processual: an account of distorted communication between agents and the social reality. Characteristically, Freire uses grammatical metaphors—the passivity of intransitive verbs versus the active orientation of transitive ones—to convey different types of relations between subjects and the world. The model is based on a continuum: At one extreme is found relatively "intransitive" consciousness that lives passively within a given reality, and at the other, the active "transitive" consciousness that engages the world cognitively and politically.

Three stages make up this continuum. The first stage is that of the *semi-intransitive* magical consciousness of the type characteristic of a traditional peasantry where people "cannot apprehend problems situated outside their sphere of biological necessity. Their interests center almost totally around survival, and they lack a sense of life on a more historic plane" (Freire, 1973, p. 17).

In contrast, secondly, *naive transitive* consciousness, characteristic of a modernizing society in transition, involves a greater capacity to engage other people and the world with a historical consciousness. Negatively, however, this consciousness—associated with "populism" in Latin America—is limited by an oversimplification of problems and a vulnerability to sectarian irrationality and fanaticism characteristic of a "mass society." The "illogicality" of primitivism has been supplanted by the mythical qualities of distorted reason, "the fanaticized consciousness" engendered by the manipulative politics of populist mass mobilization (Freire, 1973, p. 20).

The third stage, *critical transitive consciousness*, however, points to the developmental logic of humanization—a movement toward reflexivity. He describes critical consciousness in terms that closely resemble more recent efforts to extend and revise Piaget's and other developmental categories to encompass adult thinking (e.g., Basseches, 1984):

> The critically transitive consciousness is characterized by depth in the interpretation of problems; by the substitution of causal principles for magical explanations; by the testing of one's "findings" and by openness to revisions; by the attempt to avoid distortion when perceiving problems and to avoid preconceived notions when analyzing them; by refusing to transfer responsibility; by rejecting passive positions; by soundness of argumentation; by the practice of dialogue rather than polemics; by receptivity to

the new for reasons beyond mere novelty and by the good sense not to reject the old just because it is old—by accepting what is valid in both old
and new. (Freire, 1973, p. 18)

Habermas: Communicative Competence Versus the History of Domination

The critical social psychology underlying Habermas's approach can be
analyzed in parallel fashion in terms of (1) a dialogical theory of communicative action as the basis of social life; (2) an individual (ontogenetic)
developmental model of competence, embracing cognitive, ego, moral,
and interactive dimensions; (3) a social theory of domination that illuminates the systematic ways in which the realization of human competencies
is thwarted and unequally distributed; (4) a historical model of levels of
the development of the reflexivity of consciousness; and (5) a justification
of the moral point of view as part of a discourse or communicative ethics.
The first four themes will be treated here, and the final one in the final
section.

Communicative Action. Much like Freire, Habermas belongs to a synthetic tradition of theories of action and praxis that includes the traditions
of Hegel and Marx, existentialism, social phenomenology, American pragmatism, and linguistic philosophy (Bernstein, 1971). As we have seen
in his ontological account of intersubjectivity and mutual recognition,
Habermas's account of communicative action is dialogical in nature.

Development and Competence. Habermas's multidimensional account of human development is directed toward establishing a quasi-
empirical grounding of potential human competencies in what he called
the "reconstructive sciences" oriented toward analyzing universal human
competencies. The central theme of this developmental model is the interplay among thought, language, and action in the contexts of cognitive,
linguistic, and interactive forms of development and corresponding competencies.

> This proposal signifies that for each of these dimensions, and indeed only
> for these dimensions, a specific developmental-logically ordered universal
> sequence of structures can be given. Following Piaget, I suppose that
> these general structures of cognitive, linguistic and interactive ability are
> formed in a simultaneously constructive and adaptive confrontation of the
> subject with his or her environment, whereby the environment is differen-
> tiated into outer nature, language and society. The structure-forming learn-
> ing process is also a process of self-production, insofar as in it the subject

first forms itself into a subject capable of cognition, speech and interaction. (cited in Habermas, 1986, pp. 191–192; McCarthy, 1978, p. 338)

But it is important to stress that these stages can be realized only under optimal sociocultural circumstances that are not available for most people under conditions of domination and inequality. Nevertheless, theories of development can serve as regulative ideals for learning, and the basis for a critique of existing forms of socialization.

Ideology and Distorted Communication. The obstacles to the realization of human potential are analyzed by Habermas in terms of a theory of domination and distorted communication. From his earliest writings, however, Habermas was also preoccupied with the problematic of *reification*—a process related to what Marx called "alienation" in his early writings—as a way of understanding the subjective effects of commodification. It is also in this context then we find Habermas going back to the youthful Hegel in order to formulate a conception of subject formation as the outcome of language, labor, and interaction (Honneth, 1996). In Habermas's more generalized vocabulary, this model of domination serves to illustrate the nature of *distorted communication*, as opposed to the logical possibility of the *ideal speech* involving undistorted communication.

Individual Development and the Evolution of World Views. Finally, Habermas posits a complex relationship between individual and sociohistorical development based on the evolution of learning processes. The central thesis is that there are fundamental developmental-logical "correlations" between the ontogenesis of the individual (especially in cognitive and ego development) and the historical evolution of religious systems. It should be emphasized that the arguments developed in this context were introduced as tentative hypotheses as proposals for future research.

At the societal level the theme of social development is introduced in relation to the evolution of "social formations," a term that was selected over the narrower notion of "modes of production." The key theme is that understanding societal development cannot be based exclusively on rationalization at the level of technology and production, but also must include the emergence of new capacities involving practical reason, that is, normative discourse. In other words, thresholds of social change require new types of social subjects with new capacities for critical reflection. The problematic of modern democracy is thus closely linked to the formation of subjects capable of citizenship. In premodern societies these practical learning capacities were embedded in religious traditions that defined the cultural system and constrained cognitive possibilities. From an evolutionary perspective it is possible to identify various homologies between individual ontogenetic development (i.e., emergence of egocentric, sociocentric, and reflexive perspectives in interactive competence) and those observable in the development of the basic concepts and logical structures of world views. With respect to logical structures, for example, the development of religious thought parallels capacities evident in the ontogentic development of the individual. Though mythology makes possible narrative explanation based on exemplary stories, and cosmological religion allows complex deductive arguments, it is only modern science that "permits nomological explanations and practical justifications, which the help of revisable theories and constructions that are monitored against experience" (Habermas, 1979, pp. 103–104).

To summarize, the critical social psychologies of Freire and Habermas can be compared as follows: (1) Freire's dialogical subject is complemented by Habermas's theory of communication action; (2) Freire's developmental notion of humanization as incompletion is further elaborated in Habermas's concern with cognitive, linguistic, and interactive development; (3) Freire's account of domination as the "culture of silence" provides a specific example of Habermas's notion of distorted communication; and (4) Freire's thesis postulating a dialectical progression from intransitive to transitive consciousness broadly parallels Habermas's claim that the transition to modern social formations has required a transition from mythical to scientific world views.

FROM IDEOLOGY CRITIQUE TO DIALOGICAL REFLECTION

At this point we need to consider how both authors propose to draw normative conclusions from their critical social psychology. In particular, the problem they confront is one of overcoming the dogmatic assumptions of classical ideology critique, which was grounded in untenable philosophies of history and essentializing theories of human nature.

Introduction: Domination and Emancipatory Practices

In both Freire's pedagogical ideal of critical transitive consciousness and Habermas's regulative epistemological notion of ideal speech, the problematic of ideology critique is dethroned from the requirement of an absolute or privileged epistemological standpoint from which theoretical "experts" may judge "false consciousness." To this extent, it is misleading to follow those who implicitly subsume their approaches into the framework of classical ideology critique (Guba & Lincoln, 1994). Their approaches are grounded in a communicative model of development rather than epistemological models of truth. As a consequence, the critic's expertise is limited to an analysis of the procedural aspects of the modes of reasoning employed in distorted communication, not a judgment of the ultimate validity of given interpretations of empirical and normative claims. In the case of Freire, this divergence from classical ideology critique is evident in the existentialist and dialogical premises at the heart of his conception of the pedagogical encounter; in the case of Habermas, this shift is evident in his movement away from the analogy of the psychoanalytic encounter of his early writings to the theory of communicative action of his later work. Consequently, the problematic of pathologies of communication was abandoned in the early 1970s, though he still considers these issues relevant (Habermas, 1992a). These points become evident in considering Freire's conception of dialogical (and antidialogical) action and Habermas's notion of ideal speech and distorted communication. As we shall see, the divergence in their approaches stems primarily from the different levels of abstraction at which their theories are constructed.

The following discussion will thus be framed in terms of three themes: (1) the processes through which the "culture of silence" is produced through "antidialogical action" (Freire), or how distorted communication produces relations of domination that deceive subjects (Habermas); (2) how relations of dialogue as a form of learning may contribute to a process of liberation in the form of conscientization (Freire), or how the possibility of emancipatory consciousness is grounded in the capacity for self-reflection that defines reason (Habermas); and (3) how conscientization unleashes an ethical discourse through which agents develop a capacity for social criticism (Freire), and how particular ethical reflections are not completely situated and local, but rooted in the human potential for ethical dialogue with universal dimensions as part of a discourse or communicative ethics (Habermas).

Freire: Culture of Silence to Conscientização

Antidialogical Action and the Culture of Silence. As Erich Fromm remarked after first meeting Freire, "This kind of educational practice is a kind of historical-cultural political psychoanalysis" (quoted in Freire, 1994, p. 55). Though Freire reacted enthusiastically to this characterization, its limitations provide a useful entry point for considering his theory of conscientization. Most important, the dialogical relationship between teacher and learner is quite distinct from the classic relationship between psychotherapist as expert and the neurotic client. Though there is inevitably a therapeutic dimension to pedagogical relations, critical pedagogy

should not be viewed in such purely therapeutic terms. Certain psychoanalytic constructs do enter into Freire's assumptions about the origins of
the "culture of silence," but the method of coming to give voice to silence
is quite different because the educator cannot claim to possess diagnostic
"truth" in the scientific manner of the therapist.

The term *culture of silence* serves for Freire as the equivalent of the
notion of *false consciousness*, but the shift in terminology is indicative of
a fundamentally different approach to the question. The contrast is not
epistemological in the sense of revolutionary experts who know and the
ignorant who have completely false knowledge. The assumption is that
within the culture of silence there are forms of accumulated experience
that potentially can take the form of critical knowledge through processes
of dialogical learning. The concept is used with reference to both relations
of domination within a society (Freire, 1970c, p. 97) and in metropolitan-
periphery relations of dependency. The culture of silence thus manifests
itself in the duality and ambivalence (or hybridity, in the jargon of postcolonial theory) of marginalization:

> Understanding the culture of silence is possible only if it is taken as a
> totality that is itself part of a greater whole. . . . Thus, understanding the
> culture of silence presupposes an analysis of dependence as a relational
> phenomenon that gives rise to different forms of being, of thinking, of ex-
> pression, to those of the culture of silence and those of the culture that
> "has a voice." . . . This results in the duality of the dependent society, its
> ambiguity, its being and not being itself, and the ambivalent characteristic
> of its long experience of dependency, both attracted by and rejecting the
> metropolitan society. (Freire, 1985, pp. 72–73)

The mode of consciousness dominant within the colonized culture
of silence is that of "semi-intransitive consciousness" that lacks "structural
perception": "In its quasi immersion in concrete reality, this consciousness
fails to perceive many of reality's challenges, or perceives them in a
distorted way" (Freire, 1985, p. 75). Under conditions of transition, populist movements may come to express a "naive transitive consciousness"
that local power elites can manipulate with new forms of antidialogical
action—to ensure their continuing dominance.

Four basic types of antidialogical actions are identified as mechanisms
of hegemony that form a culture of silence: (a) *conquest*, involving the
establishment of relations of domination and subordination through a
combination of force and symbolic mystification; (b) *divide and rule*, based
primarily on "a *focalized* view of problems rather than on seeing them as
dimensions of a *totality*" (Freire, 1970c, p. 138); (c) *manipulation*, which
serves the ends of conquest through the communicative distortions that

become necessary to control emergent democratic participation; and (d) *cultural invasion*, which contributes to conquest by directly penetrating the cultural contexts of groups, imposing a view of the world that deprives subordinate groups of any sense of their alternative "possibilities."

Conscientization and Cultural Action. Freire's central question, however, is not one of a theory of hegemony so much as a critical pedagogy: How is it that learners can escape from the culture of silence, take steps toward critical consciousness, and enter into authentic dialogue? The Portuguese word *conscientização*, popularized by Freire in educational environments, has been translated as *conscientization* in English. Conscientization describes the social psychological processes through which the dominated become aware of blocked subjectivities related to shared experience. But this insertion into a reality that is progressively unveiled cannot be merely intellectual or individualistic because it is essentially "social" (Freire, 1973, p. 148):

> The French "prise de conscience," to take consciousness of, is a normal way of being a human being. Conscientization is something which goes beyond the "prise de conscience." It is something which is starting from the ability of getting, of taking the "prise de conscience." Something which implies to analyze. It is a kind of reading the world rigorously or almost rigorously. It is the way of reading how society works. (Torres, 1990a)

This deeper reading of reality is identified with a form of critical consciousness that is revealed through praxis: "Conscientization, which is identified with cultural action for freedom, is the process by which in the subject-object relationship . . . the subject finds the ability to grasp, in critical terms, the dialectical unity between self and object" (Freire, 1985, p. 160). The result is a form of demystification or demythologization: "While it implies overcoming 'false consciousness,' overcoming, that is, a semi-intransitive or naive transitive state of consciousness, it implies further the critical insertion of the conscientized person into a demythologized reality" (Freire, 1970a, p. 46). The crucial psychological process required is that of using new forms of language to get "distance" from the taken-for-granted realities of everyday life:[15]

> In the process of producing and acquiring knowledge, we end up also by learning to "take distance" from objects, a contradictory way of approaching them. The establishment of distance from objects presupposes the perception of them in their relation with other objects. . . . Conscientization is the deepening of the coming of consciousness. There can be no conscienti-

zation without coming first to consciousness, but not all coming to consciousness extends necessarily into conscientization. (Freire, 1993, pp. 108–
109)

As we will see in the next chapter in the context of the techniques
of literacy training, Freire seeks to understand these processes in social
semiotic terms in relation to the "codification" and "decodification" that
accompanies the act of knowing as "critical revelation" (Freire, 1985, p.
167).

Conscientization as Ethical Reflection. But the revelatory processes
unleashed through conscientization are not only cognitive (forms of structural perception); they are also *ethical* in evaluating the consequences of
domination. For Freire dehumanization is a process through which the
truly human can come to be robbed—in the same way that the product
of labor is robbed in capitalist relations according to Marxist thought.
The five principles of Freire's moral philosophy have been usefully reconstructed as follows:

1. People ought to pursue their ontological vocation of becoming
   more fully human (through engaging in critical, dialogical praxis).
2. No person or group of people ought to knowingly constrain or
   prevent another person or group of people from pursuing the
   ontological vocation; that is to say, no person ought to oppress
   another.
3. We ought (collectively and dialogically) to consider what kind of
   world—what social structures, processes, relationships, and so
   on—would be necessary to enable (all) people in a given social
   setting to pursue their humanization.
4. All people ought to act to transform existing structures where
   critical reflection reveals that these structures serve as an impedi-
   ment to the pursuit of humanization.
5. Educators and others who assume positions of responsibility in
   the social sphere ought to side with the oppressed in seeking to
   promote a better (more fully human) world through their activities.
   (Roberts, 1998, p. 113)

To summarize these considerations, it is important to stress that
within Freire's theory of conscientization, the supposition of a human
ontological vocation constitutes the background for a "moral point of
view" that rejects skepticism, but articulates the problematic at the level
of how conscientization elicits concrete ethical reflection on practical is-

sues. At the same time, this assumption about human potential for critical consciousness—both empirical and normative—does not provide a standpoint that might allow ontological "experts," as it were, to determine abstractly the discrepancies between the "real" situation of groups and their ontological possibilities, especially as the basis for concrete prescriptions. Though the educator has a kind of generalized authority in facilitating and setting up contexts of dialogue appropriate within a given cultural and historical tradition, this authority does not extend to the process of diagnosing the "false consciousness" of subordinate groups.

Habermas: From Distorted Communication to Communicative Ethics

In this section we will be concerned with three themes in Habermas: (1) his account of distorted communication as a way of understanding phenomena previously understood as "false consciousness" and ideology; (2) his theory of knowledge interests as a justification of self-reflection as crucial to the emancipatory origins of reason; and (3) his elaboration of the problematic of a discourse or communicative ethics as an oblique practical response to the general question of strategies for facilitating the reduction of distorted communication.

Distorted Communication as Repressive Communication. Though Habermas is concerned in his early works with the problematic of distorted communication and its overcoming—a theme that parallels Freire's analysis of the culture of silence and conscientization—he does not pursue this question later, except indirectly with an analysis of the "colonization of the lifeworld" in contemporary societies. His focus shifts rather toward the normative question of justifying a general "moral point of view," as we shall see.

Nevertheless, Habermas's early writings sketch an analysis of distorted communication that resembles Freire's culture of silence; and he identifies a form of critical reflection that, like processes of conscientization, might dissolve it. These themes were elaborated in his early remarks on the psychoanalytic model of critique and the pathological character of distorted communication. The psychoanalytic model of distorted communication was held to have three defining features: (a) the rules of language are distorted at the level of semantic contents, for example, through displacement, lack of grammaticality, faulty use of words; (b) at the behavioral level, the deformed language-game appears in the stereotyped, emotion-laden actions that are not congruent with the realities of situational contexts; and (c) the discrepancies in the use of language, actions, and gestures are symptomatic of private contents that cannot be publicly communicated because they are incomprehensible to the author and cannot be expressed in the rules of public communication (Habermas, 1970b, p. 118). As a consequence, problems of communication in such contexts cannot be resolved through simple hermeneutic "translation" because "the incomprehensibility is the result of a faulty organization of speech itself" (Habermas, 1970b, p. 117). At the social level, distortions appear as a consequence of the social structure: The unequal distribution of communicative competence contributes to the deformation of mutual understanding (Habermas, 1970b, p. 144).

The notion of *socially* distorted communication is thus central to Habermas's whole project, especially as an alternative to dogmatic notions of ideology critique and false consciousness. This notion of distorted communication has been applied to distorted social discourse under the heading "repressive communication," a theme that parallels Freire's notion of antidialogical action, as follows: "If, for reasons related to the structure of communication, it is not possible for groups and individuals to locate themselves in society and to articulate their interests, repressive communication occurs" (Mueller, 1970, p. 103). For the individual, the result is a split between private and public worlds, resulting in a "distorted monologue with oneself but also in distorted communication with others" (Mueller, 1970, p. 105). The resulting distortion is reflected in the incapacity to express subjective needs fully, thus short-circuiting the development of autonomy and critical consciousness:

> The common characteristic of repressive communication is that the internalized language system permits neither the articulation of subjectively experienced needs beyond the emotive level nor the realization of maximum individuation, or, thus, implicit autonomy formation. On the psychic level, the language used represses parts of one's symbolic geography and inhibits the attainment of consciousness. On the class level the language used results in an incapacity to locate oneself in history and society. (Mueller, 1970, p. 105)

At the social level, repressive communication operates through the imposition of dominant realities, resulting in the linguistic impoverishment of dominated groups (Mueller, 1970, p. 106). This is not to say, however, that the marginalized group does not possess knowledge of its experience; the problem is rather that it is articulated in privatized ways that cannot enter into public debate: "Thus is it possible that countersymbols and definitions are kept alive and communicated even if their circulation is limited to the family or small groups" (Mueller, 1970, p. 107). Nevertheless, such groups are also more subject to the ways in which the mass media, advertising, and educational institutions colonize this experience with official interpretations: "In short, the restricted speech code shared by the lower classes does not permit them to construct a defense system against dominant legitimations" (Mueller, 1970, p. 107). Further, the mass media achieve their effects in part by avoiding complex messages, limiting new information, and repetition—techniques that encode messages in ways that anticipate predictable decodifications that operate as the antithesis of dialogical communication (Hall, 1993).

Further, Habermas offers an empirical thesis regarding the relationship between social repression and levels of distorted communication that is especially evident in dependent and underdeveloped societies characterized by high levels of authoritarianism: "The degree of repression depends on the developmental stage of the productive forces and on the organization of authority, that is of the institutionalization of political and economic power (Habermas, 1970b, p. 146).

Knowledge Interests, Self-reflection, and Ideal Speech. The analysis of distorted communication (as with antidialogical action) presupposes its opposite, that is, undistorted communication. Though Habermas does not develop a pragmatics of conscientization in Freire's sense, he does formulate his theory of knowledge interests and ideal speech as an account of critical reason that systematically justifies Freire's practice. Indeed, Habermas's explication of the self-reflection underlying the emancipatory interest of reason dovetails very closely with the objectives of conscientization as a pedagogical practice that avoids dogmatism (or what Freire often refers to as "sectarianism"):

> *Self-reflection is at once intuition and emancipation, comprehension and liberation from dogmatic dependence.* This dogmatism that reason undoes both analytically and practically is false consciousness: error and unfree existence in particular. Only the ego that apprehends itself in intellectual intuition as the self-positing subject obtains autonomy. The dogmatist, on the contrary, because he cannot summon up the force to carry out self-reflection, lives in a dispersal as a dependent subject that is not only determined by objects but is itself made into a thing. He leads an unfree existence, because he does not become conscious of his self-reflecting self-activity. Dogmatism is equally a moral lack and a theoretical incapacity. (Habermas, 1971, p. 208)

Moreover, such self-reflection is necessarily understood in the context of specific and unique life histories that take on a dramatic form that illustrates what Freire would call the dynamics of conscientization:

But in our own self-formative process, we are at once both actor and critic. In the final instance, the meaning of the process itself must be capable of becoming part of our consciousness in a critical manner, entangled as we are in the drama of life history. The subject must be able to relate his own history and have comprehended the inhibitions that blocked the path of self-reflection. For the final state of a self-formative process is attained only if the subject remembers its identifications and alienations, the objectivations forced upon it and the reflections it arrive at, as the path upon which it constituted itself. (Habermas, 1971, p. 260)

Discourse Ethics. Instead of pursuing strategies for inducing such idealized dialogues (as in Freire's theory of conscientization), Habermas shifts his strategy of inquiry as part of seeking to address the foundations of the very possibility of normative justification as a "discourse ethics" (Habermas, 1993). Without such a grounding, he argues, the project of challenging relations of domination becomes an arbitrary human activity. In part this focus responds to the moral skepticism that has challenged critical social theory from Nietzsche and Max Weber through postmodernism today.

The development of such a discourse ethics is also motivated by concerns related to the fundamental question of "what constitutes the moral basis of social cooperation" (Rehg, 1994, p. 1). As a consequence, it attempts to address questions of rational justification largely absent from Freire's more practical concern with local justice. The first part of this problematic was elaborated in the theory of validity claims and discourse theory of science discussed in Chapter 3. A second step, as we have seen in Chapter 5, was to replace the speculative assumptions of a praxis philosophy with a conception of developmental competencies rendered empirically plausible by reconstructive sciences such as developmental psychology. Though this line of argument provides a more persuasive basis for normative critiques, it does not provide a full justification of a moral perspective. As a third step, Habermas also seeks to secure a strong philosophical defense against moral skepticism through the construction of a universalistic *discourse* or *communicative ethics* that provides strong criteria of justice reasoning, a theme that has a complex history in his thinking (Ferrara, 1996).

Making sense of Habermas's position here requires understanding the technical distinction (anticipated by Hegel) that he and other proponents of communicative ethics make between "morality" (*Moralität*), grounded in appeals to universal principles, and "ethics" (*Sittlichkeit*), referring to value principles characteristic of a particular community or tradition. The tasks of a discourse ethics are thus directed toward universal moral or justice reasoning in former sense. Hence Habermas is wary of making any immediate prescriptive claims for such a procedural morality, beyond that of sensitizing participants to the logical demands of a "self-conscious conduct of life":

> But philosophy cannot take over from those concerned with the answering of substantive questions of justice, or of an authentic, non-failed life. ... Whoever goes beyond the procedural questions of a discourse theory of morality and ethics, and sets out *directly*, in a normative attitude, to develop a theory of the well-ordered emancipated society, will soon find him or herself running up against the limits of his or her own historical standpoint, and its unreflected context of emergence. (Habermas, 1992a, pp. 270–271)

What then is the strategic purpose of a discourse ethics? Above all, it is a problematic that has emerged in complex societies with highly differentiated, rationalized lifeworlds. Given the diversity of perspectives in contexts of dialogue, there is a need for minimal conditions that respect the survival of all cultures, but set procedural limits as the necessary grounds of participation: "Not every life choice of men and women, to use Walzer's language, would be admissible, but only those that comply with the conditions of tolerance or discourse" (Warnke, 1995, p. 139). Only under these conditions has it become possible to differentiate between universalizable "moral" and local or concrete "ethical" issues:

> The concrete ethical life of a naively habituated lifeworld is characterized by the fusion of moral and evaluative issues. Only in a rationalized lifeworld do moral issues become independent of issues of the good life. Only then do they have to be dealt with autonomously as issues of justice, at least initially. ... For the increase in rationality brought about by isolating questions of justice has its price. Questions of the good life have the advantage of being answerable within the horizon of lifeworld certainties. They are posed as contextual and hence *concrete* from the outset. The answers to these questions retain *action-motivating* potential of the forms of life that are presupposed in the contexts. (Habermas, 1990, p. 178)

In this context two concluding points will help situate Habermas's communicative ethics. First, to reiterate, it does not seek to replace or preclude a concrete ethics, or more specially an ethics of care such as has been developed in feminist theory (e.g., Larrabee, 1993; Noddings, 1995). Such concrete contexts preserve the "action-motivating potential" that is otherwise difficult to sustain with reference to universalistic, procedural ethics.

Second, the primary rationale for discourse ethics is theoretical and lies elsewhere. On the one hand, it serves to challenge moral relativism by defending the possibility of a universal "moral point of view" in the sense of a theory of justice. Hence, a communicative ethics does point to procedural criteria that may increasingly become part of dialogue in concrete ethical decisions, especially to challenge "local" customs (e.g., ritualistic female circumcision) that may contradict "universal" human sensibilities. On the other hand, a communicative ethics is also central to Habermas's concern with a critical theory of democracy and law (e.g., Rosenfeld & Arato, 1998). In particular, he argues that autonomous morality and law stand in a "complementary relationship" that suggests the "moral and civic autonomy are co-original" (Habermas, 1996, pp. 106–107). Within this context communicative ethics provides a universalistic framework both for law and for coordinating an intercultural understanding that protects and limits differences that threaten dialogue. A crucial aspect of contemporary pluralistic societies is that

> they promote and even mobilize the multiplicity of individual life-plans and the unfolding of different religious worldviews and life-orientations. These different conceptions of the *good* life, however, must be able to coexist with equal rights. That is why we need norms for a *just* way of living together that guarantee the integrity of each and every person within the context of their own life-forms. (Habermas, 1997a, p. 85)

COMPARATIVE DISCUSSION: FROM IS TO OUGHT

In concluding, we can now review comparatively the essential assumptions of the shared postfoundationalist "humanism" of Freire and Habermas:

- The *dialogical presupposition* that human understanding and identity is grounded in intersubjective, communicative interaction.
- The *reconstructive developmental claim* that there are quasi-empirical bases for positing species-specific potentials for humanization.
- The *revelatory empirical analysis of the effects of domination* that constrain the realization of developmental potentials.
- The *emancipatory proposition* that dialogical processes involving distanciation (conscientization, critique) from given and taken-for-granted realities are decisive for unleashing transformative cognitive and affective processes required for resistance against domination.
- The *necessity of a moral point of view* that justifies a universalistic discourse and concrete communicative ethics.

The Dialogical Presupposition

Since the theme of the dialogical basis of communication has already been taken up in Chapter 3 under the heading of ontologies of the subject-objective dialectic, it does not need to be detailed again here. As we concluded previously, though Freire casts his argument in terms of a philosophy of praxis, it is reconstructed in terms of a subject-subject dialogue that broadly complements Habermas's more elaborated thesis regarding communicative action and a critique of theories of praxis. The primary difference is that Habermas anchors his formulation in communicative linguistic models rather than in an intersubjective account of the master-slave dialectic. Yet, as we will see in the next chapter, Freire actually employs a linguistic model in literacy training that points in the direction of Habermas's approach.

The Developmental Subject

For Freire the positive, developmental dimension involves a notion of "humanization" as an "ontological vocation," hence potentials are not defined in terms of a specific telos, but are defined counterfactually as "incompletion." For Habermas this problematic shifts to an analysis of the acquisition of general "communicative competences" as a developmental process that can be illuminated by reference to diverse forms of developmental research. The primary difference between these two strategies is that Freire's discourse originated in the traditional essentializing categories of Christian existentialism. Yet his existentialism is inflected with a communicative account of humanization as an open-ended vocation of freedom, along with developmental themes from Piaget, Vygotsky, and Fromm. This basic strategy is elaborated in a more systematic way with Habermas's evolutionary models of the rationalization of normative reason, as well as his more rigorous use of developmental models as a form of reconstructive science. Accordingly, Habermas translates this problematic into a theory of communicative competence that can draw on the empirical research of cognitive, ego, moral, and interactive development.

The Analysis of Domination

The negative dimension of development is analyzed by Freire in terms of antidialogical action and the resulting culture of silence and symbolic violence that reflect the internalization of relations of domination. For Habermas the negative dimension is characterized by a general model of

"distorted communication" linked to the ideological effects of socialization and contrasted to the model of "ideal speech." With respect to the
question of domination, in short, Freire focuses practically on the dominated subject as part of a specific pedagogical strategy originating in
literacy training in peripheral societies, whereas Habermas is concerned
with a systematic analysis of distorted communication in terms of the
psychoanalytic analogy and related conceptions of ideology critique,
alienation, and reification. As well, his account of the colonization of the
lifeworld seeks to specify the emergent forms of domination in advanced
capitalism.

A minor difference is that Habermas would probably be reluctant to
trace oppressive behavior to necrophilic or authoritarian personality
types, at least beyond the classic phase of early industrialization and the
initial breakdown of closed societies. As he stresses, with the advent of
advanced capitalism the compulsions of technology and administration
work autonomously: "Sociopsychologically, the era is typified less by
the authoritarian personality than by the destructuring of the superego"
(Habermas, 1970a, p. 107). In other words, in the context of multi-role
identities in complex societies, individuals may be cast in the role of
implementing oppressive professional obligations by day and being loving, democratic parents by night. To participate in relations of domination
under these conditions does not typically presuppose an "authoritarian
personality" any more than capitalism continues to rely on the Protestant
ethic.

The Possibility of Emancipatory Self-Reflection

Both Freire and Habermas propose that Kant's definition of enlightenment
in terms of individual autonomy can be reframed in terms of both the
history of the species and individual development. But they share with
Hegel and Marx a concern with the specific sociocultural and depth-
psychological obstacles to the realization of autonomy and how these
might be overcome through a pedagogy of reflexivity. In the case of Freire
these themes are introduced in his historical distinction—based on adults
in peripheral societies—between semi-intransitive, naively transitive, and
critical transitive consciousness. A central concern is that dependent modernization—illustrated by the case of Brazil—does not necessarily unleash
the critical consciousness required for authentic modernization. His critical pedagogy—based on the possibilities for conscientization—seeks to
address these concerns in the context of educational reform.

In contrast, Habermas works with developmental models based on
child development and the evolution of world views. In this scheme the

relation between egocentric perspectives and myth approximates what Freire calls semi-intransitive consciousness; the affinities between socio-centric perspectives and universalistic religions parallels naively transitive consciousness; and most important, the link between universalistic reflexive perspectives and modern science provides a more systematic basis for what Freire calls critical transitive consciousness, though without elaborating the pedagogical implications.

In short, Freire's concern with the origins of domination is directed toward constructive pedagogical strategies that can be "generated in the womb of the culture of silence itself" (Freire, 1970a, p. 4). In contrast, in focusing on the idealized and procedural bases of dialogue as communicative action, Habermas seeks to shift the debate to the level of scientific legitimation to challenge the dominant assumptions of philosophy and academic institutions as part of a reconstruction of the theory of rationality.

Universalistic Versus Concrete Ethics

Finally, what for Freire is primarily a matter of faith, conviction, or practice is given rigorous philosophical justification in Habermas's discourse ethics. For Freire the notion of *conscientization* provides a framework for understanding and facilitating the situated awakening of ethical reflection—it is thus a concrete ethics. For Freire ethics also involves the assumption of a universal theory of justice that can be recognized immanently through situated communicative relations involved in conscientization: "The critical position holds that by gaining a certain epistemological distance from the concrete world, I can know it better and make the dream of a better world a reality. . . . This is a process of struggle strongly rooted in ethics" (Freire, 1996, p. 187).

In the case of Habermas, the focus of a discourse ethics shifts to a universalistic philosophical justification of the "moral point of view" that backgrounds concrete ethical reflection. Yet this strategy does not claim to provide directive or binding substantive, situated moral claims. As opposed to communitarian moral theorists who would exclusively locate the grounds of value in local traditions, Habermas seeks to preserve a universalistic dimension for normative theory, though at the same time specifying the *limits of universalism*. The biographical basis for his position can be linked to his experience with Nazi Germany: "So the problem becomes one of finding a way to anchor an ethics in the dilemmas of modernity while at the same time avoiding the potentially destructive influence of essentially corrupt and distorted cultural traditions" (Rasmussen, 1990, p. 57). More recently, he has criticized postmodern skepticism as opening the door to similar abuses of "local" reason (Habermas, 1987a). Similarly, Freire's origins in the traditional, closed society of Pernambuco makes him wary of any ethics without universalistic dimensions; in this respect he points to the *limits of the particular*.

In short, the differences between the two authors closely parallel those defined by the feminist critique of Habermas developed in particular by Seyla Benhabib (1986), and in a somewhat different way by Axel Honneth (1995). As Benhabib argues, Habermas's theorizing is developed primarily at the level of the "universal" other of interaction and moral reasoning, but this concern needs to be complemented by attention to the situated "concrete" other. Habermas addresses this problem with the distinction between the "justification" of certain types of moral questions (e.g., relating to justice) that can be universalized, as opposed to questions of "application" where contextualization involves criteria of appropriateness (Habermas, 1993, p. 154). As we argue, this latter problematic is central to Freire and results in a strategy that is complementary to that of Habermas. In the final analysis, as McCarthy's (1978) careful reconstruction shows, Habermas's project is based on the assumption of the primacy of the *practical moment* of communication—the central theme of Freire's pedagogy:

> Even when it is theoretically grounded in a universal-pragmatic, developmental-logical account of speech and action, the critical interpretation of concrete social phenomena has an irreducibly "practical" moment. The interpreter cannot assume a purely subject-object relation to the *interpretandum* but must retain the peformative attitude of a participant in communication. . . . His position is not unlike that of a reflective partner in dialogue. . . . Even armed with this theory, the critical theorist can claim no monopoly on truth; critique cannot be pursued in isolation from the attempt to come to an understanding with others. In short it remains the case that "in a process of enlightenment there can only be participants." (p. 357)

Taken together, therefore, the positions of Freire and Habermas redefine a critical social psychology as an integral part of a critical theory of society. As we have sought to demonstrate, their complementary positions with respect to normative theory provide a strategy for linking the universal and the particular in productive ways. For example, their approach reinforces theoretically those defenders of universal rights who stress that human rights practices should have a dialogical relation to local actors (Preis, 1996). In the next chapter we turn to the more specific implications of such a critical social psychology for the organization of educational practices.

6

Critical Pedagogy and the Organization of Educational Enlightenment

From Dialogical to Collective Learning

For dialogue to be a method of true knowledge, the knowing subjects must approach reality scientifically in order to seek the dialectical connections which explain the form of reality.

—Freire, 1970a, p. 18

Linguistic communication has a double structure, for communication about propositional content may take place only with simultaneous meta-communication about interpersonal relations. . . . Language functions as a kind of transformer. . . . This transformation produces the distinction, rich in consequences, between the subjectivity of opinion . . . on the one hand, and the utterances and norms that appear with *a claim to generality*. . . . Reflexive *learning* takes place through discourses in which we thematize practical validity claims that have become problematic or have been rendered problematic through institutionalized doubt, and redeem or dismiss them on that basis of arguments.

—Habermas, 1975, pp. 10, 15

Having outlined the theory of society and critical social psychology underlying Freire's and Habermas's perspectives, we can now turn to the implications for strategies of learning and the organization of educational enlightenment. In this context Freire has considerably more to say, given that his primary concern is with educational practices. Our discussion will therefore focus on Freire's critical pedagogy. Though specifically pedagogical issues are rarely addressed by Habermas, they are implied by his general understanding of reflexive learning and the dialogical basis of ideal speech.

FROM THEORY TO PRACTICE

As an initial caution, it should be stressed that Freire's critical pedagogy does not claim to provide a comprehensive theory of learning or teaching. Yet its focus on the effects of marginality, dependency, and domination give it a strategic significance for mediating between the critical sociology of education and everyday life in the school wherever inequalities—of whatever kind—stunt human potential for learning. Accordingly, both Freire and Habermas give privileged positions to *vulnerable* social subjects as the frame of reference for questions about learning. In the case of Freire, the adult illiterate, the "popular" classes, and the dependent society provide the exemplars, whereas for Habermas it is the helpless child, the adolescent in a motivational crisis, the working class, or in the case of the public sphere, the manipulated citizen. These different points of departure have implications for the focus of their respective concerns, though not the goal: the conditions of possibility of individual autonomy.

The initial foundational premise of Freire and Habermas is that human autonomy and higher levels of cognitive and moral reasoning can be realized only through interactive learning processes. Rationality is not ultimately a property of an isolated ego or self (as implied by behavioral and traditional humanist theories), but rather the cumulative outcome of communities of inquiry and embodied social practices. Freire locates the originary site of learning in face-to-face dialogue and the acquisition of literacy. In contrast, Habermas's focus shifts to the broader context of democracy itself as a learning process.

A second shared premise is that becoming self-conscious of educational activities marks a decisive phase of human evolution because it unleashes previously suppressed possibilities for reflexivity. But neither author limits learning to formal educational institutions, nor do they—as social critics—locate the primary significance of informal and formal learning in its relation to revolutionary struggle in the traditional sense. Rather, to use Habermas's terminology, the evolutionary significance of mass education resides in its potential for facilitating the development of higher-level capacities for reflexive learning that open up new historical possibilities for change. Or in Freire's terms, critical literacy provides a means for "reading the world" in ways that may cumulatively challenge the existing political order.

A third shared premise is that both Freire and Habermas emphasize the interplay between *oral speech* (understood as dialogue or communicative action) and *written language* (understood as a text or discourse claiming validity) in the formation and transformation of human consciousness. Though the possibility of critique is initially anticipated in the dialogical situation of communicative understanding, its full possibilities can be realized only through forms of competence involving forms of abstraction based on writing. Freire's preoccupation with illiteracy and Habermas's conception of theoretical discourse as the context for the rational redemption of validity claims share a common premise: that *written speech* as a mode of communication has strategic evolutionary significance as a medium of critical discourse, a thesis echoed by historical anthropology (Goody, 1977).

Because critical literacy poses a danger for existing systems of power, however, elites have sought to actively attempt to manage knowledge for purposes of domination (Bourdieu, 1991). From the Enlightenment onward the project of literacy was burdened by conservative claims to textual authority on the part of experts and intellectuals, partly because of the anxieties unleashed by democratization. Given the precariousness of knowledge as a pawn in social struggles, a "critical" conception of literacy must therefore be wary of any technical determinism in linking literacy and reflective consciousness: "What literacy makes possible is far more than it makes necessary" (de Castell, 1995, p. 251). Consequently, a central task of critical theory has been to reconnect in theory and practice the *potential* links between literacy and emancipatory reflection.

In this chapter we will consider Freire's conception of *critical literacy* in four contexts that can be broadly linked to Habermas's theory of communication: (1) the claims of theories of critical literacy (Freire) and communicative competence (Habermas) as general frameworks for understanding the conditions of possibility for the formation of autonomous social agents; (2) the characteristics of Freire's dialogical literacy training as a pedagogical practice, a theme largely absent in Habermas, though anticipated in the concept of reflexive learning; (3) the generalizability of Freirean strategies for schooling—both formal and informal—as a realization of reflexive learning of the type presupposed by Habermas; and (4) the relationship between education and the democratic public sphere, a theme present in both authors.

CRITICAL LITERACY AS COMMUNICATIVE COMPETENCE

Freire: Critical Literacy and Dialogue

Freire's understanding of the critical functions of literacy was developed as part of both a historical argument about the development of critical consciousness and an educational proposition about the relationship of "reading the word" and "reading the world." Freire sometimes formulates the historical question in terms of a somewhat simplistic Enlightenment developmental model based on the distinction between "closed" and "open" societies, a distinction attributed to the philosopher Karl Popper (Freire, 1973, p. 8). Viewed in terms of forms of consciousness, Freire sees this "opening" up as involving a shift away from submersion in the historical process based on a "semi-transitivity of consciousness" in which people "fall prey to magical explanations because they cannot apprehend true causality" (Freire, 1973, p. 19).

But the crucial problem for Freire the educator is the question of how to facilitate the acquisition of critical literacy. As he was acutely aware, critical consciousness could not be created by propaganda or the imposition of ideas. Following from his initial ontological and epistemological assumptions about subject-subject dialogue, Freire was naturally influenced by Socratic "maieutics," that is, the method of bringing to consciousness the latent thoughts of others. Nevertheless, the Freirean method differs from Socratic maieutics in important respects in rejecting "Socratic intellectualism" as anti-empirical. What was revealed through dialogue was not knowledge that had been forgotten at birth, as opposed to the social forgetting imposed by socialization: "For dialogue to be a method of true knowledge, the knowing subjects must approach reality scientifically in order to seek the dialectical connections which explain the form of reality" (Freire, 1970a, p. 18).

Though arrived at independently through reflecting on his practice, his initial premises regarding the dialogical foundations of literacy later found a theoretical rationale in developmental psychology, most importantly in his discovery of the work of the Russian psychologist Lev Vygotsky (1896–1934). In reacting against behaviorism, Vygotsky pointed to the significance of literacy as a skill that requires translating internal thinking into a public discourse: "Vygotsky concluded that the child has to start from speech 'for himself' and transform it into speech 'for others'" (Van der Veer & Valsiner, 1991, p. 331). Consequently, teaching cannot simply impose the written discourse of others: "To implant [something] in the child ... is impossible ... it is only possible to train him for some external activity" (quoted in Van der Veer & Valsiner, 1991, p. 331). Much of the initial difficulty of literacy thus stems from the impersonal and abstract character of writing, which requires that the child become conscious of its own speaking. Since writing is addressed to absent or imaginary persons, it produces "a situation new and strange to the child. Written speech is monologous; it is a conversation with a blank sheet of paper" (Vygotsky, 1986, p. 181). Not only does this approach justify the use of dialogical techniques to bridge between oral and written skills as practical activities; it points to how, in Freire's terms, rereading the "word" creates the capacity to "read the world," transforming literacy training into "cultural politics" (Freire & Macedo, 1987, p. viii).

Critical literacy is thus the foundation of possible forms of "conscientization" that break through the "culture of silence." There is, however, a pedagogical paradox involved in conscientization that derives from the complex relationship between oral and written speech. From the perspective of the dialogical encounter, texts initially appear monological and without meaning; and at the point they come to have meaning, they threaten the security provided by taken-for-granted realities of the culture of silence.

The most obvious place to begin the study of literacy is in children, as in Piaget and Vygotsky's classic studies. But as Freire's work suggests, there is obviously something to be gained from the study of adult learners, especially those who are in important respects culturally deprived. Much as Piaget was drawn to the problematic of developmental psychology by observing that otherwise obviously intelligent children missed questions on tests, Freire was struck by how otherwise intelligent peasants had difficulty learning to read. In both cases, it was only by phenomenologically entering the cognitive worlds respectively of the child and the peasant that the dynamics of learning invisible to behavioral theories could be revealed.

The thesis of critical literacy thus provides the foundational framework for critical pedagogy. The initial assumption is that social actors are neither dupes nor fully autonomous actors capable of exercising successfully the "weapons of the weak." Critical literacy thus implies the kinds of skills required by C. Wright Mills's notion of "sociological imagination" and its relation to the capacity to link history and personal biography, private problems and public issues (Lankshear & McLaren, 1993b, pp. 28–29). Nor is critical literacy merely a capacity to read words:

> In the broadest political sense, literacy is best understood as a myriad of discursive forms and cultural competencies that construct and make available the various relations and experiences that exist between learners and the world. In a more specific sense, critical literacy is both a narrative for agency as well as a reference for critique. (Giroux, 1987, p. 10)

Habermas: Learning Processes

Freire and Habermas share a concern with the obstacles to, as well as the conditions of possibility of, learning. Yet they begin from virtually the opposite ends of the problematic of critical literacy. Freire begins with the question of the elementary pedagogical relations involving *not learning*: marginalized adult illiterates. Habermas's exploration of related issues has been concerned with the learning processes involved in the *highest forms* of learning, that is, the self-reflexive discourses of collective learning. In a sense, his concern with critical literacy shifts to the problematic of learning as the basis of a societal competence, hence from individual or local "empowerment" to that of societal empowerment. On the one hand, Habermas's theory of social evolution is premised on the suggestion that the institutionalization of critical discourses (e.g., in science, education) has been a leading force in social change. On the other hand, his multidimensional notion of "communicative competence" serves to identify the competencies of the social subjects required to further the processes of social rationalization, especially in relation to democratization.

LEARNING AS PEDAGOGICAL PRACTICES

Freire: The Methodology of Thematic Investigation

At this point we need to consider the origins of Freire's pedagogy in his specific method of literacy training. The point of departure for Freire's theory of learning is a shift from a behavioral transmission communication model of learning to an interactionist and dialogical discourse model. He thus characterizes traditional educational practices as a form of "banking" education that views learning as a process of accumulation of bits of knowledge presented as a "gift" from the teacher. Or sometimes the image is that of a "digestive" or "nutritional" conception of knowledge that is to be "deposited" in the undernourished (Freire, 1970a, p. 7). This theme is illustrated by referring to the one-directional "narrative character" of banking education: "The relationship involves a narrating Subject (the teacher) and patient, listening objects (students). . . . Education is suffering from narration sickness" (Freire, 1970c, p. 57). He invokes the master-slave analogy to reinforce this relationship of domination: "The students, alienated like the slave in the Hegelian dialectic, accept their ignorance as justifying the teacher's existence—but, unlike the slave, they never discover that they educate the teacher." The violence of these educational relations, in short, "mirror[s] oppressive society as a whole" (Freire, 1970c, p. 59).

The task of a critical pedagogy is thus to facilitate a transition from "magical consciousness" to "critical consciousness." Such facilitation requires three components: a critical and dialogical method, a changed curriculum content, and specific techniques to "codify" and "decodify" messages (Freire, 1973, p. 45). The focus in the present discussion will be the basic principles of Freire's method as elaborated in the early 1960s in literacy training in Brazil, rather than various adaptations to other contexts (e.g., Freire, Fraser, Macedo, & Stokes, 1997; Shor, 1987). Further, our presentation is based on an *idealized* version of the method that often has not been realized by those ostensibly using "Freirean" techniques. The primary difficulty is not so much the technical aspect of training as "the creation of a new attitude—that of dialogue, so absent in our upbringing and education" (Freire, 1973, p. 52)

The distinctive aspect of Freirean literacy training *as problem-posing education* lies in the way in which the content is defined through interaction with subjects, then translated through group participation into a form of communication comprehensible to illiterate participants. The general pedagogical principle involved here is *active participation* and *not* that teachers should never have expertise to communicate or that classroom interaction should always and everywhere take the immediate form of a dialogue. For example, in the quite different context of science learning for active groups without major problems, the imperative of participation may require only the occasional use of everyday examples and discovery-oriented methods to complement standard presentations.

In the case of illiteracy, however, crucial obstacles to learning are a passivity and a deference to authority that undermine *at the outset* the process of active participation. The general pedagogical principle involved, therefore, would be the assumption that every learning context has distinct obstacles to participation that can be overcome only through participatory dialogue. Once an overall dialogical relation has been established, however, *then* selective use of more traditional "mechanical" techniques (e.g., memorization, skill learning through exercises, etc.) has a place.

The dilemmas of illiterates are representative of the general category of the "oppressed." An initial assumption is that such learners need more than just skills (or abstract knowledge) because they lack the capacity for the kind of personal autonomy and confidence required for effectively linking thought and action. The case of basic literacy is thus the paradigm for a more generalized problem of overcoming dependent learning through "critical literacy":

> To acquire literacy is more than to psychologically and mechanically dominate reading and writing techniques. It is to dominate these techniques in terms of consciousness. . . . Acquiring literacy does not involve memorizing sentences, words or syllables—lifeless objects unconnected to an existential universe—but rather an attitude of creation and re-creation, a self-

transformation producing a stance of intervention in one's context. (Freire, 1973, p. 48)

In the case of literacy training, therefore, curriculum content should not be determined externally by experts, but should be discovered through an interactive process of "thematic investigation" through which teachers become aware of the basic terms of everyday life of the learners in question. For this reason, the preparation of "primers"—even in the name of Freirean techniques—becomes problematic because it short-circuits the process of participation, hence "donating to the illiterate words and sentences which really should result from his own creative effort" (Freire, 1973, p. 49).

Such literacy training has been understood in terms of three overlapping stages: (1) the investigative, (2) the pragmatic, and (3) the pedagogical (Fiori, 1968). The content is defined in the investigative stage through facilitating subjects to speak about the existential preoccupations of their everyday lives. Program content is thus based on an "anthropological concept of culture" (Freire, 1973, p. 46). Note that this content is *not* ideological (especially Marxist) in a strong sense; rather it requires presenting some of the basic distinctions and concepts that are the foundations of the interpretive social sciences:

> the distinction between the world of nature and the world of culture; the active role of men *in* and *with* their reality; the role of mediation which nature plays in relationships and communication among men; culture as the addition made by men to a world they did not make; culture as the result of men's labor, of their efforts to create and re-create; the transcendental meaning of human relationships; the humanistic dimension of culture; culture as a systematic acquisition of human experience (but as creative assimilation, not as information-storing); the democratization of culture; the learning of reading and writing as a key to the world of written communication. In short, the role of man as Subject in the world and with the world. (Freire, 1973, p. 46)

A key aspect of the method, however, is that illustrations of these themes are constructed locally through the use of interactive ethnographic strategies involving facilitators and small groups. The "circle of investigation" is responsible for the first phase of thematic investigation, which precedes the formation of "circles of culture" where more intensive pedagogical dialogue takes place (the pragmatic and pedagogical phases). Within these circles, commonsense insight into social relations is elicited through the local identification of paradigmatic "situations" that can be represented visually (with pictures, slides, etc.) and then explored verbally

through "generative words" that allow exploration of the power of the
written word.

The outcome of these preliminary investigative processes is a short list
of typical life situations that can be visually represented (most typically, a
set of drawings) as the basis for discussions that precede or accompany
immersion in actual writing. The objective here is to begin with an oral
discourse with which learners have some confidence and to initiate the
practice of dialogue. Further, this phase serves to elucidate basic terms
and situations on which later writing exercises can build. In one of the
early versions employed in Northeast Brazil, 10 typical life situations
were identified and represented with drawings. These situations included
domestic scenes, hunters, work, and a concluding drawing of the learning
circle itself. Group discussions of these drawings by facilitators are oriented toward uncovering the basic distinctions implied by the generative
situational themes: nature versus culture, culture as constructed through
subject-subject dialogue, work as the transformation of the material of
nature, poetry as a mode of popular expression, cultural differences as
the basis of behavior, the cultural circle itself as a form of democratization.
To cite a simple example, the image of a hunter with bow and arrow
becomes the basis for differentiating nature and culture:

> "Culture in this picture," the participants say, "is the bow, it is the arrow,
> it is the feathers the Indian wears." And when they are asked if the feath-
> ers are not nature, they always answer, "The feathers are nature, while
> they are on the bird. After man kills the bird, takes the feathers, and trans-
> forms them with work, they are not nature any longer. They are culture"
> (I had the opportunity to hear this reply many times, in various regions of
> the country). (Freire, 1973, p. 67)

The theoretical basis of this methodology is a communication model
that applies the concepts of *reduction*, *codification*, and *decodification*. The
phase of reduction involves the processes of initially isolating the basic
themes—the vocabulary—of curriculum content. The central objective is
to identify generative words that evoke fundamental, shared cultural
experiences, as well as representing the key phonetic combinations of
languages such as Portuguese and Spanish. Codification involves the
use of representations of typical situations that provoke deployment of
generative words in the process of writing. And decodification involves
reflection on the codifications themselves. Some further details and examples are useful for understanding these three processes.

With respect to reduction, "the generative words to be used in the
program should emerge from this field vocabulary research, not from

the educator's personal inspiration, no matter how proficiently he might construct a list" (Freire, 1973, p. 50). Three criteria are used for selecting the 15 or so generative words required: (1) syllabic richness, (2) phonetic difficulty, and (3) practical-existential content, intimately associated with the social, political, cultural, and economic themes of the community in the process of acquiring literacy. One such list used in the state of Rio de Janeiro was based on the following 17 words: slum (*favela*), rain, plow, land, food, Afro-Brazilian dancing (*batuque*), well, bicycle, work, salary, profession, government, swamplands, sugar mill, hoe, brick, wealth (Freire, 1973, pp. 83–84).

The stage of codification involves the graphic symbolization in units of learning of the strategic existential situations identified with generative words. Codification can be simple, involving visual channels (graphic), sensual channels (sociodrama, audiovisuals, etc.), or auditory (stories, popular music, talks, etc.). Or it can take a more complex, compound form involving the simultaneity of channels. The objective is to provoke discussion around themes that can be explored with writing generative words. The instructional tasks of the coordinators include presenting codifications in an order of increasing phonetic difficulty and preparing "discovery cards" that break down the phonetic families illustrated by the generative words.

Finally, though decodification can occur any place along the course of literacy training, as an expression of conscientization it tends to be closely linked with the acquisition of reading skills. The process of decodification thus involves a dialectical process through which previous codifications are reflected on in ways that produce new understandings:

> Whereas the codified representation is the knowable object mediating between knowing subjects, decodification—dissolving the codification into its constituent elements—is the operation by which the knowing subjects perceive relationships between the codification's elements and other facts presented by the real context—relationships which were formerly unperceived. (Freire, 1970a, p. 15).

At the same time, in its highest form conscientization should not "be stalled" by this revealing of objective reality; it is also logically impelled by a desire to transform it: "*It is authentic when the practice of revealing reality constitutes a dynamic and dialectical unity with the practice of transforming reality*" (Freire, 1975, p. 28).

Two features of Freire's original literacy model must be stressed to differentiate from the instrumental and political uses that have been made of it. First, the strategy is explicitly based on a rejection of teachers providing political direction; the learners themselves must construct their transformative practices. Hence, there is no guarantee that the outcomes will coincide with the expectations of educators or community leaders.

Second, this nondirective approach has an elective affinity with the structuralist communications model that underlies the methodology. The terms *reduction, codification,* and *decodification* refer to how linguistic structures generate situated *logical possibilities* that have to be activated by the participants. The method is thus *generative* (but not deterministic) in that it builds on the logic of possibilities implicit in the generative themes of everyday experience. This open-ended, processual model is oriented toward learning how to *produce* knowledge. Such competence training is dramatically different from the imposition of content in behavioral models of education and propaganda.

Habermas: From Communicative Action to Pedagogical Practice

Despite his impact on adult education, Habermas has had no occasion to discuss the implications of his theory of communicative action for adult literacy training (Welton, 1995b). Our particular concern here, however, is to point to the fundamental links between the techniques designed to produce conscientization and Habermas's account of critical reflexivity and communicative action.

We would suggest that creating a Freirean cultural circle involves establishing the relations of trust—the consensus to participate in the pedagogical relations—implied by the basic four validity claims identified by Habermas in his universal pragmatics as implicit in communicative action: the comprehensibility of the utterance, its propositional truth, the appropriateness of its normative content, and the authenticity of the intentions of speakers. Instrumental appropriations and deformations of Freirean techniques can be traced back to the violation of the spirit of these validity claims.

The failure of rural literacy training in Guinea-Bissau could be attributed to the difficulties of the first requirement: comprehensibility. As Freire later noted, his method was not appropriate for teaching a second language and the use of Portuguese for an illiterate rural population with limited or no knowledge of it was destined to failure (Freire & Macedo, 1987, pp. 160–169; Torres & Freire, 1994). But the pedagogical situation requires transposing these generalized conditions of dialogue to settings involving formally "unequal" participants in a process that involves the mediation and creation of knowledge.

Dogmatic Marxism can be used to illustrate the distortion of the other three validity claims: problematic claims about propositional truth (e.g., a "scientific" theory of revolution); the inappropriate imposition of values (e.g., based on urban and middle-class biases); and cultivation of a deceptive sincerity (e.g., the use of campesinos as a tool in a larger struggle). Parallel examples could be derived from the instrumental uses of Freirean techniques on the part of neoliberal political regimes.

Two other aspects of the Habermas approach are also especially significant for understanding the dynamics of conscientization: the psychoanalytic analogy and the theory of communicative action.

For Freire, the key aspect of conscientization is that it culminates in a "structural perspective"—a view of society as a whole—that requires a rethinking of the subjects' personal history in social terms. But this formulation begs the question of what is cognitively involved in such a process of "enlightenment"—the mediations between the abstract scientific content implied by a structural perspective and the self-recognition required by conscientization. Habermas's use of the psychoanalytic analogy can be employed to address this question. He begins with a distinction between two forms of knowledge, that is, "general theories" (involving subject-object relations) and "general interpretations" (involving subject-subject relations). General theories involve the formulation, in the name of the universal "inquiring subject," of propositions (based on empirical observations) regarding the determinations producing a particular object of inquiry. As a form of inquiry oriented toward the understanding of nature or society, this relationship assumes an abstract subject-object form. Partly for this reason, formally rational "scientific" critiques of society cannot be directly apprehended as a source of enlightenment within the ordinary language and common sense of a "culture of silence."

In contrast, general interpretations (the example of the psychoanalytic encounter is employed here) are existentially oriented toward a process of self-reflection: "This application becomes *self-application* by the subject of inquiry, who participates in the process of inquiry"; in the process, those who are the object of these interpretations come to "*know and recognize themselves* in these interpretations" (Habermas, 1971, pp. 261–262). Though there are some limitations in this therapeutic model (especially the assumption of the validity of psychiatric expertise), they are not crucial for the question at hand: the recognition required for seeing oneself in relation to "structural perspectives."

Three features of this "self-application" are of particular importance, according to Habermas, for understanding what in Freire's terms would be the process of conscientization. First, though cast in the form of generalized narrative, general interpretations can be communicated only with the horizon of a "language *common* to the interpreter and his object" (Habermas, 1971, p. 262). Within ordinary language this commonality is achieved through explaining events narratively, that is, by showing how an individual (or group) subject is involved in a series of events that have a history. Ordinary language is the medium that makes possible the transition from what appears to be a unique history to one that is shared by others for reasons that can be understood in the form of general social explanations: "For only the peculiar reflexivity of ordinary language makes possible communicating what is individual in inevitably general expressions" (Habermas, 1971, p. 263). Narrative histories can be shared through common sense because they exemplify experiences that are *shared*. Though this sharing may be abstract and highly repressed for neurotic patients, it is more direct and immediate for members of oppressed groups. At the outset the dominated subject is trapped within the meanings of what is taken to be a unique personal history of self-formation that is taken for granted:

> A *general* interpretation, on the contrary, must break this spell of the historical without departing from the level of narrative representation. It has the form of a narrative, because it is to aid subjects in reconstructing their own life history in narrative form. But it can serve as the background of *many* such narrations only because it does not hold merely for an individual case. It is a *systematically generalized history*, because it provides a scheme for many histories with foreseeable alternative courses. Yet, at the same time, each of these histories must then be able to appear with the claim of being the autobiographical narrative of something individuated. How is such a generalization possible? In every history, no matter how contingent, there is something general, for someone else can find something exemplary in it. Histories are understood as examples in direct proportion to the typicality of their content. Here the concept of type designates a quality of translatability: a history or story is typical in a given situation for a specific public, if the "action" can be easily taken out of its context and transferred to other life situations that are just as individuated. We can apply the "typical" case to our own. (Habermas, 1971, p. 263)

Second, in general interpretations the method of falsification does not take the form of standard empirical "refutation" found in natural science. As a consequence, there is no direct, intersubjective basis for the "validation" of successful conscientization. The learner may in fact reject the interpretation anticipated by the liberating teaching because of either (a) resistance or (b) the fact that the teacher's interpretative expectations are inadequate. Though "the interpretation of a case is corroborated only by the successful *continuation of a self-formative process*, that is by the completion of self-reflection," this outcome cannot be unequivocally assessed on the basis of what the learner says or does (Habermas, 1971, p. 266). It is perhaps for this reason that Freire's method is open-ended in posing problems without claiming or requiring any epistemological guarantee based on the expert knowledge of the teacher. This feature also poses great difficulties for short-run "evaluation," at least beyond the direct evidence of gains in literacy.

Third, general interpretations are characterized by a combination of hermeneutic understanding and causal explanation. But the type of causality involved is distinct from that of nature because it is bound up with the forms of consciousness that produced the links between personal and social history under examination, that is, the "cultural unconscious" that is to be revealed by conscientization. At the moment of recognition, "critique as knowledge and critique as transformation" are potentially combined in that the agent can no longer naively participate in the repetitive actions of cultural reproduction. Whether this insight can be translated into enduring practices is quite another matter, and one well understood by the "oppressed." Insight into the original explanatory causes of social events is quite distinct from the open-ended process of creating a new form of society in particular circumstances.

The pedagogical failure of classical Marxism can be traced back in part to its attempt to impose a structural perspective in the form of a "general theory" (scientific Marxism) as the basis for emancipatory enlightenment. The result was rather a new form of distorted communication that undercut the dialogical basis of the learning required for linking traditional common sense with new forms of thinking. And there are good reasons for this resistance of popular culture against the latent positivism of revolutionary Marxist theory. In contrast, the model of conscientization draws on a critical hermeneutics with which the fusion of horizons between educator and learner presupposes the need for "the education of the educator."

With respect to the second contribution of Habermas to the theory of conscientization, the educational implications of Habermas's later work on the theory of communicative action remain contested. There is general agreement, however, that the fundamental distinction between communicative action and manipulatively oriented strategic action has profound implications for education. Above all, it provides a fundamental philosophical rationale for Freire's distinction between critical and banking education, as well as reinforcing the thesis that conscientization must involve self-directed reflexivity.

More contested is the question of the residual status of "strategic" interventions in teaching. For example, it has been suggested that communicative action needs to be completed with a concept of "pedagogical action" that involves a mixture of strategic control and dialogical communication: "For the relationship between the person raising a child and the child is by definition an asymmetrical one. That relationship is not identical to the fundamentally symmetrical relationship typical for adults" (Miedema, 1994, p. 198). From this perspective pedagogical action oriented toward children forms a unique mode of action that cannot be reduced to strategic *or* communicative action in that it involves both as part of a process that moves toward symmetry. But as has been persuasively argued, locating pedagogical action as a distinct action type involves a distortion of Habermas's reconstructive method (Kachur, 1998). Nevertheless, this debate suggests the importance of clarifying the potential of Habermas's categories for analyzing the effects of "dialogical" and "antidialogical" action in diverse educational settings. A tentative conclusion based on the example of Freire would be that though the "directive" side of teaching does imply a minimal use of "strategic action," this does not entail anything like a "pedagogical paradox" in the strong sense. As Vygotsky's theory suggests and recent research corroborates—here confirming Freire's intuitions—the teacher cannot "manipulate" the learner into the zone of proximal development, as opposed to guiding in the manner of reciprocal learning (Palincsar & Brown, 1984; Palincsar, Brown, & Campione, 1993).

INFORMAL AND FORMAL SCHOOLING: CULTURAL ACTION

If we move away from the concrete issues of literacy training in marginal, dependent societies, we are confronted with issues regarding the transferability or generalizability of Freirean techniques. In this context we need to consider efforts to employ Freirean techniques in formal educational contexts, as well as in more advanced, liberal democratic societies. Though Habermas has said little about these issues, a number of educational theorists have sketched out some of the possible implications.

Freire: General Principles of Dialogical Pedagogy

In posing the question of the applicability of Freire's methods to advanced societies, there is now an extensive literature discussing these issues (Carey-Webb & Benz, 1996; Freire et al., 1997; Lankshear & McLaren, 1993a; Shor, 1987, 1992; Shor & Freire, 1987), including college and university teaching (Barnes, 1992; Long, 1995). Despite considerable disagreement on a number of issues, this literature clearly establishes both the general applicability of his pedagogical principles and the need—echoed by Freire—to adapt specific techniques to each learning situation.

In the present context our discussion will not focus on the details of these diverse experiments; instead we will consider some of the general principles that underlie the universality of Freirean pedagogy beyond the general principle of subject-subject dialogue. We will discuss five themes here: (1) the strategic advantages of dialogue as a "problem-posing" method in teaching; (2) the question of domination in dialogical settings oriented toward mutual respect and a loving relationship; (3) the dialectic of authority and freedom that underlies learning; (4) the social semiotic aspect of "codification" and "decodification" as a strategy of nondogmatic cultural criticism; and (5) the need to connect language and experience.

In introducing dialogue as an ideal, the crucial question for Freire is that the project of learning is *framed* as a subject-subject relation. It is thus *problem-posing* because from the outset learners must begin to reflect on their co-participation in the process of knowing, a strategy that has been vindicated in recent educational research (Nystrand, 1997). Potentially the outcome is a kind of "third idiom": "When critical dialogue works, teachers and students reinvent their relationship and their modes of communicating. They create a dialogic relationship in a mutual inquiry. I call this invented discourse the *third* idiom because it is different from the two conflicting ones . . . nonacademic everyday speech and academic teacher-talk" (Shor, 1992, p. 255).

This should not be taken to imply turning the curriculum over to students. Once the educational encounter has been framed dialogically, then, depending on the context, teachers can assume responsibility for direction: "A professor loses his or her role when he or she leaves the role of teaching and its content up to the students" (Freire in Escobar et al., 1994, p. 128).

Second, Freire's pedagogy is based on the premise that asymmetrical relations of power constitute a fundamental obstacle to communication in learning settings. But the means to overcome these obstacles is not direct denunciation, but "to stimulate doubt, criticism, curiosity, questioning, a taste for risk-taking, the adventure of creating" (Freire, 1993, p. 50). For example, he notes in relation to his experience at Harvard in 1969 how, after reading the first chapter of *Pedagogy of the Oppressed*, the 16-year-old son of a black woman instantly recognized that "this book was written about me. . . . It's all about me" (Freire, 1994, p. 75). Relations of domination and marginality provide the basis of shared existential experience that has a universal dimension, despite variations of detail.

A third theme that relates to the general applicability of Freirean strategies is understanding the reciprocal relationship between authority and freedom. Though his approach was initially directed against the authoritarianism of traditional schooling in Brazil, he has been equally insistent on the need for authentic *authority*, as opposed to mere anarchism or laissez-faire. As he puts this issue in terms of child-rearing generally, parental leadership is crucial to point the way, but only the child can translate this into a new form of autonomy (Horton & Freire, 1990, p. 187).

Built into this methodology is a complex tension between the *direction* that educators inevitably contribute and the openness to the learners that invites co-participation despite the counterfactual condition of asymmetrical relations of power and knowledge. In short, "to refuse to give direction is tantamount to rejecting education as a rigorous transmission of knowledge.... What I reject is how knowledge is transferred or transmitted from one subject to another that, in this case, would passively receive the 'gift' given to him or her" (Freire, 1993, p. 117). As he notes in response to Ira Shor's suggestion that in a liberating classroom the teacher's primary role is to "withdraw as the director of learning, as the directive force":

> But, look, Ira, for me the question is not for the teacher to have less and less authority. The issue is that the democratic teacher never, never transforms authority into authoritarianism. He or she can never stop being an authority or having authority. Without authority it is very difficult for the liberties of the students to be shaped. Freedom needs authority to become free. [Laughs] It is a paradox but it is true. The question nevertheless is for authority to know that it has its foundation in the freedom of others, and if the authority denies this freedom and cuts off this relationship, this *founding* relationship, with freedom, I think that it is no longer authority but has become *authoritarianism*. (Shor & Freire, 1987, p. 91)

A fourth principle is based on the link between problem-posing and the social semiotic aspects of codification and decodification. Though the specific techniques of literacy training cannot be directly extended beyond related problems in remedial writing, the basic presuppositions of the communications model utilized do relate to a wide range of learning issues. The codification-decodification model—widely employed in critical communications research—uses a structuralist account of translation as a process taking place between different levels of speech within a single language (Hall, 1980).

Finally, Freire is concerned with the linkages among experience, language, and power. He has mixed feelings about abstract concepts when they don't have the "weight" of reality, and he is particularly concerned about the distance between elaborated codes as articulated in the universities and commonsense (restricted) codes as developed by marginalized groups. The language of the classroom ought to relate to differences of experience, without abandoning the concepts of analytical discourse: "No, these concepts are absolutely important for us! . . . My question is not to deny them, but rather how to use them in such way that they are put next to concreteness" (Shor & Freire, 1987, pp. 148–149).

Habermas: Traditional Versus Reflexive Learning

Habermas has not been concerned with pedagogical practice, partly because of the marginal place of education in the older Frankfurt tradition (Morrow & Torres, 1995, ch. 8). Though some of his earliest work was on students and educational reform (Habermas, 1969), this interest was never followed up. Moreover, the German reception of his early work on knowledge interests was politicized in problematic ways, and the implications of his later theory of communicative action were not extensively explored. In short, the impact of critical theory on educational practices in Germany was largely negligible (Young, 1989, p. 99).

Nevertheless, a central theme of Habermas's project is a distinction between traditional and reflexive learning. The central implication of Habermas's theory of communicative action is that instructional practices based on a curriculum tied to the logic of instrumental and strategic action constitute a form of *nonreflexive learning,* or what Freire would call "banking education." But what remains ambiguous in Habermas's generalized characterization of reflexive learning is how to assess the specific problems of the reflexive criticism of practical validity claims. Based on the model of scientific communities, Habermas's distinction between nonreflexive and reflexive learning remains essentially *cognitive,* relating to outcomes based on better arguments:

> *Non-reflexive learning* takes place in action contexts in which implicitly raised theoretical and practical validity claims are naively taken for granted and accepted or rejected without discursive consideration.

> *Reflexive learning* takes place through discourses in which we thematize practical validity claims that have become problematic or have been rendered problematic through institutionalized doubt, and redeem or dismiss them on that basis of arguments. (Habermas, 1975, p. 15)

DEMOCRATIC LEARNING: CULTURAL ACTION, EDUCATION, AND THE PUBLIC SPHERE

Whereas the primary focus of Freire's conception of emancipatory practice is the micro, interactional context of pedagogical practice, for Habermas the focus has been the question of transferring these principles to the level of larger-scale collective agents. As we shall see, however, Freire's focus on the possibility of constructing a provisional, mini-public sphere as the interactive basis of emancipatory education broadly parallels Habermas's historical discussion of the origins of this democratic model in the 17th and 18th centuries.

Freire: Education, Revolution, and Democracy

Three aspects of Freire's account of the relationship between education and social change must be emphasized. First, he has always insisted that educational institutions, as products of society and its power relations, cannot be primary levers of social change. As a consequence, aside from his brief experiences in Chile and Africa, his educational activities have always been in the context of radical reformist educational projects. Though fundamental, educational practice "is not in itself the key to transformation": "Dialectically, education is not the key to transformation, but transformation is, in itself, educational" (Freire in Torres, 1998b, pp. 103–104). Transformative action requires struggle on two fronts: "The ideal is to fight against the system taking the two fronts, the one internal to the schooling system and the one external" (Horton & Freire, 1990, pp. 202–203).

Second, it is important here to reiterate that Freire's initial concerns with the relationship between education and *conscientização* were linked not to a theory of revolution in the Leninist or even the classic Gramscian sense, but to the question of fundamental democratization as defined by Karl Mannheim in the 1940s (Freire, 1973, p. 41). Though he does embrace the possibility of revolutionary transformation in the early 1970s, this stance is always linked to revolutionary change as part of a process of authentic democratization. Within this process of transition, education has a very specific responsibility: "Only an education facilitating the passage from naive to critical transitivity, increasing men's ability to perceive the challenges of their time, could prepare people to resist the emotional power of the transition" (Freire, 1973, p. 32). The goal, in short, is not a particular ideological perspective but the formation of a more general capacity for critical thinking.

Third, Freire's comments on and relation to political movements have shifted with the very different contexts of action—a sign of inconsistency or opportunism for some critics. Such criticism does not do justice to how he contextualizes each situation of action, not in opportunistic terms, but with respect to testing concrete "limit situations" (Aronowitz, 1993). From this perspective his association with the reformist World Council of

Churches in Geneva in the 1970s is as consistent as was his earlier involve-
ment in Brazilian literacy training, agrarian reform in revolutionary Chile,
or later support for the socialist workers movement in Brazil. Given this
contextual approach, Freire's reflections in the context of political action
and education have taken several different, if interrelated forms: (1) the
discussion of the possibility of revolutionary change as a learning process;
(2) the national project of popular education in which the school is envisioned as a site of progressive change, whether as a formal or an informal
institution; (3) participatory action research as part of strategies of community development; and (4) social movements as a new location for educational activity. What unites all of these is a conception of the formation
of active democratic citizens.

   Revolutionary Processes. In his early writings, Freire considered revolutionary processes as a kind of pedagogical relation between leaders and
the people. But it is important to differentiate between two different
contexts in which these formulations are employed. On the one hand,
usually, in response to his revolutionary critics, he does relate his pedagogical model (as we have seen) to the classic Marxist question of revolution
as action involving a national seizure of power. Yet his formulations take
the form of a general discussion of general leadership and transformative
principles rather than one of revolutionary strategy. On the other hand,
throughout his career he more typically uses the term *revolutionary* in
relation to any situated process that involves conscientization as a form
of learning and significant forms of progressive change in transformative
social movements.

   The revolutionary leadership model is defined in explicitly anti-Le-
ninist terms that evokes the more populist category of "people" rather
than class in the strictly Marxist sense. The Marxist Georg Lukács is
criticized for viewing the process of reflection in revolutionary leadership
as a process of "explaining to" rather than "dialoguing with the people"
(Freire, 1970c, p. 38). Such revolutionary leadership betrays contradictions
that undermine its purpose when as "victim of a fatalist concept of history,
it tries to domesticate the people mechanically to a future which the
leadership *knows a priori*, but which it thinks the people are incapable of
knowing" (Freire, 1970a, p. 43). Such theory is separated from practice,
a "simple verbalism," "a blind activism": "That is why there is no authentic
praxis outside the dialectical unity, action-reflection, practice-theory"
(Freire, 1985, p. 156). Several key pedagogical principles underlie this
unity of theory and practice, which invokes the Hegelian master-slave
metaphor in the context of a process of reconciliation.

   First, liberation cannot be handed to marginalized groups as a "gift" as if they were "objects," whether the paternalism is that of the oppressor or self-appointed revolutionary leaders: "They cannot enter the struggle as objects in order *later* to become men" (Freire, 1970c, p. 55). In this connection he cites Hegel's contention that freedom cannot be obtained with the risk required for independent self-consciousness (Freire, 1970c, pp. 20–21).

Second, it is held that domination dehumanizes the ruler as well as the ruled, hence fundamental change has liberating effects for the previous dominators who were dehumanized by dehumanizing others: "As the oppressed, fighting to be human, take away the oppressors' power to dominate and suppress, they restore to the oppressors the humanity they had lost in the exercise of oppression" (Freire, 1970c, p. 42). The contradiction can be resolved only by a "new man": "neither oppressor nor oppressed, but man in the process of liberation." The oppressed cannot regain their humanity simply by repressing their oppressors (Freire, 1970c, p. 42).

Third, the dominated must come to be a "class for itself" by means of a process through which they begin to move "in accord with their being" and begin not only to "know in a different way what they knew before, but they also begin to know what before they did not know. . . . It is born in and through action on reality" (Freire, 1985, p. 162). But this potential "being" of the class-for-itself cannot be known beforehand, primarily because it can be constructed, realized, and understood only retroactively by the participants themselves.

Finally, such consciousness formation cannot be realized either through the duality of leaders as "thinkers" and the oppressed as mere "doers" or through hatred or destruction of the other; otherwise the result is a "sectarian climate" and bureaucratization, resulting in a "spirit more revanchist than revolutionary" where the aspiration for revolution becomes "a means of domination, rather than . . . a road to liberation" (Freire, 1970c, pp. 121–122). Humanizing change can take place only through a process involving love and solidarity:

> The pursuit of full humanity, however, cannot be carried out in isolation or individualism, but only in fellowship and solidarity; therefore it cannot unfold in the antagonistic relations between oppressor and oppressed. No one can be authentically human while he prevents others from being so. Attempting *to be more* human, individualistically, leads to *having more*, egoistically: a form of dehumanization. Not that it is not fundamental *to have* in order *to be* human. Precisely because it *is* necessary, some men's *having* must not be allowed to constitute an obstacle to other's *having*, must not consolidate the power of the former to crush the latter. (Freire, 1985, pp. 73–74).

Whatever the merits of these formulations as an attempt to extend dialogical pedagogical principles to the idealized dynamics of transformation, they bear little resemblance to strategic realism of Marxist revolutionary theory.

National Popular Education. With the decline of revolutionary movements in the early 1970s, Freire's concerns refocused on applying these general pedagogical principles to national projects of popular education, participatory action research at the level of communities, and the possibilities for educational activity in social movements (Gadotti & Torres, 1994).

Popular education has previously existed as political-pedagogical projects, with the state being the driving force in the construction of a new democratic citizenship. An early example is what came to be known as "socialist education" in Mexico in the mid-1930s; more recent examples include Chile, Cuba, Nicaragua, and other cases of "socialist" experimentation where Freire has been an important influence (Carnoy & Samoff, 1990; Morales-Gómez & Torres, 1990). Though these experiments have varied with respect to the degree to which they employed dialogical and reflexive strategies of learning, they cannot easily be dismissed by reference to the authoritarianism of the Soviet and Maoist models of popular education.

Participatory Action Community Research. Beyond such national programs of formal and informal popular education, Freirean pedagogy also has had an impact on participatory action research as a form, in effect, of community education (Torres, 1995b, pp. 35–53). Such projects assume professionals with the type of fundamental commitments required of change agents (Freire, 1968b, 1968c). As an educational project, participatory research was connected especially to the agrarian reform projects developed in the early 1960s in Latin America (Fals-Borda & Rahman, 1991; Gajardo, 1982). Members of the Institute for Cultural Action (IDAC), a research and pedagogical action center founded in the 1970s in Geneva, formed a European version of participatory action research. Such Freirean participatory approaches seek to design nonschool, nonstate alternatives to community development within the civil society. Many of the representatives of this pedagogy have worked, politically and professionally, very close to political parties, universities, and research centers as well as with organizations that have originated in, or are linked to, churches (Torres, 1990b).

Education and Social Movements. Finally, Freire later links liberating education to the practices within social movements:

But there is another place for the existence and the development of liberation education which is precisely in the intimacy of social movements. For
example, the women's liberation movement, the environmental movements, the housewives' movement against the cost of living, all these
grassroots movements will have emerged into a very strong political task
by the end of this century. In the intimacy of these movements we have
aspects of liberating education sometimes we don't perceive. (Shor &
Freire, 1987, p. 38)

What underlies these educational activities in such diverse contexts
is the problematic of democratization. The crucial thesis here is the suggestion that there is an internal link between the ontological vocation of
humanization and democratization: "There is, then, an ontological and
historical foundation for the political struggle around democracy and its
permanent improvement" (Freire, 1996, p. 146).

In this context the formation of citizens becomes strategically important: "Citizenship is a social invention that demands a certain political
knowledge, a knowledge born of the struggle for and reflection on citizenship. The struggle for citizenship generates a knowledge indispensable
for its invention" (Freire, 1996, p. 113). A further contribution of Freire
is his thesis that the pedagogical subjects of the educational process are
not homogeneous citizens but culturally diverse individuals; hence, the
subjects of education are not fixed, essential, or inflexible—that is, the
teacher can be a student and the student a teacher. Moreover, these principles can also be applied to multicultural education and its relationship
to democratic citizenship (Torres, 1998a).

Habermas: Revitalization of the Public Sphere

Whereas Freire's preoccupation has been with the general question of the
link between critical literacy and possible democratization in experimental
Third World contexts, Habermas has focused on analyzing the conditions
of possibility of further expansions of democratization in more advanced,
liberal democratic societies. Habermas's social theory is not directed specifically to pedagogy in the narrow educational sense or to the strategic potential of educational systems to contribute to processes of radical change. The
context of crisis he addresses in the theory of communicative action is that
of rethinking Enlightenment "reason" and the implications for "collective
learning," that is, the general process through which human societies have
successfully mastered new challenges to further human possibilities.

Three educational issues have been of particular concern to Habermas
in this context: (1) the historical significance of the institutionalization of

discourses; (2) the general relation between education and the democratic public sphere, especially the role of the university; and (3) the significance of "new" social movements as forms of collective learning related to a revitalization of the public sphere.

Institutionalizing Critical Discourses. Habermas is particularly interested in the question of translating the theory of practice from the microinteractive level to that of the organization and institutionalization of self-reflection and enlightenment. He gives a strategic evolutionary status to "discourses," by which he means institutional spheres (based in part on the model of scientific communities) characterized by dialogue and consensus generated through rational argumentation: "Only when certain domains of discourse are *institutionalized* to such an extent that under specifiable conditions a general expectation exists, that discursive conversations will be initiated, can they become systematically relevant mechanism of learning for a given society. (Habermas, 1973, p. 25)

From this perspective educational institutions are part of a complex of discourses that contribute to the overall process of collective learning. In evolutionary terms, other dramatic examples of such institutionalization of discourses include the theological questioning of mythical and religious interpretations; the systematic testing of the validity claims of profane (scientific) knowledge and related professional ethics; and the emergence of a public sphere that could question political representation, that is, "bourgeois democracy."

Educational Systems and the Public Sphere. Habermas has not spoken in detail about the potential relation of educational systems to the expansion of the public sphere. Yet early in his career, he advocated educational reform to enhance educational opportunities and to deal with specifically German problems of democratization related to overcoming the Nazi heritage. Nevertheless, in the late 1960s his critique of the German student movement rejected the thesis that a revolutionary process could be carried out through the school system or led by students. This is not to say that he concluded that school reform was without strategic importance. For example, mass education transformed traditional patterns of socialization that were "set free by the psychologizing of children's education and the planning of school curricula according to cultural policy, and rendered accessible to general practical discourse by means of a process of 'scientization'" (Habermas, 1973, p. 26). In the early 1970s he proposed that "in advanced capitalism changing the structure of the general system of education might possibly be more important for the organization of enlightenment than the ineffectual training of cadres or the building of impotent parties" (Habermas, 1973, pp. 31–32).

Habermas's limited comments on educational questions have focused on the role of universities. His early critique of science and technology sought "to illuminate the interrelationships of methodologies, global background assumptions, and objective contexts of application," holding out the hope this might contribute to the "enlightenment of the political public sphere" (Habermas, 1989b, p. 118). Though conceding that these university reform proposals in Germany largely failed, he still contends that the university retains a strategic role. Despite their failings, universities preserve their importance as examples of communicative rationality and creativity as "specialized internal public spheres" that carry "the promissory note of the surprising argument . . . at any moment a new viewpoint may emerge, a new idea appear unexpectedly" (Habermas, 1989b, pp. 124–125).

The institutionalization of such discourses is largely taken for granted in advanced societies, but remains highly contested. Currently, the general movement associated with the notion of cultural studies could be viewed as a further development of such discursive reflexivity. Critical pedagogy can also be viewed as a response to the problems produced by such scientization in the context of inadequately developed democratic public spheres.

New Social Movements as Collective Learning Processes. More recently, Habermas has provided some suggestive observations about the contradictory emancipatory potential of new social movements that "arise along the seams between system and lifeworld" (Habermas, 1987b, p. 393). Central to this conception is the notion that such movements initiate processes of collective learning with far-reaching consequences for dominant normative systems. In contrast to the classic welfare state pattern of conflicts over distribution, the new social movements are more concerned with "defending and restoring endangered ways of life. In short, the new conflicts are not ignited by distribution problems but by questions having to do with the grammar of forms of life" (Habermas, 1987b, p. 392). Among these, "only the feminist movements stand in the tradition of bourgeois-socialist liberation movements," whereas the others offer a complex spectrum of possibilities, some of which are suggestive of emancipatory potentials, whereas others are indicative of mere defensive "resistance and withdrawal" (p. 393). Habermas's contributions have been a key influence on recent debates about new social movements, civil society, and democratization (e.g., Benhabib, 1996b; Dryzek, 1990; Forester, 1985;

Haacke, 1996). Though the problematic of the public sphere has increasingly influenced Latin American discussions of democratization, in Brazil it has been proposed that Habermas be used to understand social movements in terms of a process of social learning that can be evaluated in terms of "a comparative scale to gauge 'political development'" (Krischke, 1998, p. 417).

COMPARATIVE DISCUSSION

Forms and Contexts of Emancipatory Learning

The preceding discussion can be summarized in terms of four general themes that link the otherwise disparate preoccupations of Freire and Habermas in the context of organizing educational enlightenment:

- The *thesis of critical literacy*, which argues that critical consciousness depends crucially on a form of literacy that facilitates a "structural perspective" for understanding social reality, a process that formally parallels the notions of communicative competence and collective learning that underlie Habermas's theory of society.
- A *dialogical understanding of the pedagogical practices* required for acquiring critical communicative competence, as illustrated practically in Freire's account of the methodology of thematic investigation and illuminated by Habermas's account of the logical and linguistic character of the "general interpretations" involved in social knowledge.
- The *generalizability of the basic principles of Freirean pedagogy* to formal and nonformal settings in all types of societies, a suggestion consistent with Habermas's general distinction between reflexive and nonreflexive learning.
- The *intimate interrelationships between reflexive learning, the formation of critical citizenship, and the potential revitalization of democratic public spheres* in diverse settings.

Though this chapter raises many controversial issues that require further research and discussion, we will limit ourselves to three concluding questions: (1) the sense in which Freire's pedagogy is "revolutionary"; (2) some of the ways in which theory and research could and have reinforced and "reinvented" Freirean understandings of dialogical principle in teaching; and (3) the manner in which Freire's critical pedagogy provides a foundation for the missing theory of pedagogical practices in Habermas's account of collective learning.

Revolutionary Pedagogy?

Much of the confusion surrounding Freire's political stance stems from references to his "revolutionary pedagogy." This term can be taken in at least four different senses: First, the term may imply that his pedagogy is innovative in a revolutionary—novel—way relative to that of his predecessors; second, that it is a pedagogy oriented toward creating a revolution; third, as a qualification of the second possibility, hence that his pedagogical principles contain a theory of revolutionary leadership; and fourth, that it is a pedagogy oriented toward transformations of consciousness that have revolutionary potential in very specific contexts or in an expanded sense of the term. Each of these possibilities requires brief comments.

The first sense in which Freire's pedagogy is revolutionary is valid if we accept the originality of his pedagogical practices. To be sure, Freire was always careful to point to his predecessors and not make extravagant claims to originality. But taken as a whole, his overall project can easily be characterized as having revolutionary implications for educational theory.

The second characterization is false in that it involves a simplistic interpretation of his method as a form of political "revolutionary" mobilization either in the Leninist or even the Gramscian sense. This label has been perpetuated by both the Brazilian reactionaries who wanted to undermine his credibility and revolutionary Marxists attempting to apply his ideas in an instrumental way. He has insisted that education is not the lever of revolutionary social change: "Let me begin again with the important point I became clear on after the coup: education per sé is not the lever of revolutionary transformation. The school system was created by political forces whose center of power is at a distance from the classroom" (Shor & Freire, 1987, p. 33). Indeed, this is partly the basis for Freire's personal preference for working outside the official educational system.

As some critics complain (as against the fears of the leaders of the Brazilian coup of 1964), there is little evidence that literacy training provides a direct catalyst for agrarian revolts: "For years I have been searching for an instance in which peasants have broken out of their oppression, even at a local level, but I have found none. When I asked Freire, he admitted that neither has he" (MacEoin quoted in Taylor, 1993, p. 80). And as Freire's Marxist critics have suggested again and again, this reflects his lack of "true" class analysis. But all of these criticisms overlook the more limited and longer-term understanding of empowerment that Freire had in mind for educational settings. This point is reconfirmed in the few systematic accounts of the practice of Freirean literacy training (Purcell-Gates & Waterman, 2000; Stromquist, 1997).

The third theme of the tasks of revolutionary leadership, was in fact important to Freire from the late 1960s through the early 1970s in relation to his Chilean and African experience, as well as events in Cuba, Nicaragua, and Grenada (Carnoy & Samoff, 1990; Hickling-Hudson, 1988). On the one hand, he was simply responding to the questions of those activists who were attempting to build revolutionary movements in Latin America. His conclusion was basically that the relationship between leaders and masses had to be authentically democratic if the means of revolution were to be consistent with its ends. On the other hand, he also saw his literacy method as an important resource for postrevolutionary governments, most effectively in Nicaragua (Arnove, 1986). More problematic was his engagement with literacy training in Guinea-Bissau and Cabo Verde. That experience pointed to various difficulties advising a revolutionary regime as an outsider, particularly the contradictions involved in attempting to use his method as a form of second language training. The imposition of Portuguese as a "national" language had the effect of undermining the intimate relationship between experience and language that was the basis of the method (Freire & Macedo, 1987, p. 103)

Given these experiences, his earlier writings contain some abstract formulations of the logic of revolutionary transformations. But today these same passages could equally well be read as the basis of a theory of democratic leadership of the kind represented by the socialist movement in Brazil today, along with the "re-visioning" of Latin American social movements generally (Alvarez, Dagnino, & Escobar, 1998). Consequently, evoking poetically (and anachronistically) Freire's affinities with the guerrilla revolutionary Che Guevara may appeal to leftist nostalgia, but it obscures the specificity of his more modest conception of transformative struggle (McLaren, 2000).

The fourth interpretation—that the method may be revolutionary in specific contexts or in an expanded understanding of the term—does capture the spirit of his method as one that involves empowerment of marginalized groups. Further, in Freire's more recent writings the term *revolutionary consciousness* is used in a loose way relating mobilization of various kinds:

> The ideal is to promote revolutionary consciousness, which despite being more difficult to attain, continues to be essential and possible. Just look at

the advancement of popular movements throughout the 1980s and 1990s, a decade [*sic*] seen as lost by many. Look at the advances made by the landless; their victories in claiming land rights, cooperatively developing the land, and creating settlements. Look at the homeless and schoolless. Victories exist side by side with the sacrifices of lives. (Freire, 1996, p. 119)

From a very different perspective, Freire's "political" conception of education has led some to characterize his approach as merely a sophisticated approach to "indoctrination." As one critic puts it, "Yet is there not a subtle manipulation built into this method, given the lack of education in the students and the obvious political purposes of the teachers?" (Elias, 1994, p. 133). Two basic responses can be given to this charge. First, though Freirean techniques may be abused for purposes of indoctrination, their essential logic is based on a very different notion of the "political," one that rejects any form of indoctrination as inauthentic, antidialogical communication. Second, though demands for "objectivity" and "rational argumentation" are important for the construction of rational discourses, most existing ways of organizing these goals in educational settings are biased at the outset. The meanings of these terms must be reexamined in a reflexive manner that takes into account the history of domination that backgrounds all educational encounters, a question that is, after all, the central theme of both Freire's theory of conscientization and Habermas's critique of distorted communication.

Reinventing Freire

We would like to conclude this discussion of Freirean pedagogy by considering some of the contexts in which his strategy has been and could be "reinvented": (a) the problematic of the generalizability of the critical literacy model; (b) a consideration of this pedagogical relationship in social semiotic terms as a process of communication that seeks to reverse the process of hegemonic imposition; and (c) the ways in which various forms of research have broadly illuminated or confirmed aspects of his general approach.

We have already addressed the question of the generalizability of Freire in relation to several themes: the value of dialogue in problem-posing education; the benefits of overcoming hierarchical relations in teaching without undermining authority altogether; the dialectic of freedom and authority as the foundation of socialization oriented toward critical competence; the value of codification-decodification strategies as part of a methodology of social and cultural criticism; and mutual learning that results from linking experience and language in concrete ways.

Many of these general principles can and have been translated in the context of classroom teaching in North America and elsewhere (Freire et al., 1997; Shor, 1992; Shor & Freire, 1987; Shor & Pari, 2000). Such adaptations inevitably give rise to questions about what the "true" method is. Some of those close to Freire (e.g., Donaldo Macedo) have criticized much of what passes for Freirean pedagogy on the grounds that in the name of liberation pedagogy it is translated into a method that merely exoticizes lived experience without relating it to a political project. Perhaps the fundamental question here relates to the sociohistorical differences in the kinds of social subjects that are the target of emancipatory educational projects:

> Reinvention requires of me that I recognize that the historical, political, cultural, and economic conditions of each context present new methodological and tactical requirements, so that it is always necessary to search for the actualization of . . . ideas with every new situation. In other words, the way that I struggle against machismo in Northeast Brazil cannot be possibly the same way that one should fight against machismo in New York City. (Freire, 1997c, p. 326)

Beyond adapting critical pedagogy to different types of oppressed groups in the context of multiculturalism (Leistyna, 1999), proponents of Freire in advanced societies argue that the problematic of illiteracy can be extended metaphorically to those who fail to "read the world" even though they can read "words": "As part of the larger and more pervasive issue of cultural hegemony, illiteracy refers to the functional inability or refusal of middle- and upper-class persons to read the world and their lives in a critical and historically relational way" (Giroux, 1987, p. 12). How processes of conscientization are to be unleashed in the relatively privileged, however, remains a problematic goal to the extent that the model of conscientization presupposes that the target group suffers from a lack of significant forms of mutual recognition. In any case, the use of testimonials—as in the case of Nobel Peace Prize winner Rigoberta Menchú—offers a promising model of how relations of sympathy can be created between privileged and oppressed groups (Carey-Webb & Benz, 1996). Testimonials provide the basis for a subject-subject relation between victims and witnesses, giving rise to conscientization on the part of many who simply never had an occasion to personally reflect on the plight on distant others. Nevertheless, a *pedagogy of the privileged* remains to be invented.

A second way in which Freire might be reinvented through generalizing his method is through further development of the model of reflexivity and the social subject that underlies the counterhegemonic codification-decodification model. Communications research in cultural studies has also drawn on an encoding-decoding model developed by Stuart Hall (Hall, 1980, 1993). Hall's distinctions between dominant-hegemonic, nego-tiated, and oppositional readings of media messages bear some resem-blance to the communicative dynamics of banking versus liberatory edu-cation. A related question is the task of overcoming the verbal bias of existing work on critical literacy through the development of strategies oriented toward the visual bias of popular culture (e.g., Kellner, 1998; Morrow, 1990).

It has also been argued that Freire's understanding of conscientization can be illuminated by an analysis of the implicit parallels between linguis-tic mastery and structural understanding: "The demystification of the structure of language implies . . . a parallel potential demystification of social-political-cultural structuration, and agential control over the ele-ments of language intimates a similar control over social elements" (Jan-mohamed, 1994, p. 243). Finally, though Pierre Bourdieu's theory of educa-tional reproduction could be viewed as a critique of Freire's populism, Bourdieu's account of the "habitus"—the practical and embodied charac-ter of the dominated subject—in fact provides insight into the cautious realism of Freire's method. In contrast to idealistic pleas for the revolution-ary "raising of consciousness," Freire's approach, it could be argued, is based on an understanding of the "extraordinary inertia which results from the inscription of social structures in bodies" (Bourdieu, 2000, p. 172).

Third, there are other contexts in which aspects of Freire are being "reinvented" by relating his approach to existing, complementary research in education. An ethnographic study of the use of Freirean methods with rural women in El Salvador provides one of the few empirical attempts to understand his techniques in relation to existing research on learning (Purcell-Gates & Waterman, 2000). Without necessarily invoking his name, recent research on reading, writing, and instructional discourse has begun to work out more systematically the kind of dialogical discourse model underlying Freire's method (Nystrand, 1997). As well, there have been attempts to draw on Vygotsky and Mikhail Bakhtin to develop a sociocul-tural and dialogical understanding of the formation of the subject that complements and extends the problematic of the dialogical and develop-mental subject (Morrow, 1998; Sampson, 1993; Wertsch, 1991, 1998). More specifically, it has been argued that Bakhtin's thought converges with participatory action research (Hajdukowski-Ahmed, 1998).

Bringing Habermas Down to Earth

The theme of this chapter has been that Freire's dialogical pedagogy provides some of the most important clues to the theory of pedagogical practices implied by Habermas's overall theory of collective learning and fundamental conception of the role of reflexivity in human cognition. At the same time, Freire's more existential analysis provides an important corrective to Habermas's cognitive focus, as well as drawing attention to the deeper implications of Habermas's own formulations. For example, his account of the developmental subject implies that the maturation of the pupil—a movement through various stages of competence—requires a balanced relation between cognitive, ego, moral, and interactional development. In short, Habermas's understanding of development contains a theory of embodiment that is not so obvious in his reconstruction of communicative action as a form of rationality. Only through the cultivation of a multiplicity of competencies does education contribute fully to the capacity for "critical literacy" that is required of democratic citizens capable of resisting the manipulative strategies of governments and the mass media. In the next chapter we will more systematically consider the question of both Habermas's contribution to Freire and Freire's to Habermas.

7

Critical Social Theory as Critical Pedagogy

The Freirean Contribution

Modernity is for many (for Jürgen Habermas or Charles Taylor, for example), an essentially or exclusively European phenomenon. . . . Modernity is, in fact, a European phenomenon, but one constituted in a dialectical relation with a non-European alterity that is its ultimate content. Modernity appears when Europe affirms itself as the "center" of a *World* History that it inaugurates; the "periphery" that surrounds this center is consequently part of its self-definition. . . . Modernity includes a rational "concept" of emancipation that we affirm and subsume. But, at the same time, it develops an irrational myth, a justification for genocidal violence. The postmodernists criticize modern reason as a reason of terror; we criticize modern reason because of the irrational myth it conceals.

—Dussel, 1993, p. 66

Having established the broad complementarities between Habermas and Freire at the levels of metatheory, theory of society, critical social psychology, and pedagogical theory, it is appropriate to draw out more sharply how their respective *differences* are mutually illuminating. After all, complementarity implies differences, but of a particular kind: those that are not in principle antagonistic, but are potentially reconcilable in theory and/or practice, or suggestive of new research agendas. Further, complementarity also suggests a process of mutual informing, selective revision, and deepening of approaches, perhaps even their synthesis. In the case at hand, the strategy of appropriation is that of incorporating Freire more explicitly and directly within the more general framework of Habermas's critical theory of society and communicative action, and fleshing out the latter in terms of issues raised by Freire's project. The question of the contributions of Habermas to Freire's project can be treated more briefly, primarily because the issues have already been discussed fairly extensively and go beyond our educational focus. In both cases our remarks are intended only to be suggestive and do not claim to provide anything like a definitive response to the issues that we highlight.

HABERMAS: A POSTFOUNDATIONAL FRAMEWORK

As we have argued in the preceding chapters, Habermas's social theory and the traditions it engages provide a framework within which Freire's critical pedagogy can be incorporated without having to claim to be a self-sufficient theoretical project. This shifts the burden of much criticism away from Freire the individual to the critical theory tradition as defined by Habermas and others. Habermas's theory of communicative action and critique of praxis philosophy also point to some of the risks involved in the language of Freire's humanism. Though Freire's concepts of praxis and the subject-object dialectic are clearly grounded in a dialogical, intersubjective model of action, they lend themselves to essentializing misinterpretations about the nature of "man." It remains an open question whether the language of praxis theory should be abandoned altogether, as Habermas sometimes suggests (Honneth, 1991, p. xxxii). Interpreted from the perspective of Habermas's theory of communicative action, for example, Freire's use of praxis theory has a continuing rhetorical appeal.

In the context of a critical social psychology, Habermas shifts the focus of legitimation from an ontology of humanization to one based on an integral theory of developmental competencies based on reconstructive sciences. This strategy has the advantage of drawing on empirical knowledge to justify a theory of humanization that otherwise remains potentially abstract and essentializing in Freire's framework. Nevertheless, the practical outcome remains broadly complementary and builds on developmental themes very much central to Freire's approach.

In several other respects Habermas provides a point of departure for deepening or expanding on themes cursorily touched on by Freire. Habermas's general philosophy of social science and his conception of crisis theory and of the colonization of the lifeworld are suggestive of the kind of theory of society that remains sketchy in Freire. In particular, Habermas's reflections on the public sphere and the mass media have provided a framework for a deliberative or proceduralist theory of democracy that can illuminate the general democratic understanding that has guided Freire's practical relation to socialist movements.

Finally, Habermas's concern with a critique of postmodernist thought (a topic to be taken up in the final chapter) and a conception of communicative ethics provides a rejoinder to simplistic characterizations of Freire as a "humanist" and "essentialist" thinker, pointing toward an alternative strategy of understanding of the Enlightenment as an "incomplete" project.

Though Freire consistently invokes ethical claims and links them to the practice of critical pedagogy, he has largely avoided any effort to justify his value priorities in a more systematic, philosophical way. The response of postmodernist critical theory has been to dismiss the residual universalism of such efforts as a modernist illusion, inviting teachers to construct a purely situated theory of ethics: "Both the discourse of rights and cognitive moral reasoning fail to situate a theory of ethics in a notion of the good life that is attentive to the aspirations and hopes of those subordinate and marginal groups who occupy particular historical and social contexts" (Giroux, 1988, p. 58).

Yet there are some serious problems with this type of criticism from Habermas's perspective, especially the conclusion that a radical theory of ethics necessarily rejects concern with the universalistic dimensions of moral theory. Above all, it is not clear why this question needs to be formulated in oppositional, either-or terms, especially if one differentiates the perspectives of Rawls and Kohlberg from the critical appropriation of these issues in the work of Habermas, Apel, and others (Dussel, 1994). The version of discourse ethics proposed by critical theory does not understand the rights-bearing citizens independently of social contexts. For this very reason, it argues in dialogical terms that the ethical visions of particular standpoints must be able to potentially justify themselves *in relation to* universal principles of justice reasoning (Benhabib, 1992, 1995; Benhabib & Dallmayr, 1990).

WHAT CAN FREIRE DO FOR HABERMAS?

In the discussion that follows we will focus on several responses to how Freire dialogically poses problems for Habermas, and how, in the process, he points toward the further development and self-correction of Habermas's project. In a sense, then, the following discussion takes the form of an imaginary dialogue in which Freire poses questions without pretending to give answers. The general theme will be that confronting Freire's thought requires shifting the focus from issues of communicative action in general to the specifics of pedagogical practices, and from a formal to a concrete ethics immanent in dialogical relations. Moreover, Freire focuses on a particular type of "oppressed" social subject that has inherited the problematic claim of universalism given by Marxism to the European working class: the postcolonial oppressed of peripheral societies. While not justifying a teleological theory of history based on a supposed "universal" class, this theme does provide the basis for a material, concrete ethics with urgent global dimensions and an antidote to the relativistic effects of pure postmodernist identity politics.

This chapter will briefly discuss a number of themes relating to Freire that address these silences in Habermas.

First, Freire's preoccupation with the relationship between ethics and dialogue points to some fundamental problems stemming from Habermas's focus on the anticipation of consensus based on the model of scientific communities. For Habermas the paradigmatic experience of mutual understanding derives from the model of ideal speech exemplified in scientific communities or a reconstruction of the universal structure of language. But this approach neglects the problem of mutual understanding in contexts where the "otherness" of the marginalized inhibits dialogue and the formation of ethical consciousness. The problematic of conscientization, reframed in terms of a conception of radical "otherness" (or alterity) as sketched by Enrique Dussel (1997), provides a basis for reconsideration the ethical foundations of a critical theory.

Second, we will consider how Habermas has generally neglected the question of pedagogical practice, even though it is implicit in his theory of developmental competence and reflexive learning. But what is missing here is an adequate account of the moral dimension of learning. In this context it will be argued that Axel Honneth's (1996) reconstruction of the moral grammar of mutual recognition provides a strategy for reconnecting Freire's effort to link love to pedagogy with a multiple conception of mutual recognition.

Third, the focus on concrete experience of mutual recognition provides the basis for a critique of postmodernist cynicism that lies prior to rational argumentation, hence a strategy that complements Habermas's focus on the latter.

Fourth, the preceding insights also point to returning to the theme of liberation theology, the context out of which Freire's thought first took shape. Above all, it points to the need for Habermas to take into account the significance of public and liberation theology in certain historical contexts for the resistance to the colonization of the lifeworld that underlies his political project.

Fifth, we will consider how Freire's questions open up again the problematic of the utopian content of critical theory, a theme present, but subdued, in Habermas.

And finally, Freire points to a way of conceiving the question of alternative modernities in a manner that challenges Eurocentrism without succumbing to the illusions of postmodernism or some of the contradictions of postcolonial theory.

Conscientization and Dialogue: The Other as Critical Alterity

As a regulative concept, Habermas's conception of ideal speech is grounded in the model of scientific communities, hence it does not adequately address the practical obstacles to procedural rationality in other contexts. Similarly, the tasks of an idealized discourse ethics of justice are quite distinct from those of an ethics concerned with the substantive "good life" of a particular community. In short, Habermas's consideration of ideal speech focuses primarily on idealized forms of dialogue at the expense of concrete social relations. As Burbules (1993) constructively suggests, Habermas's theory of dialogue does not adequately address the communicative implications of relating to a concrete other, and hence needs to incorporate the emotions and experiences that facilitate communication. He suggests that Habermas's "sincerity" condition of communication might be broadened to include emotional authenticity and empathy as "communicative virtues" (p. 77).

In contrast, much of the force of Freire's early formulation of the pedagogy of the oppressed stemmed from how it addressed dialogue within the specific historical context of the *absolute domination* experiences of rural and urban illiterate proletarians. Here the formal principle of ideal speech is linked to a multiplicity of dialogical strategies, as well as a context that provides an initial orienting universalistic ethical principle. This specific historical experience of domination has an unequivocal, universalizing ethical content that contrasts sharply with the "postmodern condition" where the privileged have the freedom from necessity to entertain ethical relativism and even nihilism.

In contrast, Freire's concept of conscientization is oriented toward the concrete "other" of practical ethics rather than the abstract intersubjective "other" of scientific communities or a discourse ethics. In other words, as a form of practical "critique," conscientization not only involves a social psychological process of consciousness transformation; it is also linked to ethical reflection. The popularization of the notion of conscientization, however, led to its abuse. At worst, conscientization became associated with popular psychological notions of "consciousness raising" or, at best, general social psychological formulations such as a transformation theory of adult learning (Mezirow, 1995). As Freire acknowledged in reacting to these tendencies, he stopped using the term long ago:

> You inquired about my having stopped making direct reference to the word *conscientization*. It is true. The last time I expanded on this topic was in 1974—it had already been four years, more or less, since I had stopped using it. . . . Naturally, however, in not using the word for a time, I did not refute its signification. . . . During the seventies . . . people would

speak or write about conscientization as if it were a magical pill to be
applied in different does with an eye toward changing the world. (Freire,
1993, pp. 110–111)

In popular psychology the problematic of consciousness raising so
dilutes the content of the concept that the original context of reference in
a class-divided, dependent society was lost. The dilemma then is that *not
all* coming to consciousness extends necessarily into conscientization in
Freire's sense of the term. If all forms of distorted communication are not
equal, how do we differentiate them? For Freire the polemical notion of
"oppression" has a paradigmatic status in the grounding of concrete ethical
reflection in dialogue. As an extreme limit case of domination, the category
of the "oppressed" has a foundational function that becomes obscured by
the tendency—evident in the rise of identity politics in liberal democra-
cies—for every real and imagined form of oppression to claim an equal
status. Though these residual forms of domination need to be subjected to
social criticism, they cannot simply be equated with the absolute forms of
oppression associated historically with slavery, traditional patriarchy, racial
apartheid, authoritarian class oppression, and totalitarianism generally.
What is at stake then is the identification of the universalistic core of the
theory of conscientization, hence of establishing relative priorities with
respect to various ways in which mutual recognition is withheld.

It is instructive here to follow the suggestions of Enrique Dussel
(1997), a social theorist and liberation philosopher originally from Argentina who has worked for many years in Mexico. His more recent work
seeks to revitalize the concept of emancipation as part of an non-Eurocen-
tric liberation ethics. In its first moment, this strategy involves a universalistic appeal to French philosopher Emmanuel Levinas's oppressed "other"
as a degraded subject totally deprived of recognition: "The majority of
this humanity finds itself sunk in 'poverty,' 'unhappiness,' 'suffering,'
domination, and/or exclusion" (p. 285). It is in this context that Dussel
turns to Freire's concept of conscientization as a description of the processes within which liberation ethics unfolds not only in the consciousness
of the oppressed, but also in those who have shared experience with
the dominated and/or excluded (p. 286). In other words, the process of
conscientization has two moments relating to both the oppressed and the
witnesses to oppression who elaborate this as "explicit thematic critique"
for the global community.

Mutual Recognition: What's Love Got to Do with It?

Dussel's (1997) formulations bring us back to the question of the existential
origins of ethical critique and the personal dimensions of dialogue—

themes neglected by Habermas. Nevertheless, it has been argued that his account of aesthetic experience points to such unexplored possibilities. Though our feelings and emotions "are not normally shaped *directly* by the force of arguments," rational discourse "can serve to 'open our eyes' to the values disclosed or discredited in certain exemplary experiences"; this process could be extended to "the transformative power of experiences of significant others, life crises, alien cultures, countercultures, nature, and the sacred, among other things" even though they "remain bound to the context of action and experience in a way that, according to Habermas, discourses do not"(McCarthy, 1992, p. 57).

From this vantage point it can be argued that it is precisely here—in focusing on the dialogical contexts of action and experience—that Freire complements Habermas's preoccupation with formal argumentation in the context of theoretical and practical discourses. To have focused on the experiential contexts involving pedagogical practices would have forced Habermas to confront the question of a theory of pedagogical action, as well as such related questions as the status of "love" in critical theory (Bertilsson, 1991), the issues posed by feminist theories of "caring" (Larrabee, 1993), and the role of "moral feelings" generally. In putting love at the center of the pedagogical relation, Freire (1970a) and Dussel (1997) make explicit a theme that is otherwise marginalized in, though not absent from, Habermas's discourse. Though he acknowledges that "feelings make us sensitive to moral phenomena," it is argued that "in questions of the grounding and applications of norms they have, in addition, an invaluable heuristic function. But they cannot be the *ultimate* authority for the judgment of the phenomena which they reveal" (Habermas, 1992a, p. 270). Still, without this "heuristic" function there would be no moral phenomena to experience and evaluate.

For this reason Freire insists on the practical importance of love as a dimension of pedagogical relations and dialogue generally. This theme does not appear in Habermas except indirectly in relation to one of the four validity claims that implicitly underlie communicative action: The criterion of sincerity could be taken to imply something about relations of care. But Freire's consideration of love as a dimension of dialogue remains ambiguous, resulting in various possible interpretations. For example, Joel Spring (1994) connects this theme with Freire's use of Fromm's theory of social character and argues that like Wilhelm Reich, his pedagogy is eros-driven (pp. 164–165). Interpreting Freire in terms of an "Eros-driven teacher," however, is problematic on various grounds. He does follow Fromm's authoritarian-personality thesis as a general way of understanding domination in traditional class societies, especially the link between sexual repression and aggression. But his central concern is with the formation of open personalities capable of empathy with the oppressed. It is not so clear that his conception of "critical transitive consciousness" depends directly on sexual liberation in Wilhelm Reich's sense. Certainly, his understanding of conscientization in the context of literacy training does not depend directly on the sexual liberation of the campesino, though it is linked with the possibility of more egalitarian relations between the sexes. Though cognizant of the erotic dimension of teaching, Freire's critical pedagogy cannot be adequately understood in terms of a purely psychoanalytic model of liberation.

Then what does love have to do with pedagogical dialogue? A more persuasive way of addressing this question would be to consider the conception of mutual recognition that underlies Freire's dialogical model of learning and identity formation that derives from his appropriation of Hegel. Here again, Dussel's (1997) more recent formulations extend Freire's intuitions. For Dussel, the foundational principle of liberation ethics is initiated in a process of mutual recognition that acknowledges the existence of those who are excluded from rational argumentation (p. 288). Further, this recognition is grounded in a form of love that *precedes* criticism: "The recognition of the Other, the 'originary-ethical reason' [of Levinas], is prior to critique and prior to argument [to discursive or dialogical reason]. (pp. 288–289)

This point can be further illustrated by reading Freire's theory of conscientization from the perspective of Axel Honneth's (1996) reconstruction of the moral grammar of social conflicts in terms of patterns of mutual recognition. Though developed as a critique of Habermas's focus on the competence model of learning at the expense of a moral learning model, Honneth's discussion also provides—we would argue—a theoretical justification of the primacy of love and mutual recognition in Freire's pedagogical practice.

Drawing on the early Hegel and the American pragmatist social psychologist Mead, as well as Dewey's theory of emotions, Honneth (1996) develops a model of three patterns of intersubjective recognition respectively following the logic of "love," "rights," and "solidarity." Each of these involves a context of how forms of social integration are mediated by different types of social relations, that is, "emotional bonds, the granting of rights, or a shared orientation toward values" (p. 96). Each of these patterns of mutual recognition also involves specific types of moral development and self-relations, but love as a form of mutual recognition has a distinctive originary status:

> Thus in speaking of recognition as a constitutive element of love, what is meant is an affirmation of independence that is guided—indeed, supported—by care. . . . Although this means that love will always have an

> element of moral particularism to it, Hegel was nonetheless right to discern within it the structural core of all ethical life. For it is only this symbolically nourished bond . . . that produces the degree of basic individual self-confidence indispensable for autonomous participation in public life. (p. 107)

The second form of mutual recognition concerned with rights is based on the principles of respect and legal universality and has a fundamentally different content. As opposed to the particularism of love, the mutual recognition of respect conveyed through legal rights involves a capacity for taking the "perspective of the 'generalized other' which teaches us to recognize the other members of the community as the bearers of rights. Only here can we also understand ourselves as legal persons, in the sense that we can be sure that certain of our claims will be met" as part of a universalistic (and modern) conception of morality (Honneth, 1996, p. 108). The empirical basis for justifying the universalism of claims for respect can be derived primarily from evidence of its negative forms, that is, disrespect and degradation.

Finally, the third form of recognition is based on the distinction between legally defined "respect" as a universal quality of equal treatment given to personhood, as opposed to social "esteem" that "involves not the empirical application of general, intuitively known norms but rather the graduated appraisal of concrete traits and abilities" (Honneth, 1996, p. 113). By contrast, such social esteem does not have a universal structure because it is shaped by culturally variable conceptions of the relative worth of different contributions—based on personal differences—to the social division of labor. Whereas in corporatively stratified societies (e.g., feudalism) esteem was defined in terms of group-based forms of "honor," in modern societies esteem is increasingly based on individual achievement, though having increasingly plural forms as bases for "prestige" (p. 125). To be sure, this pluralism is accompanied by the tension of cultural conflict over assessments of relative worth. But within cultural groups there is a basic "solidarity" that "can be understood as an interactive relationship in which subjects mutually sympathize with their various different ways of life because, among themselves, they esteem each other symmetrically" (p. 128). In modern societies social solidarity depends on the ways in which social esteem is distributed and organized despite inequalities in the distribution of rewards: "To the extent to which every member of society is in a position to esteem himself or herself, one can speak of a state of societal solidarity" (p. 129).

In a remarkable way this typology of forms of mutual recognition parallels the objectives of conscientization as derived from the practice of literacy training. For Freire the point of departure is to create conditions of dialogue based on love and trust that give the insecure illiterate immersed in traditional society a basis for sharing a common humanity. Through the processes of codification and decodification, the linguistic basis for translating suppressed needs and aspirations into rights-based claims for self-respect becomes possible. Finally, conscientization ideally produces a capacity to relate various claims for social esteem as part of a broader solidarity that negates any simplistic sectarian conception of a death struggle between social classes, but does require a fundamental redistribution of esteem, and in highly inegalitarian societies, rewards as well.

Freire's focus on love is thus best understood in terms of an ethics of care oriented toward the three faces of mutual recognition: love, rights, and solidarity. The differentiated analysis of the three modes of mutual recognition helps restore the universal core of the theory of conscientization. From this perspective it becomes possible to avoid both the pseudo-universalism of class essentialism and the arbitrary and relativistic dilution of claims for recognition through the politics of identity. Though rejecting any notion of a calculus for establishing priorities, this strategy does provide a shared language for comparing and evaluating diverse forms of the experience of degradation.

The Ethical Critique of Postmodernism

The question of Freire's relationship to *postmodernism* remains controversial. It was not a topic to which he had the occasion or time to give any sustained attention. In his later writings he occasionally applied the term to his own approach, apparently under the influence of commentators who have linked critical pedagogy with postmodernism (Giroux, 1991; McLaren, 1986). With this in mind, we can understand his offhand use of the term. For example, in referring to his early days in Brazil, he suggests that "without knowing it, at the time, we were already—each in his or her own way—postmodern! In fact, in our mutual respect, we were actually experiencing the rock-bottom foundation of politics" (Freire, 1994, p. 13). Or again he identifies his method with "the postmodern progressive viewpoint" (1994, p. 81) and urges teachers "to become postmodernly progressive" (Freire, 1998b, p. 12). In criticizing Latin American Marxists, he suggests that they "get over their smug certainty that they are *modern*, adopt an attitude of humility in dealing with the popular classes, and become *postmodernly* less smug and less certain—progressively postmodern" (p. 96). In short, he essentially assimilates the concept into his own position: "the progressive postmodern, democratic outlook in which I take my position," a characterization that implies the possibility perhaps of a "nonprogressive" postmodern outlook (p. 132). Yet toward the end of his life he became sensitized to some of the limitations of his understanding of the term. For example, with respect to the seeming inevitability of the power of the powerful, he suggests that "one of the most important tasks for progressive intellectuals is to demystify postmodern discourses with respect to the inexorability of the situation" (Freire, 1997b, p. 36). As a consequence of this selective understanding of the term, Freire was not in a position to see those aspects and forms of postmodernism that offered a fundamental challenge and threat to his critical pedagogy.

Nevertheless, Freire's thinking contains the basis of a critique of aspects of postmodernist thought. Whereas Habermas provides a powerful philosophical critique of skeptical postmodernism, Freire's concrete ethics of dialogue provides a different kind of rejoinder. It is in this context that Enrique Dussel (1994) again becomes important as the basis of a reconstruction of conscientization in terms of a materialist liberation ethics that complements a formalist discourse ethics. For Dussel the discourse ethics of Habermas and Karl-Otto Apel are effective as a refutation of the moral skeptic, but fail with respect to the cynic who simply refuses to enter into the process of discursive argumentation, a tactic characteristic of much postmodernist theory. The dilemma of transcendental-pragmatic justification of Apel or even of Habermas's theory of communicative action is that the philosopher "who argues in the face of the skeptic finds him/herself already within a system where cynical reason reigns" (Dussel, 1996, p. 68). A conscientizing liberation ethics, according to Dussel, provides an alternative strategy that bypasses strategically the focus on rational argumentation. Drawing on Levinas, Dussel attempts to ground liberation philosophy in a nonargumentative a priori of the Other of ethical consciousness.[16] Accordingly, a liberation ethics supplements discourse ethics here as a concrete as opposed to a universalistic claim: "Liberation philosophy confronts the cunning of such a *strategic rationality grounded in Power*" by insisting on the testimonial power of the "other" in a face-to-face relation, as a dialogical praxis illustrated by Freire's concept of *conscientização* (Dussel, 1996, pp. 68–69).

The Theological Moment: Liberation Ethics

Consistent with Freire's links with liberation theology, Dussel's argument also couples the principle of critical alterity to specific religious traditions as the reference point for a "concrete" ethics. On the one hand, the Freirean pedagogical method is sufficiently open-ended to generate concrete ethi-

cal debate within diverse traditions (including non-Christian ones) because it builds directly on the universal experiences of learners and degraded subjects. On the other hand, the Freirean method does have an
elective affinity with the Latin American Catholic traditions of its origins
(Schutte, 1993, pp. 141ff.). For this reason, it is plausible to link Freire
with liberation theology (Oldenski, 1997), though this *is not a necessary*
link. It is well known that in the early years Freire learned tolerance in
being brought up by a Catholic mother and a non-Christian father with
spiritualist leanings. Yet in his early 20s he left the Catholic Church for
a year: "Because of the distance—which I could not understand because
of my naiveté—between real life and the commitment it demands,
and what the priests were saying in their Sunday sermons; I distanced
myself from the Church—but never from God" (quoted in Franco, 1979,
p. 47).

Consequently, Freire's work has from the beginning been regarded
as a resource for Christian social activism, a relationship elaborated
through the numerous studies of Freire from a theological perspective
(e.g., Elias, 1994; Schipani, 1984). The early *Educational Practice of Freedom*
(1973) quickly became in the mid-1960s the most popular book for Christian teachers in Brazil. His book *Pedagogy of the Oppressed* (1970c), however,
is credited with being one of the first pedagogical expressions of liberation
theology in tune with the documents of the Medellin Conference (1968),
which actualized the teachings of the Catholic Church for Latin America
after the Second Vatican Council. But Freire never pursued the specific
connections between his educational theory and liberation theology. In
stressing that churches cannot be neutral, he necessarily sides with the
prophetic conception of religious practice found in theologies of liberation
that draw on his critical pedagogy (Freire, 1985, pp. 121–142). In short,
Freire's personal perspective opens the way for a critical embracing of
both "Marx" and "Jesus":

> I got the conviction that people were sending me to Marx. The people
> never did say, "Paulo, please why do you not go to read Marx?" No. The
> people never said that, but their reality said that to me. The misery of the
> reality. . . . But what is interesting in my case—this is not the case of all
> the people whose background is similar to mine—my "meetings" with
> Marx never suggested to me to stop "meeting" Christ. I never said to
> Marx: "Look, Marx, really Christ was a baby. Christ was naive." And also
> I never said to Christ, "Look, Marx was a materialistic and terrible man."
> I always spoke to both of them in a very loving way. You see, I feel com-
> fortable in this position. Sometimes people say to me that I am contradic-
> tory. . . . If you ask me, then if I am a religious man, I say no. . . . They un-

derstand religious as religion-like. I would say that I am a man of faith.
(Horton & Freire, 1990, pp. 245–246)

In short: "This is how I have always understood God—a presence
in history that does not preclude me from making history, but rather
pushes me toward world transformation, which makes it possible to
restore the *humanity* of those who exploit and of the weak" (Freire, 1997b,
pp. 103–104). And it is in this context that it is possible to develop a rather
different vantage point for assessing the problematic foundationalist ontological claims of Freire's theory of humanization and philosophy of praxis.
We would suggest that there are three plausible grounding strategies for
Freirean pedagogy. A first possibility, popular in Brazil, is to reaffirm the
links between Freire and the Marxist tradition understood in terms of a
general dialectical philosophy or pedagogy of conflict and praxis (Gadotti,
1996). A second leads in a post- or antifoundationalist direction along the
lines of convergence with Habermas (as we have argued), or from a
slightly different perspective, the resistance postmodernism of Henry
Giroux (1993) and Peter McLaren (1994). The third direction is to renew
the links between Freirean pedagogy and the liberation theology with
which it was associated at its birth. This latter option is largely closed
to the secular interpretations of Freire that inform critical pedagogy in
advanced societies. But many have pointed to the need for a theological
moment in critical theory, especially given its Hegelian origins (Baum,
1975). But Habermas remains resistant to pursuing such theological questions (Habermas, 1992d, 1997b) even though his theory of communicative
action has stimulated the rethinking of fundamental theology (Browning & Fiorenza, 1992; Peukert, 1984) and has been viewed as complementary to liberation theology (Campbell, 1999). For Habermas, however:

> Communicative reason neither announces the absence of consolation in a
> world forsaken by God, nor does it take it upon itself to provide any con-
> solation. . . . As long as no better words for what religion can say are
> found in the medium of rational discourse, it will coexist abstemiously
> with the former, neither supporting it nor combating it. (1992c, 145)

Yet theological questions remain inevitable for those caught up in
transforming the way of life through which their identity was formed.
The vast majority of oppressed groups retain strong religious beliefs as
part of their popular culture. One of the weaknesses of the critical modernism of Habermas and others has been its ambivalence toward the diverse
forms of religious revival that have become apparent in the context of

resistance to globalization and the postmodern condition. The practical question is whether critical modernism can sustain a productive dialogue with revitalized religious traditions that are consistent with the emancipatory impulses of critical social theory informed by Freirean pedagogy (Habermas, 2001b, pp. 78–89). The fraternal relation between the Zapatista National Liberation Army and liberation theology in Chiapas, Mexico, provides an illustration of such possibilities, as well as the tensions (Johnston, 2000).

The Utopian Moment of Critical Theory

Freire's historical anthropology, as well as his theory of conscientization, also draws attention to the motivational importance of the utopian dimension of praxis theory. This theme is obscured in Habermas's focus on formal aspects of justice reasoning, as well as his focus on advanced societies. In his essay "the crisis of the welfare state and the exhaustion of utopian energies," the explicit frame of reference is the time consciousness of modern "Western culture" (Habermas, 1989b, p. 284). Though disputing the postmodern claim that the apparent exhaustion of utopian energies reflects a new *Zeitgeist*, he concedes that the relative success of the welfare state has fundamentally changed the context of politics because the vast majority is relatively affluent. However plausible as a characterization of those forms of society that enjoy something like a liberal democratic welfare state, *this formulation simply ignores the fact that the majority of humanity does not have such opportunities.* It is in this context that Dussel's (1997) effort to incorporate the concerns of peripheral societies into the conception of critical rationality assumes pivotal importance for an *alternative conception of utopian energies.* Freire also offers a valuable complement to Habermas by explicitly linking critical philosophy and the practice of freedom as part of a "utopian enterprise" (Freire, 1970a, p. 47).

This utopian factor implies a double tension: "denunciation" and "annunciation." Insofar as the educator carries out his or her utopian role, he or she is turned into a dangerous prophet for the system. Rather than performing the role of the functionary who reproduces the elements of the ideological consciousness of the mode of production, the educator becomes a cultural critic:

> In this sense the pedagogy which we defend, conceived in a significant area of the Third World, is itself a utopian pedagogy. By this very fact it is full of hope, for to be utopian is not to be merely idealistic or impractical but rather to engage in denunciation and annunciation. Our pedagogy

cannot do without a vision of man and of the world. It formulates a scientific humanist conception which finds its expression in a dialogical praxis in which the teachers and learners together, in the act of analyzing a dehumanizing reality, denounce it while announcing its transformation in the name of the liberation of man. (Freire, 1970a, p. 20)

It is also in this context that we need to consider Freire's important concept of "untested feasibility" as he puts it in suggesting that "we need critical hope the way a fish needs unpolluted water" (Freire, 1994, p. 9). The terms *limit situations* and *untested feasibility* are central to Freire's pragmatic utopianism. Limit situations are what social actors perceive to be obstacles or barriers to change and freedom in their lives. The question of transformation is thus ultimately about how people come to view those situations as "realities," whether as something impossible to change, something that is feared to be changed, or perhaps something that could be changed. But for the most part immersion in everyday life does not encourage reflection on such issues, does not allow the distance and detachment necessary. And yet it is only through such critical reflection that "limit acts" that might initiate change and a process of dialogical action become possible.

From Modernity to Trans-modernity

Finally, a Freire informed by Dussel (1996) provides a corrective to Habermas's neglect of peripheral societies. At the same time, it suggests a somewhat different strategy than that of assimilating Freire into "resistance postmodernism" in the manner of Giroux (1993) and McLaren (1994). Dussel's alternative strategy is to acknowledge that the concept of enlightenment as used from Kant to Habermas "inherits an Eurocentric point of departure"; but for Dussel this residual ethnocentrism does not altogether negate its potential universality (Dussel, 1996, p. 51). Dussel reconstructs the logic of its degeneration as a sacrificial myth from the Valladolid dispute of 1550 with the confrontation between Ginés de Sepúlveda and Bartolomé de las Casas, who defended the Indians of the New World against Eurocentric claims of superiority. From this perspective he calls for a *trans-modernity* that articulates the *role of the periphery in constituting modernity from its origins*. From this perspective the critique of modernity was evident at the outset in its selectivity, one-sidedness, and incompletion. At the same time, the "emancipatory rational nucleus" of this project remains indispensable for those who have yet to enjoy its benefits. For Dussel, "Liberation Philosophy, going beyond post-Marxism (but returning to Marx 'himself') and post-modernity (from the 'other face' of modernity)" provide a positive, future-oriented discourse directed toward the majority of humanity (Dussel, 1996, p. 14). This formulation provides a helpful interpretation of Freire's position on the relationship among modernity, postcolonialism, and dependency, as well as a position that is consistent with Habermas's account of the selectivity of modernity. The concept of trans-modernity envisions recognizing and reconciling the multiple modernities implied equally by Habermas's conception of the selectivity of modernity and Freire's understanding of the incompletion of humanization.

8

Conclusion

In Defense of Critical Theory as Educational Theory

I think that I'm, in that sense, a Gramscian—that every moment of decon-struction is also a moment of reconstruction. That reconstruction is no more permanent than the previous one, but it is not just pulling the text apart. . . . You can't get out of the fact that to say something is to pull apart an existing configuration of meaning and to begin to sketch out another configuration.

—Hall, 1994, p. 264

Postmodernist critiques of moral universalism too often simply ignore the fact that it is precisely notions of fairness, impartiality, respect for the integrity and dignity of the individual, and the like that undergird respect-ful tolerance of difference by placing limits on egocentrism. Typically such notions are simply taken for granted in anti-universalist invocations of otherness and difference—which are, it evidently goes without saying, to be respected, not obliterated.

—McCarthy, 1990, p. xiii, n. 12)

Critical theory and related forms of the sociology of education and critical pedagogy have been typically subjected to at least five types of attack that are generally well known: (1) From the direction of positivist educational theory, it has been rejected as impractical, romantic, and without any empirical basis; (2) from the Marxist Left, it has been condemned for idealism, subjectivism, and romanticism, a perspective most common in Latin America; (3) from the direction of conservative hermeneutic and phenomenological approaches, it has been received with ambivalence because of its "Westernizing" politicization of education at the expense of the lifeworld and tradition; (4) in the name of radical environmental critiques it has been charged with normative anthropomorphism; and (5) under the labels of postmodernist, poststructuralist, and postcolonial the-ory, it has been questioned for its modernist rationalist bias, normative universalism, conception of an autonomous subject, and lack of attention to questions of difference.

We will not take up in detail the first four lines of criticism here. In various ways these types of criticism have been addressed in the preceding chapters. With respect to positivist critics, we have argued that the pluralist methodological approach shared by Freire and Habermas does not preclude selective use of empirical methodologies any more than they would reduce educational research to a narrowly defined empiricism. As for Marxist criticism, in a post-Marxist context the need for radical reconstruction is self-evident: The projects of both Freire and Habermas can be understood as immanent critiques of the Marxist tradition from the perspective of a theory of intersubjectivity and communication. Further, such a critical theory of communicative action provides a powerful critique of conservative hermeneutic defenses of the lifeworld that ignore the cumulative effects of domination that distort existing traditions and their ongoing need for critical renewal.[17] Finally, it must be acknowledged that though this issue is not taken up by Freire and Habermas, the vision of "education for integral human development" should be expanded to include nature (O'Sullivan, 1999: 208ff).

In concluding, we will focus rather on several interrelated questions relating to the issue of critical theory's "modernism." First, we will argue that the perspectives of Freire and Habermas incorporate a postfoundationalist critique of Enlightenment modernist thought. From this perspective, we will introduce some cautions with respect to the attempt to appropriate Freire as a "resistance postmodernist." Second, we will suggest that extending critical theory to educational issues in peripheral and dependent societies in the context of globalization provides important insights into the limitations of postmodernist critiques of universalism. Third, we will argue that in important respects critical theory and postmodernism are complementary. And finally, we will consider the ways in which Freire and Habermas's conception of the responsibility of intellectuals responds to the challenge of postmodern critiques of modernist theorizing.

CRITICAL THEORY'S RADICAL "MODERNISM"

In taking up the vexed question of modernity versus postmodernity, we accept the role of postmodernist thinking at its best as having an important therapeutic function, but contend that it abdicates the problems of positive reconstruction embraced in complementary ways by Habermas and Freire. As a diffuse philosophical tendency, postmodernism is closely associated with a poststructuralist interpretation of the so-called *linguistic turn* in philosophy that stresses that all knowledge is a linguistic construction. As Habermas has suggested, there are three basic strategies for dealing with the linguistic turn in postmetaphysical or postfoundationalist social theory: communications-theoretic, structuralist, and poststructuralist. It is *the communications-theoretic conception of language* that defines the shared reconstructive perspectives of Habermas and Freire. From this perspective, the intersubjective construction of reality has a pragmatic relation to historical contexts of action that is mediated by technical and social rationalities that can become the basis of contingent, yet universalizing, knowledge. Whereas structuralism simply dissolves the subject, poststructuralist theory reduces it to pure contingent discourses, thus undermining any emancipatory reference points:[18]

> When the *poststructuralist* thinkers surrender this scientistic self-understanding, they also surrender the only moment that was still retained from the concept of reason developed in the modern period. They follow the lead of the later Heidegger. . . . *All* validity claims become immanent to particular discourses. They are simultaneously absorbed into the totality of some one of the blindly occurring discourses and left at the mercy of the "hazardous play" among these discourses as each overpowers another. (Habermas, 1992c, p. 208)

Freire and Habermas share a postfoundationalist conception of the communicative subject that attempts to provide a defensible strategy of critique that is based on neither a teleological philosophy of history nor a positivist conception of ideology critique. From this perspective there have always been oppositional elements within modernity, hence an immanent critique of the Enlightenment based on viewing modernity as an "unfinished project." The *critical modernist* sensibility thus derives from a strategic option: "We can either celebrate the death of the modernist subject or seek to transform the embattled self of modernity into a new self than can appreciate otherness without dissolving in it, that can respect heterogeneity without being overwhelmed by it" (Benhabib, 1996a, p. 337). This critical modernist position has sometimes been characterized as "between" modernism and postmodernism. Consequently, the diffuse and contradictory uses of the term *postmodern* give considerable leeway for interpreting Freire (and to a certain extent even Habermas) as a "resistance postmodernist." Our suggestion is that it would be less confusing to locate Habermas (and Freire) in terms of a distinctive *postfoundationalist critical social theory*.[19] It is in this context that we must evaluate their continuing concern with "reason" and "universality." As Habermas puts it, the unconcealed horrors of existing unreason have eliminated the last remnant of an essentialist trust in reason. Yet so far as we can see, there still exits no alternative to a modernity that is now conscious of its own contingencies. . . . There is neither a higher nor a lower reason to which we can appeal, only a procedurally sobering reason—a reason that proceeds solely on sufficient grounds; a reason that puts itself on trial. That is what Kant meant: the critique of reason is reason's proper task. . . . The work of self-critical reason consists in overcoming its own unreasonable projections. (Habermas, 1997a, p. 61)

From the perspective of such a postfoundationalist critical theory, it is crucial to differentiate between different forms of universalism. Most importantly, Habermas distinguishes the moral universalism that postulates "an exclusive truth claim for a certain doctrine and for an exemplary way of life" from a *procedural universalism* that is oriented toward the validity of outcomes. For example, a procedural universalism does not claim to rule on the question of whether abortion is in some abstract sense right or wrong; nor does it provide a method for determining whether a particular woman should have an abortion. All it can do is assess the extent to which a particular process of moral decision is characterized by self-reflexive processes of deliberation that adequately include self and others:

This procedural rigor has nothing overpowering about it. It merely spells out the idea of equal rights and reciprocal recognition that also lies at the heart of any critique of the rape of the particular by the general. Because moral universalism demands equal respect for each and every person, it facilitates individualism—that is, the acknowledgement of the individual and the particular. The critics' category error is connected with their choice of the wrong model; namely, the normalizing, leveling interventions of a bureaucracy insensitive to uniqueness and to individual rights in individual cases. (Habermas, 1997a, pp. 78–79).

In short, the historicist or contingent universalism of Habermas and Freire is not abstract and ahistorical. It is open to particularity and difference, though within procedurally defined limits. In other words, transitorily realized mutual understanding is guaranteed procedurally because "the unity of reason only remains perceptible in the plurality of its voices" (Habermas, 1992c, p. 117). For example, though neither theorist has adequately treated issues of gender and race, developing bodies of criticism have productively explored the issues of enlarging the theory of domination and emancipation to encompass such issues for Habermas (Benhabib,

Butler, Cornell, & Fraser, 1995; Meehan, 1995), and Freire (Freire et al., 1997; Weiler, 1994, 1996), or with reference to both (Burbules, 1993, 1995; Burbules & Rice, 1991; Kohli, 1995).

Furthermore, reading Freire in relation to Habermas cautions against attempts to assimilate Freire into some kind of "resistance" or "emancipatory" postmodernism. At some points Freire's critical modernism does not seem to be in doubt, as when it is suggested that "Freire stands, like Habermas, as a modernist, though not, we would argue against postmodernist critics, to be seen as a 'disappearing species' within a 'dying class'" (McLaren & Lankshear, 1993, p. 3). But elsewhere McLaren (1994) suggests that Freire's work "stands at the borderline of modernist and postmodernist discourse" and draws him into the cause of a resistance postmodernism that is not politically debilitating because it is based on a materialist politics concerned with "a critique of the totality of regimes of exploitation in its various guises" (p. 204). The key postmodernist element in Freire is the rejection of theoretical totalization: He serves as "both a modernist reminder that people still suffer pain, oppression, and abandonment and a postmodernist strategy for destabilizing totalizing regimes of signification" (McLaren, 1994, p. 210).

The problem with this definition is its equation of "postmodernism" with "destabilizing totalizing regimes of signification," thus ignoring the fact that this theme has long been central to some forms of modernist thought (e.g., Dewey's pragmatism, Wittgenstein's linguistic philosophy, and Adorno and Habermas in the Frankfurt School tradition). If Freire is to be labeled a postmodernist in this sense, these other figures must be included, but then the term becomes totally ambiguous as a reference point. To then link this resistance postmodernism with Freire's "critical utopianism" even further dilutes the connection with what generally passes for postmodernism—a decidedly anti-utopian tendency.

Similarly, Henry Giroux (1993) locates Freire on the border of modernist and postmodernist thinking, though this point is also transformed into a biographical thesis that characterizes the early Freire as overly totalizing and afflicted by essentializing binary oppositions between oppressor and oppressed, and so forth, as opposed to the later Freire who "pushes against those boundaries that invoke the discourse of the unified, humanist subject, universal agents, and Enlightenment rationality" (p. 181). In these later writings and conversations, Freire shares an "affinity with emancipatory strands of postmodern discourse" given "his refusal of a transcendent ethics, epistemological foundationalism, and political teleology" and "a provisional political and ethical discourse subject to the play of history, culture and power" (Giroux, 1993, p. 182). Within the educational literature, as a consequence, it has become common to refer to Freire's work as a "postmodern moral pedagogy" (Tappan & Brown, 1996).

We have several reservations about this kind of argument. First, as our preceding analysis suggests, we find greater continuity in Freire's thinking, but would acknowledge a shift in his later recognition of the radicalness of his own ideas, especially the extent to which they involved an ambivalent relation to aspects of the classical Marxist tradition. Second, Freire's personal thinking (as opposed to the specific principles of his pedagogy) retained a link with Christian and liberation theology, as we have noted; hence, he does not altogether abandon "political theology" as a resource for practice. Third, Freire's primary concern is with a practical pedagogy, but he views his work as part of a division of labor within a critical social science. Accordingly, he acknowledges the importance of a wide variety of strategies for gaining knowledge about social reality and consistently refers to the importance of scientific credibility, despite the historical origins of all knowledge. Fourth, the notion of an "affinity" with postmodernism obscures the distance of Freire from many typical postmodernist positions, other than a shared antifoundationalism.

In short, vaguely situating Freire in terms of an emancipatory postmodernism does not suffice to adequately locate and specify the ways in which he persisted in making generalizable validity claims for ethical, epistemological, and emancipatory concerns: He seeks to rationally justify ethical discourse (though not in transcendental terms), to ground empirical knowledge in scientific practices (though in constructivist rather than foundationalist terms), and to imagine a utopian future (though not in terms of teleological inexorability). The comparison with Habermas provides resources for reinforcing and complementing Freire's position on the border between modernism and postmodernism, but anchored in both critical social theory and the experience of marginalized societies. As we have argued, it is through Habermas's unique postfoundationalist strategy that Freire can most effectively ground the intuitions underlying his dialogical pedagogy. For these kinds of reasons we prefer to characterize the shared approaches of Freire and Habermas as an *emancipatory postfoundationalism* rather than an emancipatory postmodernism.

CRITICAL THEORY AND POSTCOLONIAL WORLDS

On the other hand, we fully agree when Giroux (1993) argues that "what has been increasingly lost in the North American and Western appropriation of Freire's work is the profound and radical nature of its theory and practice as an anti-colonial and postcolonial discourse" (p. 177), though this theme must be defined in terms of the unique "postcolonial" context of Latin America (De la Campa, 1995; Klor de Alva, 1995). Yet we would argue that assimilating Freire into contemporary postmodernism forgets how his thought *precedes* postmodernism as a part of the *underside of modernity on the periphery*. In this respect he embodies Foucault's (1984) concern with the "countermodernity" (p. 39) that has been a part of modernity from the outset. Postmodernists may counter that such a critique of modernity still "implies repressive totalization," but "critique is not a question of the arbitrary and coercive espousal of premises and precepts, but rather of commitment to that coherence of thought which alone ensures its emancipatory power" (Dews, 1987, p. 242).

A key issue of debate is the applicability of procedural universalism and the critique of domination as selective rationalization of the type proposed by Freire and Habermas to understand postcolonial and underdeveloped contexts. Standard criticisms of theories of psychological development, for example, suggest that developmental psychology merely "functions as a tool of cultural imperialism through the reproduction of Western values and models within post-colonial societies" (Burman, 1994, p. 185). Similar difficulties have plagued Western feminists in their failure to adequately contextualize their critique or to include adequate participation on the part of Third World women. At the level of societal rationalization, the application of "Western" technologies has been labeled a failure on human and ecological grounds. Taken together these types of sentiments have increasingly been radicalized under the heading "postdevelopment" theory (Rahnema, 1997). But others argue that such critiques "overstate their case and offer no alternatives." At most they vaguely appeal to "people's culture, indigenous culture, local knowledge and culture" even though they can "lead, if not to ethnochauvisnism, to reification of both cultural and locality or people" (Nederveen Pieterse, 1998, p. 366).

A critical or "reflexive" modernist perspective holds that theories of domination and development may be European in origin but their import is universal (Beck, 1992; Beck, Giddens, & Lash, 1994). As Habermas notes,

> this normative idea of equal respect for everyone was developed in Europe, but it does not follow that it is merely a narrow-minded expression of European culture and Europe's will to assert itself. Human rights also depend on the reflexivity that enables us to step back from our own tradition and learn to understand others from their point of view. Europe produced more than a colonialism and an imperialism whose ugliness cannot be papered over. Occidental rationalism also produced the cognitive posi-

tions that allow us to take a self-critical attitude toward Eurocentrism. That of course does not mean that Europeans and Americans do not need members of Arabic, Asiatic, or African cultures to enlighten them concerning the blind spots of their potentially selective ways of reading the meaning of human rights. (1997a, pp. 85–86)

But mutual understanding requires conditions of symmetry that are difficult to meet: "Europeans can also learn from Africans—though it is difficult to fulfill such conditions for symmetry when the asymmetric conditions of exchange in the world economy reach into all aspects of life" (Habermas, 1997a, p. 85). For similar reasons, it is plausible to apply Frankfurt critical theory to African issues (Bidima, 1993) or imagine African applications of—and equivalents to—Freire (Gitau, 1982; Manzo, 1995).

Yet it should also be stressed that this universalism is understood in historicist terms, not as a transcendental a priori beyond time: "Moral universalism is a *historical result* . . . not something that can safely be left to Hegel's absolute spirit. Rather, it is chiefly a function of collective efforts and sacrifices made by sociopolitical movements" (Habermas, 1990, p. 208). For this reason, Habermas acknowledges, "any universalistic morality is dependent upon a form of life that *meets it halfway*" in the sense that it facilitates abstract, flexible ego identities and complementary, responsive institutions (Habermas, 1990, p. 208). Once these thresholds have been crossed, local and concrete ethical reflection cannot ignore dialogue with universal questions.

In short, our account of Freire and Habermas provides a warning for those ignoring the practical consequences of a postmodernizing "postdevelopment" theory in Latin America and elsewhere that tends to dismissively label all universalistic claims—whether technical or normative—as hopelessly Eurocentric (e.g., Crush, 1995; Rahnema, 1997). Critical social theory recognizes the selectivity and limits of much of what has passed as "development theory," yet proposes a reflexivity that does not annihilate the universal in the name of the "local." Like postdevelopment theory, the postmodernist debates have had a salutary deconstructive influence but also falter as constructive alternatives. For example, it is widely acknowledged that the influence of postmodernism in Latin America has had some positive effects: self-criticism on the Marxist Left, a new appreciation of democracy, and awareness of the one-sidedness of European-style modernization based primarily on instrumental rationality. But this appropriation runs into contradictions to the extent that it assumes something like the surpassing of modernity by postmodernity:

> Such a supposedly postmodern conception requires a certain univeralism as a foundation for institutionalizing and guaranteeing the possibility of exercising those liberties, of letting difference live. . . . Without such universalism, there would be no categories with which to evaluate cultural practices, to take positions; that is to say, a pure appreciation of plurality, of difference, does not leave any evaluative instruments for condemning practices or cultural traditions and/or policies that precisely oppose the values of tolerance and plurality. But the sad consequence is that accepting tolerance has its limits, that plurality must have its limits—if both do not want to sow the seeds of their own destruction. (Schwenn, 1998, p. 73)

Processes of globalization are de facto creating a unification of the planet that will require minimal, species-specific criteria for adjudicating disputes between different forms of civilization and ways of life, as well as their impact on nature. The fundamental tensions between the concrete and universalistic dimensions for evaluating knowledge and values cannot be wished away, but they can be understood and dealt with more effectively. Critical social theory in the versions advocated by Freire and Habermas builds awareness of this tension into the theory itself, thus arguing that "difference" cannot defensively ignore demands for minimally accommodating to universal principles, any more than "universality" can be adequately articulated independently of particular groups in specific historical contexts. These practical dilemmas are largely evaded by the postmodernist mantra of wishing away dualities, or the tendency of some forms of postcolonial and postmodernist theory to gloss over the human consequences of traditional forms of domination in the name of difference or resisting Eurocentrism. For such reasons, Edward Said (1994)—one of the founders of postcolonial theory who is often labeled a postmodernist—does not flinch in asserting that the responsibility of intellectuals is to "speak the truth to power" and to criticize "on the basis of universal principles: that all human beings are entitled to expect decent standards of behavior concerning freedom and justice" (p. 11). Similarly, the French philosopher Jacques Derrida (1996)—whose deconstructionist philosophy is often held to culminate in a skeptical postmodernist relativism—sees his ultimate objectives very differently:

> I refuse to renounce the great classical discourse of emancipation. I believe that there is an enormous amount to do today for emancipation, in all domains and all the areas of the world and society. . . . Even if I say that "I don't believe in truth" or whatever, the minute I open my mouth there is a "believe me" at work. . . . And this "I promise you that I am speaking the truth" is a messianic a priori, a promise which, even if it is

not kept, even if one knows that it cannot be kept, takes place and *qua* promise is messianic. And from this point of view, I do not see how one can pose the question of ethics if one renounces the motifs of emancipation and the messianic. Emancipation is once again a vast question today and I must say that I have no tolerance for those who—deconstructionist or not—are ironical with regard to the grand discourse of emancipation. (p. 82)

And, as Michel Foucault—often characterized as a postmodern relativist—noted in a statement, "Confronting Governments: Human Rights," just before his death: "there exists an international citizenship that has its rights and its duties, and that obliges one to speak out against every abuse of power, whoever the author, whoever its victim" (Foucault, 2000, p. 474).

POSTMODERNISM AS THE "OTHER" OF REASON

What these commitments of some "postmodernist" authors to principles such as "truth," "emancipation," and "rights" suggest is that in many respects the fundamental opposition between critical theory and postmodernism has been misconceived, a theme of some important recent work in educational theory (Popkewitz & Brennan, 1998; Popkewitz & Fendler, 1999). And, to be sure, Habermas has contributed to this tendency by his own aggressive critique of French thought (Passerin d'Entrèves & Benhabib, 1997), despite acknowledging that "'posties' are not only deft opportunists with their noses to the wind; as seismographers tracking the spirit of the age, they must also be taken seriously" (Habermas, 1992c, p. 4). A more promising way of framing these oppositions has been suggested by the insightful comparison of the dilemmas of Kant and Habermas as "comprehensive" theorists (Strong & Sposito, 1995). From this perspective, Kant was confronted with the paradox of his own comprehensiveness, that is, being both original and comprehensive at the same time. We can present only some the basic themes of this complex critique. The point of departure is the assumption that any constructivist and historicist position that understands its own limits is confronted with the need for a "metacritique of pure reason" of the type developed by Herder against Kant. Herder's relativizing culturalism sought to show that Kant's pure reason was ultimately embedded in historical contexts, a possibility Kant only hints at, Strong and Sposito conclude, in his own *Critique of Judgment*:

> The insight of the metacritique of pure reason is that the comprehensiveness of a system of reason cannot be predicated on comprehensiveness itself, and that a certain amount of *incomprehensibility* is necessary to make "systematic" or "complete" comprehension possible. The "other of reason," understood as that which stands outside of, or is precluded by, an existing system of reason, is the *ground* of reason in that in order to make sense, individuals must be oriented such that they can in fact understand each other. The orientation itself cannot come from within the system since the system itself is predicated on it. (Strong & Sposito, 1995, p. 274)

Similarly, Habermas's paradigm shift is confronted with the same dilemma: "Kant, like Habermas, is confronted with the upholders of the possibility of incomprehensibility—for Kant Schlegel, Herder, and the others; for Habermas the postmodernists" (Strong & Sposito, 1995, p. 279). Habermas's total denunciation of postmodernists contributes to his failure to engage them adequately on many issues. What Habermas forgets is that "the we of universalizability is thus dependent on that availability of the nonuniversal—not just the particular, but that which cannot be comprehended in terms of that world" (Strong & Sposito, 1995, pp. 280–281). From a similar perspective, it has also been argued that "communicative reason and discursive democracy need supplementing by an appreciation of the prediscursive and non-discursive levels on which power and alterity circulate, such that postmodern decodings and strategies are an essential dimension of any emancipatory politics" (Coole, 1997, p. 221). A number of recent discussions of the relationship between critical and poststructuralist theory (especially Foucault) have reflected a similar strategy of mediation (Ashenden & Owen, 1999; Benhabib et al., 1995; McCarthy, 1996; Popkewitz & Brennan, 1998). It is in this context that critical pedagogy needs to be confronted with the "impossibility" of education, demystification, and justice in Derrida's sense of impossibility releasing the possible (Biesta, 1998). We anticipate that the reformulation of these confrontations within the context of educational theory relating to questions of power, knowledge, and difference will be a productive basis for rethinking many current positions.

LAST WORDS: THE EDUCATION OF THE EDUCATORS

This study has attempted to bring together versions of critical social theory linked respectively with the center and periphery, as well as North and South. Despite the great contrast of theoretical style and forms of practice, Freire and Habermas reconnect Latin America and critical social theory in a manner that was ironically prefigured in the endowment that made the Frankfurt School of social research possible. It was an Argentinian Jewish exporter whose funds established the Frankfurt Institute for Social Research in the early 1920s. Paradoxically, "it was the value produced by the labor of the gauchos and peons of the pampa, objectivized in wheat or beef and appropriated by the great landowning and merchant families of Argentina that, transferred to Germany, gave birth to the Frankfurt School." (Dussel, 1996, p. 66)

In its more recent incarnations, critical social theory has been premised on a conception of the nature of social theory and the intellectual that departs dramatically from the classic leftist understanding of the "legislative" intellectual of the type personified by Jean-Paul Sartre (Bauman, 1987). As "interpretive" intellectuals, both Freire and Habermas view themselves with great humility and a sense of limits. Freire was fond of saying, citing Dewey, that originality did not stem from "the extraordinary and fanciful" as opposed to "putting everyday things to uses which had not occurred to others" (Freire, 1973, p. 57, n. 24). As he notes, he did not even invent the term *conscientization*, which was rather the anonymous product of a working group in 1964, though it was first diffused internationally in the work of Helder Cámara. Similarly, Habermas's synthetic strategy—standing on the shoulders of Kant, Hegel, Marx, Mead, and so forth—proves illuminating in showing how already well known theories can elucidate old problems in novel ways.

Given such an attitude toward their own creative powers, Freire and Habermas have given theoretical and practical flesh to Marx's poignant but problematic dictum: "The materialist doctrine that men [*sic*] are products of circumstances and upbringing, and that, therefore, changed men are products of other circumstances and changed upbringing, forgets that it is men who change circumstances and that it is essential to educate the educator" (Marx & Engels, 1978, p. 144). But what does it really mean "to educate the educator"? In important respects, this whole book has been directed toward this question as one of the central questions of education and social theory. As Freire cautions, "By talking about 'illumination,' it is very important for the liberating educators to know they are not properly the 'illuminators.' I think that liberating education implies illumination of reality, but the illuminators are the agents together in this process, the educators and the educatees together" (Freire & Macedo, 1987, p. 49).

In a parallel fashion, Habermas strongly limits the claims of experts and intellectuals in social struggles and rejects inflated claims for the status of philosophy and philosophers. Accordingly, his conception of the intellectual "rejects the claim for leadership and exclusive knowledge" but "holds on to a paradigm of rational pedagogy" based on the procedures of "dialogue and immanent criticism" (Hohendahl, 1997, pp. xxiii–xxiv). As Habermas (1997a) notes in addressing the question of what we can learn from history, "history may at best be a critical teacher who tells us how we ought *not* to do things. Of course, it can advise us in this way only if we admit to ourselves that we have failed" (p. 13).

Habermas's social theory is animated by a foundational lesson of "how we ought not to do things" that is implicit in his theory of practice: first, that "in a process of enlightenment there can only be participants"; and second, that whatever general orientation theory can provide in justifying the validity claims of discourse about moral truth, it cannot prescribe actual forms of life that can be realized only through participants in dialogue. For this reason he strongly qualifies the claims of discourse ethics and a critical theory of society:

> However, this perspective comprises *only* formal determination of the communicative infrastructure of *possible* forms of life and life-histories; it does not extend to the concrete shape of an exemplary life-form or a paradigmatic life-history. Actual forms of life and actual life-histories are embedded in unique traditions . . . communication free of domination can count as a necessary condition for the "good life" but can by no means replace the historical articulation of a felicitous form of life. (Habermas, 1982, p. 228)

A crucial consequence of this position is a rejection of the assumption that emancipation can be legislated from above as imagined by traditional socialist conceptions of the uses of state power: "You can no more conjure a liberal political culture out of your hat than you can employ a network of voluntary associations to create an activist society of citizens. The idea that history could be fabricated was an illusion of the philosophy of history. Administrative power is not the right medium for the creation or even the production of emancipated life-forms," which require "culturally mobilized public spheres" (Habermas, 1997a, pp. 76–77).

Further, Habermas has a very limited conception of the tasks of philosophy and social theory in pointing to the formation of ethical sensibilities: "I don't believe that we can change moral intuitions except as educators—that is, not as theoreticians and not as writers" (Habermas, 1992a, p. 202). And in speaking of his own ambitions as a writer, he challenges those who sustain the pretensions of classical metaphysics: "The thinker as lifestyle, as vision, as expressive self-portrait is no longer possible. I am not a producer of a *Weltanschauung*; I would really like to produce a few small truths, not the one big one" (Habermas, 1992a, p. 128). Instead, Habermas rejects as mythical any elitist, individualistic conception of truth:

One should not try, as Heidegger and Adorno both did, to produce truths outside of the sciences and to wager on a higher level of insight, on the thinking of Being or on a mindfulness of tormented nature. . . . For my own part, in any case, I have said goodbye to the emphatic philosophical claim to truth. This elitist concept of truth is a last remaining piece of myth, and you know that I do not want to return to where the *Zeitgeist* is heading today. (Habermas, 1992a, pp. 126–127)

What are the guiding principles of these "small truths"? They culminate in a conceptual motive and a fundamental intuition:

I have a conceptual motive and a fundamental intuition. . . . The motivating thought concerns the reconciliation of modernity which has fallen apart, the idea that without surrendering the differentiation that modernity has made possible in the cultural, the social and economic spheres, one can find forms of living together in which autonomy and dependency can truly enter into a non-antagonistic relation, that one can walk tall in a collectivity that does not have the dubious quality of backward-looking substantial forms of community.

The intuition springs from the sphere of relations with others; it aims at experiences of undisturbed intersubjectivity. These are more fragile than anything that history has up till now brought forth in the ways of structures of communication—an ever more dense and finely woven web of intersubjective relations that nevertheless make possible a relation between freedom and dependency that can only be imagined with interactive models. Wherever these ideas appear, . . . they are always ideas of felicitous interaction, of reciprocity and distance, of separation and of successful, unspoiled nearness, of vulnerability and complementary caution. All of these images of protection, openness and compassion, of submission and resistance, rise out of a horizon of experience, of what Brecht would have termed "friendly living together." *This* kind of friendliness does not exclude conflict, rather it implies those human forms through which one can survive conflicts. (Habermas, 1992a, pp. 125–126)

Despite his concern about the erosion of utopian ideas in the West, Habermas persists in defending a nontotalizing utopian stance:

Utopias have a practical function to the extent that they enter into social movements in the form of orientations. Bloch, for example, used the formula "walking tall" with the gaze of a utopian. Society should be such that everyone can walk tall, even the long-suffering and the heavy-laden, the deprived and degraded. In this context the use of utopian images serves to introduce a precisely defined conception, namely that of human dignity. . . . One should only speak of socialism in the sense of an attempt, in the historical conditions in which one finds oneself, to indicate the necessary conditions which would have to be fulfilled in order for emancipated life-forms to emerge—whatever they may be. Totalities only appear in the plural, and this pluralism cannot be anticipated in theory. (Habermas, 1992a, pp. 144–145)

The unifying postfoundationalist premise that ultimately unites Freire and Habermas despite all of their apparent differences is that moral truth cannot be delivered by "intellectuals' dream dances" from without: "All we can do is reconstruct the Ought that has immigrated into praxis itself" (Habermas, 1997a, p. 145). For Freire, however, the focus is not on theoretically reconstructing this "ought," but rather on practically engaging participants to discover for themselves the full meaning of their praxis through a process of conscientization. As Freire repeats again and again in various ways, his theory is not derived from without, but "is rooted in concrete situations" that have revealed the latent possibilities of human experience (Freire, 1970c, p. 21).

Let us give Freire the last word stemming from the speech announcing his resignation as Secretary of Education for São Paulo. Though Habermas would never define himself with quite these prosaic words—directed as they are to members of a social movement—they equally well express his intellectual commitments. Those who would dismiss this as naive, humanistic sentimentalism need to bear in mind Freire's psychoanalytic and theological reminder that the opposite of "love is not, as often thought, hate, but rather the fear to love which is the fear of being free" (in Torres, 1978b, p. 103):

To write and read represent, as important moments, part of my struggle. I put this love of reading and writing at the service of a certain societal design whose realization, with a large number of colleagues, I, within the limits of my possibilities, have been working to create. . . . My love for reading and writing is directed toward a certain utopia. This involves a certain course, a certain type of people. It is a love that has to do with the creation of a society that is less perverse, less discriminatory, less racist, less *machista* than the society that we now have. This love seeks to create a more open society, a society that serves the interests of the always unprotected and devalued subordinate classes, and not only the interests of the rich, the fortunate, the so-called "well-born." (Freire, 1993, p. 140)

Notes

1. For a brief preliminary version of our project, see Morrow & Torres, 1998a, 1998b.

2. The diffuse impact of Freire on practice-oriented professionals and activists is not directly evident in the sheer quantity of related academic publications. Beyond the educational literature cited later, see also contributions in fields such as the following: participatory action research and community development (Fals-Borda & Rahman, 1991; Latapí, 1988; Montero, 1997; Richards, Thomas, & Nain, 2001; Torres, 1995b); nursing (Fulton, 1997); health promotion (Barnes & Fairbanks, 1997; Brunt, Lindsey, & Hopkinson, 1997; Eakin, Robertson, Poland, & Coburn, 1996; Travers, 1997; Wallerstein, 1993; Wang & Burris, 1994); mental health (Mussell, Nicholls, & Adler, 1991); social work (Avalos, 1992; Leonard, 1993; Sachs, 1991); work and trade unions (Bräuer, 1985; Szell, 1985); the disabled (Lynd, 1992; Marsh, 1999); liberation psychology (Martín-Baró, 1996); and gender and race studies (Freire et al., 1997; Henderson, 1987). In this applied literature Habermas is often also mentioned. Perhaps the richest presentation of themes linking aspects of Habermas and Freire, however, can be found in a stimulating proposal for linking "critical psychology and pedagogy" (Sullivan, 1990).

3. Neither the *Cambridge Companion to Habermas* (White, 1995a) nor the *Handbook of Critical Theory* (Rasmussen, 1996) indexes topics such as education or pedagogy. The six volumes of "critical assessments" of the Frankfurt school do not contain a single item on education (Bernstein, 1994). Despite precedents for viewing Freire as a critical theorist (e.g., Leonard, 1990), he is virtually ignored in standard treatments of critical theory.

4. Some indication of Freire's intellectual depth is evident in the list of the 572 books he acquired—despite meager wages—from 1942 to 1955. This list also suggests that he began reading Spanish in 1943, French in 1944, and English in 1947 (Freire, 1996, pp. 225–226). The remarkable international cast of writers suggests a person of immense and diverse erudition, though this was not usually apparent in his actual writings.

5. On the question of the relationship between Gramsci and Freire, see Coben, 1998, and Mayo, 1999. Whereas Coben's account of Freire is very problematic, Mayo provides a valuable corrective.

6. For pioneering Latin American discussions of the influence of Hegel on Freire, see Torres, 1976a, 1976b.

7. This rejection of a labor-based ontology can be traced in the Brazilian

context to father Enrique Vaz, S.J., who wrote: "Man is not defined essentially by labor, but by the communication of consciences, i.e. not by its relation to nature, but its relation with the other" (Paiva, 1982, p. 144, n. 101). This theme is also echoed in Nicol's (1965) philosophy, though in a more systematic and nontheological way.

8. For a more detailed account of this quasi-transcendental, pragmatic strategy, see Cooke, 1994, and Habermas, 1998c.

9. As he described this shift away from epistemological grounding in 1982: "This is a prospect I no longer entertain. The theory of communicative action that I have since put forward is not a continuation of methodology by other means. It breaks with the primacy of epistemology and treats the presupposition of action oriented to mutual understanding *independently* of the transcendental preconditions of knowledge" (Habermas, 1988, p. xiv).

10. In his early writings on Freire, Carlos Alberto Torres made a sometimes· problematic attempt to reconstruct Freire's methodology as a "historical structural" approach that took the logical form of "objective dialectics" as opposed to empiricism, formalism, and voluntarism (Torres, 1978b, pp. 75ff.). Freire can now be better understood, however, in terms of the interpretive structuralist methodologies and critical hermeneutics of the critical theory tradition (Morrow, 1994a; Torres, 1995a, pp. 29–34).

11. On Roy Bhaskar's critical realism as a perspective for understanding Habermas, see Morrow, 1994a, and Outhwaite, 1987.

12. It should be noted that the lifeworld versus system distinction has drawn extensive criticism from some of Habermas's otherwise sympathetic critics. Most important, this distinction glosses over the communicative aspects of systemic relations, as well as obscuring the latent power relations in the lifeworld (Honneth, 1991, pp. 298–301).

13. Apparently Habermas delayed the translation of this book because of a long-standing intention to revise it extensively, an intention that never was realized (Calhoun, 1992, p. 5). Consequently, Habermas acknowledges the validity of much of the criticism (e.g., feminist) that has been directed toward this early formulation, but continues to defend its basic premises (Habermas, 1992b). Otherwise sympathetic critics have argued, however, that the procedural and communicative focus of the public-sphere concept must be supplemented with a focus on the struggles for mutual recognition within civil society, as well as alternative communicative strategies (Chambers, 1996; Dean, 1996; Marshall, 1994; McAfee, 2000).

14. In Habermas's terms, as we have seen, there are forms of "reconstructive sciences" that resemble transcendental arguments of the Kantian type in some respects, but he gives them a quasi-empirical status: "The expression *transcendental*, with which we associate a contrast to empirical science, is thus unsuited to characterizing, without misunderstanding, a line of research such as universal pragmatics" (Habermas, 1979, p. 25).

15. A parallel notion of "distanciation" is the foundation of Paul Ricoeur's conception of critical hermeneutics, which, as John Thompson (1981) has argued, converges with Habermas's use of the psychoanalytic analogy. At other points this process is characterized by Freire in terms such as *ad-miration* and *recognition* (Freire, 1970a, pp. 15–16).

16. For a similar effort to use Levinas (via Derrida) to link a universalistic and concrete ethics to Habermas, see Honneth, 1995.

17. For example, Bowers (1983) has criticized Freire's pedagogy for its Western hegemonic imposition of critical values on nontraditional cultures. But Peter Roberts (1996) has provided an incisive rejoinder.

18. Against Habermas's dismissal of the poststructuralist linguistic turn, it has been forcefully argued, however, that by incorporating a "revised Foucauldian version of disclosure within discursive formations or styles of reasoning, Habermas can better account for the plurality of cultural worlds that his own hermeneutic perspective demands. In these cases, a less restrictive notion of disclosure enriches Habermas's own theory of meaning and interpretive methodology" (Bohman, 1997, p. 215).

19. To be sure, postfoundationalisms come in many varieties: "Certainly postfoundationalism can take relativist forms. But it need not do so unless, unhelpfully, one simply defines the repudiation of foundations as a form of relativism"; such a definition can be taken to include figures as diverse as Kuhn, Lakatos, Feyberabend, Wittgenstein, Dewey, Rorty, Heidegger, Gadamer, Derrida, Habermas, etc. (Blake, 1998, p. 25).

References

Alvarez, S. E., Dagnino, E., & Escobar, A. (Eds.). (1998). *Cultures of Politics/Politics of Cultures: Re-Visioning Latin American Social Movements*. Boulder, CO: Westview.

Archibald, W. P. (1989). *Marx and the Missing Link: 'Human Nature'*. London: Macmillan.

Arnove, R. (1986). *Education and Revolution in Nicaragua*. New York: Praeger.

Aronowitz, S. (1993). Paul Freire's Radical Democratic Humanism. In P. McLaren & P. Leonard (Eds.), *Paulo Freire: A Critical Encounter* (pp. 8–24). London and New York: Routledge.

Aronowitz, S., & Giroux, H. A. (1991). *Postmodern Education: Politics, Culture and Social Criticism*. Minneapolis and Oxford: University of Minnesota Press.

Ashenden, S., & Owen, D. (1999). *Foucault contra Habermas: Recasting the Dialogue between Genealogy and Critical theory*. Thousand Oaks, CA: Sage.

Austin, R. (1997). Freire, Frei, and Literacy Texts in Chile, 1964–1970. In C. A. Torres & A. Puiggrós (Eds.), *Latin American Education: Comparative Perspectives* (pp. 323–348). Boulder: Westview Press.

Avalos, B. (1992). Education for the Poor: Quality or Relevance? *British Journal of Sociology of Education, 13*(4), 419–436.

Bakhtin, M. M. (1981). *The Dialogic Imagination: Four Essays* (M. Holquist, Trans.). Austin: University of Texas Press.

Barnes, M. D., & Fairbanks, J. (1997). Problem-Based Strategies Promoting Community Transformation: Implications for the Community Health Worker Model. *Family and Community Health, 20*(1), 54–65.

Barnes, N. (1992). The Fabric of a Student's Life and Thought: Practicing Cultural Anthropology in the Classroom. *Anthropology and Education Quarterly, 23*(2), 145–159.

Barreiro, J. (1974). *Educación y proceso de conscientización*. Mexico, D.F.: Siglo Veintiuno.

Basseches, M. (1984). *Dialectical Thinking and Adult Development*. Norwood, NJ: Ablex.

Baum, G. (1975). *Religion and Alienation: A Theological Reading of Sociology*. New York: Paulist Press.

Bauman, Z. (1987). *Legislators and Interpreters: On Modernity, Post-Modernity and Intellectuals*. Ithaca, NY: Cornell University Press.

Baynes, K. (1992). *The Normative Grounds of Social Criticism: Kant, Rawls, and Habermas*. Albany: State University of New York Press.

Beck, U. (1992). *Risk Society: Towards a New Modernity* (M. Ritter, Trans.). London and Thousand Oaks: Sage.

Beck, U., Giddens, A., & Lash, S. (1994). *Reflexive Modernization: Politics, Tradition and Aesthetics in the Modern Social Order.* Stanford, CA: Stanford University Press.

Beisiegel, C. d. R. (1982). *Concepçao e Educaçao Popular.* São Paulo: Editora Atica.

Benhabib, S. (1986). *Critique, Norm and Utopia: A Study of the Foundations of Critical Theory.* New York: Columbia University Press.

Benhabib, S. (1992). *Situating the Self: Gender, Community and Postmodernism in Contemporary Ethics.* New York: Routledge.

Benhabib, S. (1995). Feminism and Postmodernism. In S. Benhabib et al. (Eds.), *Feminist Contentions: A Philosophical Exchange* (pp. 17–34). New York and London: Routledge.

Benhabib, S. (1996a). Critical Theory and Postmodernism: On the Interplay of Ethics, Aesthetics, and Utopia in Critical Theory. In D. M. Rasmussen (Ed.), *Handbook of Critical Theory* (pp. 327–339). Oxford and Cambridge, MA: Blackwell.

Benhabib, S. (Ed.). (1996b). *Democracy and Difference: Contesting the Boundaries of the Political.* Princeton, NJ: Princeton University Press.

Benhabib, S., Butler, J., Cornell, D., & Fraser, N. (1995). *Feminist Contentions: A Philosophical Exchange.* New York and London: Routledge.

Benhabib, S., & Dallmayr, F. (Eds.). (1990). *The Communicative Ethics Controversy.* Cambridge, MA, and London: MIT Press.

Bernstein, J. (Ed.). (1994). *The Frankfurt School: Critical Assessments.* London and New York: Routledge.

Bernstein, R. J. (1971). *Praxis and Action: Contemporary Philosophies of Human Activity.* Philadelphia: University of Pennsylvania Press.

Bertilsson, M. (1991). Love's Labour Lost? A Sociological View. In M. Featherstone, M. Hepworth, & B. S. Turner (Eds.), *The Body: Social Process and Cultural Theory* (pp. 297–324). London: Sage.

Bidima, J. G. (1993). *Théorie Critique et modernité négro-africaine: De l'École Francfort à la 'Docta spes africana'.* Paris: Publications de la Sorbonne.

Biesta, G. J. J. (1998). Say You Want a Revolution . . . Suggestions for the Impossible Future of Critical Pedagogy. *Educational Theory, 48*(4), 499–511.

Blake, N. (1998). *Thinking Again : Education after Postmodernism.* Westport, CT: Bergin & Garvey.

Boer, T. D. (1983). *Foundations of Critical Psychology* (T. Plantinga, Trans.). Pittsburgh: Duquesne University Press.

Bohman, J. (1996a). Critical Theory and Democracy. In D. M. Rasmussen (Ed.), *Handbook of Critical Theory* (pp. 190–215). Oxford and Cambridge, MA: Blackwell.

Bohman, J. (1996b). *Public Deliberation: Pluralism, Complexity, and Democracy.* Cambridge, MA, and London: MIT Press.

Bohman, J. (1997). Two Versions of the Linguistic Turn: Habermas and Poststructuralism. In M. Passerin d'Entrèves & S. Benhabib (Eds.), *Habermas and the Unfinished Project of Modernity: Critical Essays on The Philosophical Discourse of Modernity* (pp. 197–220). Cambridge, MA and London: MIT Press.

Bourdieu, P. (1991). *Language and Symbolic Power* (Gino Raymond and Matthew Adamson, Trans.). Cambridge, MA: Harvard University Press.

Bourdieu, P. (2000). *Pascalian Meditations* (R. Nice, Trans.). Stanford, CA: Stanford University Press.

Bourdieu, P., & Wacquant, L. J. D. (1992). *An Invitation to Reflexive Sociology*. Chicago and London: University of Chicago Press.

Bowers, C. A. (1983). Linguistic Roots of Cultural Invasion in Paulo Freire's Pedagogy. *Teachers College Record, 84*(4), 935–953.

Bräuer, R. (1985). *Soziale Konstitutionsbedingungen politischen Lernens in der Theorie Paulo Freires: Eine Auseinandersetzung mit der Theorie Freires unter dem Aspekt ihrer Übertragbarkeit auf Arbeiterbildung in der Bundesrepublik*. Frankfurt am Main: Haag+Herchen Verlag.

Broughton, J. M. (Ed.). (1987). *Critical Theories of Psychological Development*. New York and London: Plenum Press.

Browning, D. S., & Fiorenza, F. S. (Eds.). (1992). *Habermas, Modernity, and Public Theology*. New York: Crossroad.

Brunt, J. H., Lindsey, E., & Hopkinson, J. (1997). Health Promotion in the Hutterite Community and the Ethnocentricity of Empowerment. *Canadian Journal of Nursing Research, 29*(1), 17–28.

Buck-Morss, S. (1980). Piaget, Adorno, and the Possibilities of Dialectical Operations. In H. J. Silverman (Ed.), *Piaget, Philosophy and the Human Sciences* (pp. 103–137). New Jersey and Sussex: Humanities Press/Harvester Press.

Buck-Morss, S. (1987). Piaget, Adorno and Dialectical Operations. In J. M. Broughton (Ed.), *Critical Theories of Psychological Development* (pp. 245–274). New York and London: Plenum Press.

Burbules, N. (1995). Reasonable Doubt: Toward a Postmodern Defense. In W. Kohli (Ed.), *Critical Conversations in Philosophy of Education* (pp. 82–102). New York and London: Routledge.

Burbules, N. C. (1993). *Dialogue in Teaching: Theory and Practice*. New York and London: Teachers College.

Burbules, N. C., & Rice, S. (1991). Dialogue Across Differences: Continuing the Conversation. *Harvard Educational Review, 61*(4), 393–416.

Burman, E. (1994). *Deconstructing Developmental Psychology*. London and New York: Routledge.

Buss, A. R. (1979). *A Dialectical Psychology*. New York: Irvington.

Calhoun, C. (1992). Introduction: Habermas and the Public Sphere. In C. Calhoun (Ed.), *Habermas and the Public Sphere* (pp. 1–50). Cambridge, MA, and London: MIT Press.

Calhoun, C. (1995). *Critical Social Theory*. Oxford and Cambridge, MA: Basil Blackwell.

Campbell, M. M. (1999). *Critical Theory and Liberation Theology: A Comparison of the Initial Work of Jürgen Habermas and Gustavo Gutiérrez*. New York: P. Lang.

Carey-Webb, A., & Benz, S. (Eds.). (1996). *Teaching and Testimony*. Albany: State University of New York Press.

Carnoy, M., & Samoff, J., et al. (1990). *Education and Social Transition in the Third World*. Princeton, NJ: Princeton University Press.

Carr, W. (1995). *For Education: Towards Critical Educational Inquiry.* Buckingham and Philadelphia: Open University Press.

Carr, W., & Kemmis, S. (1986). *Becoming Critical: Education, Knowledge and Action Research.* London and Philadelphia: Falmer Press.

Castañeda, J. G. (1993). *Utopia Unarmed: The Latin American Left After the Cold War.* New York: Knopf.

Castells, M. (1996). *The Rise of the Network Society* (Vol. 1). Oxford: Blackwell.

Chambers, S. (1996). *Reasonable Democracy: Jürgen Habermas and the Politics of Discourse.* Ithaca and London: Cornell University Press.

Chandler, M. (1997). Stumping Around for Progress in the Post-Modern World. In E. Amsel & K. A. Renninger (Eds.), *Change and Development: Issues of Theory, Method, and Application* (pp. 1–27). Mahwah, NJ: L. Erlbaum.

Coben, D. (1998). *Radical Heroes: Gramsci, Freire, and the Politics of Adult Education.* New York: Garland Pub.

Cohen, J. L., & Arato, A. (1992). *Civil Society and Political Theory.* Cambridge, MA, and London: MIT Press.

Comstock, D. E. (1994). A Method for Critical Research. In M. Martin & L. C. McIntyre (Eds.), *Readings in the Philosophy of Social Science* (pp. 625–640). Cambridge, MA, and London: MIT.

Cooke, M. (1994). *Language and Reason: A Study of Habermas's Pragmatics.* Cambridge, MA, and London: MIT Press.

Coole, D. (1997). Habermas and the Question of Alterity. In M. Passerin d'Entrèves & S. Benhabib (Eds.), *Habermas and the Unfinished Project of Modernity: Critical Essays on The Philosophical Discourse of Modernity* (pp. 221–244). Cambridge, MA and London: MIT Press.

Crush, J. (Ed.). (1995). *Power of Development.* London and New York: Routledge.

de Castell, S. (1995). Textuality and the Designs of Theory. In W. Kohli (Ed.), *Critical Conversations in Philosophy of Education* (pp. 241–258). New York and London: Routledge.

De la Campa, R. (1995). On Latin Americanism and the Postcolonial Turn. *Canadian Review of Comparative Literature/Revue Canadienne de Littérature Comparée, 22*(3–4), 745–771.

Dean, J. (1996). *Solidarity of Strangers: Feminism After Identity Politics.* Berkeley, Los Angeles, and London: University of California Press.

Derrida, J. (1996). Remarks on Deconstruction and Pragmatism. In S. Chritchley & C. Mouffe (Eds.), *Deconstruction and Pragmatism* (pp. 77–88). London and New York: Routledge.

Dewey, J. (1957). *Reconstruction in Philosophy* (enlarged ed.). Boston: Beacon.

Dews, P. (1987). *Logics of Disintegration: Post-Structuralist Thought and the Claims of Critical Theory.* London and New York: Verso.

Dryzek, J. S. (1990). *Discursive Democracy: Politics, Policy, and Political Science.* Cambridge: Cambridge University Press.

Dussel, E. (1993). Eurocentrism and Modernity (Introduction to the Frankfurt Lectures). In J. Beverly & J. Oviedo (Eds.), *The Postmodernism Debate in Latin America* (pp. 65–76). Durham: Duke University Press.

Dussel, E. (Ed.). (1994). *Debate en torno a la ética del discurso de Apel: Diálogo filosófico Norte-Sur desde América Latina*. México, D.F.: siglo xxi/Universidad Autónoma Metropolitana-Iztapalapa.

Dussel, E. (1996). *The Underside of Modernity: Apel, Ricoeur, Rorty, Taylor and the Philosophy of Liberation* (E. Mendieta, Trans.). Atlantic Highlands, NJ: Humanities Press.

Dussel, E. (1997). The Architechtonic of the Ethics of Liberation: On Material Ethics and Formal Moralities. In D. e. a. Batstone (Ed.), *Liberation Theologies, Postmodernity, and the Americas* (pp. 273–304). London and New York: Routledge.

Eakin, J., Robertson, A., Poland, B., & Coburn, D. (1996). Towards a Critical Social Science Perspective on Health Promotion Research. *Health Promotion International, 11*(2), 157–165.

Elias, J. L. (1994). *Paulo Freire: Pedagogue of Liberation*. Malabar, FL: Krieger Publishing.

Escobar, M., Fernández, A. L., Guevara-Niebla, G., & Freire, P. (1994). *Paulo Freire on Higher Education: A Dialogue at the National University of Mexico*. Albany: State University of New York Press.

Ewert, G. D. (1991). Habermas and Education: A Comprehensive Overview of the Influence of Habermas in Educational Literature. *Review of Educational Research, 61*(3), 345–378.

Fals-Borda, O., & Rahman, M. A. (Eds.). (1991). *Action and Knowledge: Breaking the Monopoly with Paticipatory Action-Research*. New York and London: Apex Press/Intermediae Technology Publications.

Fay, B. (1975). *Social Theory and Political Practice*. London: George Allen & Unwin.

Ferrara, A. (1996). The Communicative Paradigm in Moral Theory. In D. M. Rasmussen (Ed.), *Handbook of Critical Theory* (pp. 119–137). Oxford and Cambridge, MA: Blackwell.

Fiori, J. L. (1968). Dialéctica y libertad. Dos dimensiones de la investigación temática. In P. Freire, R. Veloso, & J. L. Fiori (Eds.), *Educação e conscientização: Extensionismo rural* (pp. 6/1–6/12). Cuervavaca: CIDOC (Centro Intercultural de Documentación), Cuaderno No. 25.

Forester, J. (Ed.). (1985). *Critical Theory and Public Life*. Cambridge, MA and London: MIT Press.

Foucault, M. (1984). *The Foucault Reader* (P. Rabinow, Ed.). New York: Pantheon.

Foucault, M. (2000). *Essential Works of Foucault 1954–1984. Volume 3: Power*. New York: New Press.

Fox, D. R., & Prilleltensky, I. (1997). Introducing Critical Psychology: Values, Assumptions, and the Status Quo. In D. R. Fox & I. Prilleltensky (Eds.), *Critical Psychology: An Introduction* (pp. 3–20). Thousand Oaks, CA: Sage.

Franco, F. (1979). Paulo Freire y su obra: Influjos idelógicos y postura religiosa. In C. A. Torres (Ed.), *Paulo Freire en América Latina* (pp. 43–49). Mexico, D.F.: Ediciones Gernika.

Fraser, N. (1994). Rethinking the Public Sphere: A Contribution to the Critique of Actually Existing Democracy. In H. A. Giroux & P. McLaren (Eds.), *Between Borders: Pedagogy and the Politics of Cultural Studies* (pp. 74–98). New York and London: Routledge.

Freire, P. (1968a). Algunas sugerencias en torno de una labor educativa que vea el asentamiento como un totalidad. In P. Freire, R. Veloso, & J. L. Fiori (Eds.), *Educação e conscientização: Extensionismo rural* (pp. 8/1–8/14). Cuervavaca: CIDOC (Centro Intercultural de Documentación), Cuaderno No. 25.

Freire, P. (1968b). El compromiso del profesional con la sociedad. In P. Freire, R. Veloso, & J. L. Fiori (Eds.), *Educação e conscientização: Extensionismo rural* (pp. 11/11–11/13). Cuervavaca: CIDOC (Centro Intercultural de Documentación), Cuaderno No. 25.

Freire, P. (1968c). El rol de trabajador social en el proceso de cambio. In P. Freire & R. Veloso & J. L. Fiori (Eds.), *Educação e conscientização: Extensionismo rural* (pp. 9/1–9/22). Cuervavaca: CIDOC (Centro Intercultural de Documentación), Cuaderno No. 25.

Freire, P. (1970a). Cultural Action for Freedom (L. Slover, Trans.). *Harvard Educational Review*, Monograph Series No. 1.

Freire, P. (1970b). *Pedagogía del oprimido* (J. Mellado, Trans.). Mexico, D.F.: Siglo Veintiuno.

Freire, P. (1970c). *Pedagogy of the Oppressed* (M. B. Ramos, Trans.). New York: Seabury.

Freire, P. (1973). *Education for Critical Consciousness* (M. B. Ramos, Trans.). New York: Seabury.

Freire, P. (1975). *Diálogo Paulo Freire-Ivan Illich*. Buenos Aires: Editorial Búsqueda.

Freire, P. (1978). *Entrevistas con Paulo Freire*. Mexico, D.F.: Ediciones gernika.

Freire, P. (1983). *Pedagogy in Process: The Letters to Guinea-Bissau* (C. S. J. Hunter, Trans.). New York: Continuum.

Freire, P. (1985). *The Politics of Education: Culture, Power and Liberation* (D. Macedo, Trans.). South Hadley, MA: Bergin & Garvey.

Freire, P. (1993). *Pedagogy of the City*. New York: Continuum.

Freire, P. (1994). *Pedagogy of Hope: Reliving the Pedagogy of the Oppressed*. New York: Continuum.

Freire, P. (1996). *Letters to Cristina: Reflections on My Life and Work* (D. Macedo, Trans.). New York and London: Routledge.

Freire, P. (1997a). *Pedagogia de la Autonomia: Saberes necessários á prática educativa*. São Paulo: Paz Terra.

Freire, P. (1997b). *Pedagogy of the Heart* (D. M. a. A. Oliveira, Trans.). New York: Continuum.

Freire, P. (1997c). A Response. In P. Freire, J. W. Fraser, D. Macedo, & W. T. Stokes (Eds.), *Mentoring the Mentor: A Critical Dialogue with Paulo Freire* (pp. 303–330). New York: Peter Lang.

Freire, P. (1998a). *Pedagogy of Freedom: Ethics, Democracy, and Civic Courage*. Lanham, MD: Rowman & Littlefield Publishers.

Freire, P. (1998b). *Teachers as Cultural Workers: Letters to Those Who Dare Teach* (D. K. Donaldo Macedo & A. Oliveira, Trans.). Boulder, CO: Westview.

Freire, P., & Faundez, A. (1989). *Learning to Question: A Pedagogy of Liberation*. New York: Continuum.

Freire, P., Fraser, J. W., Macedo, D., & Stokes, W. T. (Eds.). (1997). *Mentoring the Mentor: A Critical Dialogue with Paulo Freire*. New York: Peter Lang.

Freire, P., & Macedo, D. (1987). *Literacy: Reading the Word and the World*. South Hadley, MA: Bergin & Garvey.

Fromm, E. (1965). *Escape from Freedom*. New York: Avon.

Fulton, Y. (1997). Nurses' Views on Empowerment: A Critical Social Theory Perspective. *Journal of Advanced Nursing, 26*(3), 529–536.

Furth, H. G. (1996). *Desire for Society: Children's Knowledge as Social Imagination*. New York: Plenum Press.

Gadotti, M. (1986). *Concepção Dialética da Educação: Um estudo introdutório*. São Paulo: Cortez Editora-Editora Autores Associados.

Gadotti, M. (1996). *Pedagogy of Praxis: A Dialectical Philosophy of Education* (J. Milton, Trans.). Albany: State University of New York Press.

Gadotti, M., et al. (Ed.). (1996). *Paulo Freire: Uma Biobliografia*. São Paulo: Cortez Editora/Instituto Paulo Freire.

Gadotti, M., & Torres, C. A. (Eds.). (1994). *Educação popular: Utopia Latino-Americana*. São Paulo: Cortez Editora/Editora da Universidade de São Paulo.

Gajardo, M. (1982). *Evolución, situación actual y perspectivas de las strategías de investigación participativa en América Latina*. Santiago: FLACSO.

Gallagher, S. (1992). *Hermeneutics and Education*. Albany: State University of New York Press.

Geras, N. (1981). *Marx and Human Nature: Refutation of a Legend*. London: Verso.

Geyer, P. (1997). *Die Entdeckung des modernen Subjekts: Anthropologie von Descartes bis Rousseau*. Tübingen: Max Niemeyer Verlag.

Gibson, R. (1986). *Critical Theory and Education*. London: Hodder and Stoughton.

Giroux, H. (1988). *Schooling and the Struggle for Public Life: Critical Pedagogy in the Modern Age*. Minneapolis: University of Minnesota Press.

Giroux, H., Penna, A. N., & Pinar, W. F. (Eds.). (1981). *Curriculum and Instruction: Alternative Theoretical and Practical Perspectives for Education*. Berkeley: McCutchan.

Giroux, H. A. (1987). Literacy and the Pedagogy of Political Empowerment. In P. Freire & D. Macedo (Eds.), *Literacy: Reading and Word and the World* (pp. 1–27). South Hadley, MA: Bergin & Garvey.

Giroux, H. A. (1991). Modernism, Postmodernism, and Feminism: Rethinking the Boundaries of Educational Discourse. In H. A. Giroux (Ed.), *Postmodernism, Feminism, and Cultural Politics: Redrawing Educational Boundaries* (pp. 1–59). Albany: State University of New York Press.

Giroux, H. A. (1993). Paulo Freire and the Politics of Postcolonialism. In P. McLaren & P. Leonard (Eds.), *Paulo Freire: A Critical Encounter* (pp. 177–188). London and New York: Routledge.

Gitau, B. K. (1982). Ngugi Wa Thiongo: The African Paulo Freire? *African Journal of Sociology, 2*(1), 42–55.

Goldmann, L. (1969). *The Human Sciences and Philosophy* (Hayden White and Robert Anchor, Trans.). London: Jonathan Cape.

González, J. (1981). *La metafísica dialéctica de Eduardo Nicol* (1a ed.). México, D.F.: Universidad Nacional Autónoma de México Dirección General de Publicaciones.

Goody, J. (1977). *The Domestication of the Savage Mind*. Cambridge: Cambridge University Press.

Görtzen, R. (1982). *Jürgen Habermas: Eine Bibliographie seiner Schriften und der Sekundärliteratur 1952–1981*. Frankfurt am Main: Suhrkamp.

Görtzen, R. (1990). Jürgen Habermas: A Bibliography. In D. Rasmussen (Ed.), *Reading Habermas* (pp. 114–140). Cambridge, MA, and Oxford: Basil Blackwell.

Gottdiener, M. (1985). *The Social Production of Urban Space*. Austin: University of Texas Press.

Grundy, S. (1987). *Curriculum: Product or Praxis*. London, New York, & Philadelphia: Falmer Press.

Guba, E. G. (1990). *The Paradigm Dialog*. Newbury Park and London: Sage.

Guba, E. G., & Lincoln, Y. S. (1994). Competing Paradigms in Qualitative Research. In N. K. Denzin & Y. S. Lincoln (Eds.), *Handbook of Qualitative Research* (pp. 105–117). Thousand Oaks, CA, and London: Sage.

Haacke, J. (1996). Theory and Praxis in International Relations: Habermas, Self-Reflection, Rational Argumentation. *Millennium: Journal of International Studies, 25*(2), 255–289.

Habermas, J. (1969). *Protestbewegung und Hochschulreform*. Frankfurt am Main: Suhrkamp.

Habermas, J. (1970a). *Toward a Rational Society: Student Protest, Science and Politics* (J. J. Shapiro, Trans.). Boston: Beacon.

Habermas, J. (1970b). Toward a Theory of Communicative Competence. In H. Dreitzel (Ed.), *Recent Sociology No. 2* (pp. 114–148). New York: Macmillan.

Habermas, J. (1971). *Knowledge and Human Interests* (J. J. Shapiro, Trans.). Boston: Beacon.

Habermas, J. (1973). *Theory and Practice* (J. Viertel, Trans.). Boston: Beacon.

Habermas, J. (1975). *Legitimation Crisis* (T. McCarthy, Trans.). Boston: Beacon.

Habermas, J. (1979). *Communication and the Evolution of Society* (T. McCarthy, Trans.). Boston: Beacon.

Habermas, J. (1982). A Reply to My Critics. In J. Thompson & D. Held (Eds.), *Habermas: Critical Debates* (pp. 219–283). Cambridge, MA, and London: MIT Press.

Habermas, J. (1983). Interpretive Social Science vs. Hermeneuticism. In N. Haan, R. N. Bellah, P. Rabinow, & W. M. Sullivan (Eds.), *Social Science as Moral Inquiry* (pp. 251–267). New York: Columbia University Press.

Habermas, J. (1984). *The Theory of Communicative Action, Vol. 1: Reason and the Rationalization of Society* (T. McCarthy, Trans.). Boston: Beacon.

Habermas, J. (1986). *Vorstudien und Ergänzungen zur Theorie des kommunikativen Handelns*. Frankfurt am Main: Suhrkamp.

Habermas, J. (1987a). *The Philosophical Discourse of Modernity: Twelve Lectures* (F. Lawrence, Trans.). Cambridge, MA and London: MIT Press.

Habermas, J. (1987b). *The Theory of Communicative Action, Vol. 2: Lifeworld and System: A Critique of Functionalist Reason* (T. McCarthy, Trans.). Boston: Beacon Press.

Habermas, J. (1988). *On the Logic of the Social Sciences* (S. W. N. a. J. A. Stark, Trans.). Cambridge, MA and London: MIT Press.

Habermas, J. (1989a). *Jürgen Habermas on Society and Politics: A Reader*. Boston: Beacon Press.

Habermas, J. (1989b). *The New Conservatism* (S. W. Nicholsen, Trans.). Cambridge, MA and London: MIT Press.

Habermas, J. (1989c). *The Structural Transformation of the Public Sphere: An Inquiry into a Category of Bourgeois Society* (T. B. a. F. Lawrence, Trans.). Cambridge, MA and London: MIT Press. (Original work published in 1962.)

Habermas, J. (1990). *Moral Consciousness and Communicative Action* (C. a. N. Lenhardt & Shierry Weber, Trans.). Cambridge, MA and London: MIT Press.

Habermas, J. (1992a). *Autonomy and Solidarity: Interviews with Jürgen Habermas*. London and New York: Verso.

Habermas, J. (1992b). Further Reflections on the Public Sphere. In C. Calhoun (Ed.), *Habermas and the Public Sphere* (pp. 421–461). Cambridge, MA and London: MIT Press.

Habermas, J. (1992c). *Postmetaphysical Thinking: Philosophical Essays* (W. M. Hohengarten, Trans.). Cambridge, MA and London: MIT Press.

Habermas, J. (1992d). Transcendence from Within, Transcendence in This World. In D. S. Browning & F. S. Fiorenza (Eds.), *Habermas, Modernity, and Public Theology* (pp. 226–250). New York: Crossroad.

Habermas, J. (1993). *Justification and Application: Remarks on Discourse Ethics* (C. P. Cronin, Trans.). Cambridge, MA and London: MIT Press.

Habermas, J. (1994). *The Past as Future: Jürgen Habermas Interviewed by Michael Haller* (P. Hohendahl, Trans.). Lincoln and London: University of Nebraska Press.

Habermas, J. (1996). *Between Facts and Norms: Contributions to a Discourse Theory of Law and Democracy* (W. Rehg, Trans.). Cambridge, MA and London: MIT Press.

Habermas, J. (1997a). *A Berlin Republic: Writings on Germany* (S. Rendall, Trans.). Lincoln: University of Nebraska Press.

Habermas, J. (1997b). Israel and Athens, or to Whom Does Anamnestic Reason Belong? On Unity in Multicultural Diversity. In D. e. a. Batstone (Ed.), *Liberation Theologies, Postmodernity, and the Americas* (pp. 243–252). London and New York: Routledge.

Habermas, J. (1998a). *The Inclusion of the Other: Studies in Political Theory*. Cambridge, MA and London: MIT Press.

Habermas, J. (1998b, August). Nuestro breve siglo. *Nexos, Internet Version*, pp. 1–10.

Habermas, J. (1998c). *On the Pragmatics of Communication* (M. Cook, Ed.). Cambridge, MA, and London: MIT Press.

Habermas, J. (2001a). *The Postnational Constellation: Political Essays* (M. Pensky, Trans.). MA and London: MIT Press.

Habermas, J. (2001b). *The Liberating Power of Symbols: Philosophical Essays* (P. Dews, Trans.). MA and London: MIT Press.

Hajdukowski-Ahmed, M. (1998). Bakhtin Without Borders: Participatory Action Research in the Social Sciences. *The South Atlantic Quarterly, 97*(3/4), 511–536.

Hall, S. (1980). Encoding/Decoding. In S. Hall, D. Hobson, A. Lowe, & P. Willis (Eds.), *Culture, Media, Language* (pp. 128–138). London: Hutchinson.

Hall, S. (1993). Encoding, Decoding. In S. During (Ed.), *The Cultural Studies Reader* (pp. 90–103). London and New York: Routledge.

Hall, S. (1994). Reflections on the Encoding/Decoding Model: An Interview with Stuart Hall. In J. Cruz & J. Lewis (Eds.), *Viewing, Reading, Listening: Audiences and Cultural Reception* (pp. 253–274). Boulder, CO: Westview Press.

Hegel, G. W. F. (1971). *Early Theological Writings* (T. M. Knox, Trans.). Philadelphia: University of Pennsylvania Press.

Hegel, G. W. F. (1977). *Phenomenology of the Spirit* (1807 ed.). Oxford: Oxford University Press.

Hegel, G. W. F. (1979). *System of Ethical Life (1802/3) and First Philosophy of Spirit (1803/4)* (T. M. Knox, Trans.). Albany: State University of New York Press.

Held, D. (1995). *Democracy and the Global Order: From the Modern State to Cosmopolitan Governance*. Stanford, CA: Stanford University Press.

Henderson, P. K. (1987). Paulo Freire: Unveiling the "Culture of Silence" for Third World Women. *Social Development Issues, 11*(3), 40–51.

Hickling-Hudson, A. (1988). Toward Communication Praxis: Reflections on the Pedagogy of Paulo Freire and Educational Change in Grenada. *Journal of Education, 170*(2), 9–38.

Hinchey, P. H. (1998). *Finding Freedom in the Classroom: A Practical Introduction to Critical Theory*. New York: Peter Lang.

Hohendahl, P. (1994). Foreword. In M. Pensky (Ed.), *The Past as Future: Jürgen Habermas Interviewed by Michael Haller* (pp. vii–xxvi). Lincoln and London: University of Nebraska Press.

Hohendahl, P. U. (1997). Introduction. In J. Habermas (Ed.), *A Berlin Republic: Writings on Germany* (pp. vii–xxiv). Lincoln: University of Nebraska Press.

Honneth, A. (1991). *The Critique of Power: Reflective Stages in a Critical Theory of Society* (K. Baynes, Trans.). Cambridge, MA, and London: MIT Press.

Honneth, A. (1995). The Other of Justice: Habermas and the Ethical Challenge of Postmodernism. In S. K. White (Ed.), *The Cambridge Companion to Habermas* (pp. 289–324). Cambridge: Cambridge University Press.

Honneth, A. (1996). *The Struggle for Recognition: The Moral Grammar of Social Conflicts* (J. Anderson, Trans.). Cambridge, MA and London: MIT Press.

Honneth, A., & Joas, H. (1988). *Social Action and Human Nature* (R. Meyer, Trans.). Cambridge: Cambridge University Press.

hooks, b. (1993). bell hooks Speaking about Paulo Freire—The Man, His Work. In P. McLaren & P. Leonard (Eds.), *Paulo Freire: A Critical Encounter* (pp. 146–154). London and New York: Routledge.

Hoover, K., Marcia, w. J., & Parris, K. (1997). *The Power of Identity: Politics in a New Key*. Chatham, NJ: Chatham House Publishers.

Horton, M., & Freire, P. (1990). *We Make the Road by Walking: Conversations on Education and Social Change*. Philadelphia: Temple University Press.

Ibáñez, T. (Ed.). (1994). *Psicología social construccionista: Textos recientes*. Guadalajara: Universidad de Guadalajara.

Janmohamed, A. R. (1994). Some Implications of Paulo Freire's Border Pedagogy.

In H. A. Giroux & P. McLaren (Eds.), *Between Borders: Pedagogy and the Politics of Cultural Studies* (pp. 242–252). New York and London: Routledge.

Joas, H. (1993). *Pragmatism and Social Theory.* Chicago and London: University of Chicago Press.

Johnston, J. (2000). Pedagogical Guerrillas, Armed Democrats, and Revolutionary Counterpublics: Examining Paradox in the Zapatista Uprising in Chiapas Mexico. *Theory and Society, 29*(4), 463–505.

Kachur, J. L. (1998). Habermas's "Theory of Communicative Action" and Sibrem Miedema, Part One: The Ideological Context for Intellectual Appropriation. *Interchange, 29*(2), 207–223.

Kadt, E. d. (1970). *Catholic Radicals in Brazil.* New York: Oxford University Press.

Kanpol, B. (1994). *Critical Pedagogy: An Introduction.* Westport, CT, and London: Bergin & Garvey.

Kant, I. (1983). *Perpetual Peace and Other Essays.* Indianapolis and Cambridge: Hackett Publishing. (Original work published 1784.)

Kant, I. (1992). *Kant on Education (Ueber Pädagogik).* Bristol: Thoemmes Press.

Keane, J. (1988). *Democracy and Civil Society.* London and New York: Verso.

Kellner, D. (1998). Multiple Literacies and Critical Pedagogy in a Multicultural Society. *Educational Theory, 48*(1), 103–122.

Kelly, G. A. (1969). *Idealism, Politics and History: Sources of Hegelian Thought.* Cambridge: Cambridge University Press.

Klor de Alva, J. J. (1995). The Postcolonization of the (Latin) American Experience: A Reconsideration of "Colonialism," "Postcolonialism," and "Mestizaje." In G. Prakash (Ed.), *After Colonialism: Imperial Histories and Postcolonial Displacements.* Princeton, NJ: Princeton University Press.

Kohli, W. (1995). Educating for Emancipatory Rationality. In W. Kohli (Ed.), *Critical Conversations in Philosophy of Education* (pp. 103–115). New York and London: Routledge.

Kosík, K. (1976). *Dialectics of the Concrete: A Study on Problems of Man and World* (K. Kovanda & J. Schmidt, Trans.). Dordrecht and Boston: D. Reidel.

Krischke, P. J. (1998). Final Comments: Challenges to Cultural Studies in Latin America. In S. E. Alvarez, E. Dagnino, & A. Escobar (Eds.), *Cultures of Politics/Politics of Cultures: Re-Visioning Latin American Social Movements* (pp. 415–421). Boulder, CO: Westview.

Langman, L., & Kaplan, L. (1981). Political Economy and Social Character: Terror, Desire and Domination. *Current Perspectives in Social Theory, 2,* 87–115.

Lankshear, C., & McLaren, P. L. (Eds.). (1993a). *Critical Literacy: Politics, Praxis, and the Postmodern.* Albany: State University of New York Press.

Lankshear, C., & McLaren, P. L. (1993b). Introduction. In C. Lankshear & P. L. McLaren (Eds.), *Critical Literacy: Politics, Praxis, and the Postmodern* (pp. 1–56). Albany: State University of New York Press.

Larrabee, M. J. (Ed.). (1993). *An Ethic of Care: Feminist and Interdisciplinary Perspectives.* New York and London: Routledge.

Lash, S., & Urry, J. (1987). *The End of Organized Capitalism.* Madison: University of Wisconsin Press.

Latapí, P. (1988). Participatory Research: A New Research Paradigm? *Alberta Journal of Educational Research, 34*(3), 310–319.

Lê, T. K. (1991). *Marx, Engels et l'éducation* (1re éd.). Paris: Presses Universitaires de France.

Leistyna, P. (1999). *Presence of Mind: Education and the Politics of Deception*. Boulder, CO: Westview Press.

Leonard, P. (1993). Critical Pedagogy and State Welfare: Intellectual Encounters with Freire and Gramsci, 1974–86. In P. McLaren & P. Leonard (Eds.), *Paulo Freire: A Critical Encounter* (pp. 155–168). London and New York: Routledge.

Leonard, S. T. (1990). *Critical Theory in Political Practice*. Princeton, NJ: Princeton University Press.

Long, D. A. (1995). Sociology and a Pedagogy of Liberation: Cultivating a Dialogue of Discernment in Our Classrooms. *Teaching Sociology, 23*(4), 321–330.

Lynd, M. (1992). Creating Knowledge Through Theater: A Case Study with Developmentally Disabled Adults. *American Sociologist, 23*(4), 100–115.

Mainwaring, S. (1986). *The Catholic Church and Politics in Brazil, 1916–1985*. Stanford, CA: Stanford University Press.

Manzo, K. (1995). Black Consciousness and the Quest for a Counter-Modernist Development. In J. Crush (Ed.), *Power of Development* (pp. 228–254). London and New York: Routledge.

Marsh, D. G. (1999). *Vygotsky and Special Education: Towards a Mediated Metacognitive Resource Model*. Unpublished doctoral dissertation, Dalhousie University, Halifax, Nova Scotia.

Marshall, B. (1994). *Engendering Modernity: Feminism, Social Theory and Social Change*. Cambridge: Polity Press.

Martín-Baró, I. (1996). *Writings for a Liberation Psychology*. Cambridge, MA: Harvard University Press.

Marx, K., & Engels, F. (Eds.). (1978). *The Marx-Engels Reader* (2nd ed.). New York: W. W. Norton.

Mayo, P. (1999). *Gramsci, Freire and Adult Education: Possibilities for Transformative Action*. London: Zed Books.

McAfee, N. (2000). *Habermas, Kristeva, and Citizenship*. Ithaca, NY, and London: Cornell University Press.

McCarthy, T. (1978). *The Critical Theory of Jürgen Habermas*. Cambridge, MA, and London: MIT Press.

McCarthy, T. (1990). Introduction. In J. Habermas (Ed.), *Moral Consciousness and Communicative Action* (pp. vii–xiii). Cambridge, MA: MIT Press.

McCarthy, T. (1992). Practical Discourse: On the Relation of Morality to Politics. In C. Calhoun (Ed.), *Habermas and the Public Sphere* (pp. 51–72). Cambridge, MA, and London: MIT Press.

McCarthy, T. (1996). Critical Theory and Postmodernism: A Response to Hoy. In D. M. Rasmussen (Ed.), *Handbook of Critical Theory* (pp. 340–368). Oxford and Cambridge, MA: Blackwell.

McLaren, P. (1986). Postmodernity and the Death of Politics: A Brazilian Reprieve. *Educational Theory, 36*(4), 389–401.

McLaren, P. (1994). Postmodernism and the Death of Politics: A Brazilian Reprieve.

In P. McLaren & C. Lankshear (Eds.), *Politics of Liberation: Paths from Freire* (pp. 193–215). London and New York: Routledge.

McLaren, P. (1996). Paulo Freire and the Academy: A Challenge from the U.S. Left. *Cultural Critique, 33,* 151–184.

McLaren, P. (1997). Paulo Freire's Legacy of Hope and Struggle. *Theory, Culture and Society, 14*(4), 147–153.

McLaren, P. (2000). *Che Guevara, Paul Freire, and the Pedagogy of Revolution.* Lanham, MD: Rowman & Littlefield.

McLaren, P., & Lankshear, C. (Eds.). (1994). *Politics of Liberation: Paths from Freire.* London and New York: Routledge.

McLaren, P., & Leonard, P. (Eds.). (1993). *Paulo Freire: A Critical Encounter.* London and New York: Routledge.

McLaren, P. L., & Lankshear, C. (1993). Critical Literacy and the Postmodern Turn. In C. Lankshear & P. L. McLaren (Eds.), *Critical Literacy: Politics, Praxis, and the Postmodern* (pp. 379–419). Albany: State University of New York Press.

Meehan, J. (Ed.). (1995). *Feminists Read Habermas: Gendering the Subject of Discourse.* New York and London: Routledge.

Mezirow, J. (1995). Transformation Theory of Adult Learning. In *In Defense of the Lifeworld: Critical Perspectives on Adult Learning* (pp. 39–70). Albany: State University of New York Press.

Miedema, S. (1994). The Relevance for Pedagogy of Habermas' "Theory of Communicative Action." *Interchange, 25*(2), 195–206.

Misgeld, D. (1975). Emancipation, Enlightenment, and Liberation: An Approach Toward Foundational Inquiry into Education. *Interchange, 6*(3), 23–37.

Misgeld, D. (1981). Habermas's Retreat from Hermeneutics: Systems Integration, Social Integration and the Crisis of Legitimation. *Canadian Journal of Political and Social theory, 5*(1–2), 8–44.

Misgeld, D. (1985). Education and Cultural Invasion: Critical Social Theory, Education as Instruction, and the "Pedagogy of the Oppressed." In John Forester (Ed.), *Critical Theory and Public Life* (pp. 77–118). Cambridge, MA and London: MIT Press.

Montero, M. (1997). Political Psychology: A Critical Perspective. In D. R. Fox & I. Prilleltensky (Eds.), *Critical Psychology: An Introduction* (pp. 233–244). Thousand Oaks, CA: Sage.

Morales-Gómez, D., & Torres, C. A. (1990). *The State, Corporatist Politics, and Educational Policy Making in Mexico.* New York: Praeger.

Moreira Alves, R. (1969). *Toward a Theology of Liberation.* Princeton, NJ: Princeton University Press.

Morrow, R. A. (1982). Théorie critique et matérialisme historique: Jürgen Habermas. *Sociologie et Sociétés, 14*(2), 97–111.

Morrow, R. A. (1983). Habermas et le pragmatisme américain. *Communication et Information, 5*(2–3), 187–214.

Morrow, R. A. (1989). The Developmental Subject: Habermas and the Reproduction of the Lifeworld. *Discours social/Social Discourse, 2*(1–2), 247–266.

Morrow, R. A. (1990). Post-Marxism, Postmodernism and Popular Education in Latin America. *New Education, 12*(2), 47–57.

Morrow, R. A. (1991). Toward a Critical Theory of Methodology: Habermas and the Theory of Argumentation. *Current Perspectives in Social Theory, 11*, 197–228.

Morrow, R. A. (1994a). *Critical Theory and Methodology.* Newbury Park and London: Sage.

Morrow, R. A. (1994b). Critical Theory, Poststructuralism and Critical Realism: Reassesing the Critique(s) of Positivism. *Current Perspectives in Social theory, 14*, 27–51.

Morrow, R. A. (1994c). Mannheim and the Early Frankfurt School: The Weber Reception of Rival Traditions of Critical Sociology. In A. Horowitz & T. Maley (Eds.), *The Barbarism of Reason: Max Weber and the Twilight of Enlightenment* (pp. 169–194). Toronto and Buffalo: University of Toronto Press.

Morrow, R. A. (1998). Bakhtin and Mannheim: An Introductory Dialogue. In M. M. Bell & M. Gardiner (Eds.), *Bakhtin and the Human Sciences* (pp. 145–162). London: Sage.

Morrow, R. A., & Torres, C. A. (1994). Education and the Reproduction of Class, Gender and Race: Responding to the Postmodern Challenge. *Educational Theory, 44*(1), 43–61.

Morrow, R. A., & Torres, C. A. (1995). *Social Theory and Education: A Critique of Theories of Social and Cultural Reproduction.* Albany: State University of New York Press.

Morrow, R. A., & Torres, C. A. (1998a). Jürgen Habermas, Paulo Freire e a pedagogia crítica: Novas orientaçãoes para a educacação comparada. *Educação, Sociedade & Culturas, 10*, 123–155.

Morrow, R. A., & Torres, C. A. (1998b). Paulo Freire, Jürgen Habermas and Critical Pedagogy: Implications for Comparative Education. *Melbourne Studies in Education, 39*(2), 1–20.

Morrow, R. A., & Torres, C. A. (2001). Gramsci and Popular Education in Latin America: From Revolution to Democratic Transition. *International Journal of Educational Development, 21*(4), 331–343.

Mueller, C. (1970). Notes on the Repression of Communicative Behavior. In H. Dreitzel (Ed.), *Recent Sociology No. 2* (pp. 101–113). New York: Macmillan.

Mussell, W. J., Nicholls, W. M., & Adler, M. T. (1991). *Making Meaning of Mental Health Challenges in First Nations: A Freirean Perspective.* Chilliwack, BC: Saltshan Institute Society.

Nederveen Pieterse, J. (1998). My Paradigm or Yours? Alternative Development, Post-Development, Reflexive Development. *Development and Change, 29*(2), 343–373.

Nicol, E. (1965). *Los principios de la ciencia.* México, D.F.: Fondo de Cultura Económica.

Noddings, N. (1995). Care and Moral Education. In W. Kohli (Ed.), *Critical Conversations in Philosophy of Education* (pp. 137–148). New York and London: Routledge.

Nystrand, M. (1997). *Opening Dialogue: Understanding the Dynamics of Language and Learning in the English Classroom.* New York: Teachers College Press.

O'Cadiz, M. d. P., Wong, P. L., & Torres, C. A. (1998). *Education and Democracy:*

Paulo Freire, Social Movements, and Educational Reform in São Paulo. Boulder, CO: Westview Press.

Offe, C. (1984). *Contradictions of the Welfare State.* London: Hutchinson.

Oldenski, T. (1997). *Liberation Theology and Critical Pedagogy in Today's Catholic Schools: Social Justice in Action.* New York and London: Garland.

O'Neill, J. (1985). Decolonization and the Ideal Speech Community: Some Issues in the Theory and Practice of Communicative Competence. In John Forester (Ed.), *Critical Theory and Public Life* (pp. 57–76). Cambridge, MA and London: MIT Press.

O'Neill, J. (Ed.). (1996a). *Hegel's Dialectic of Desire and Recognition: Texts and Commentary.* Albany: State University of New York Press.

O'Neill, J. (1996b). Introduction: A Dialectical Genealogy of Self, Society, and Culture in and after Hegel. In J. O'Neill (Ed.), *Hegel's Dialectic of Desire and Recognition: Texts and Commentary* (pp. 1–28). Albany: State University of New York Press.

O'Sullivan, E. (1999). *Transformative Learning: Educational Vision for the 21st Century.* Toronto, London, & New York: University of Toronto/Zed Books.

Outhwaite, W. (1987). *New Philosophies of Social Science: Realism, Hermeneutics and Critical Theory.* London: Macmillan.

Paiva, V. P. (1982). *Paulo Freire y el nacionalismo desarrollista.* México, D.F.: Editorial Extemporáneos.

Palincsar, A. S., & Brown, A. L. (1984). Reciprocal Teaching of Comprehension-fostering and Comprehension-monitoring Activities. *Cognition and Instruction, 1,* 117–175.

Palincsar, A. S., Brown, A. L., & Campione, J. C. (1993). First-grade Dialogues for Knowledge Acquisition and Use. In E. A. Forman, N. Minick, & C. A. Stone (Eds.), *Contexts for Learning: Sociocultural Dynamics in Children's Development* (pp. 43–57). New York: Oxford University Press.

Paringer, W. A. (1990). *Dewey, John and the Paradox of Liberal Reform.* Albany: State University of New York Press.

Passerin d'Entrèves, M., & Benhabib, S. (Eds.). (1997). *Habermas and the Unfinished Project of Modernity: Critical Essays on The Philosophical Discourse of Modernity.* Cambridge, MA and London: MIT Press.

Pensky, M. (1995). Universalism and the Situtated Critic. In S. K. White (Ed.), *The Cambridge Companion to Habermas* (pp. 67–98). Cambridge: Cambridge University Press.

Pescador, J. A., & Torres, C. A. (1985). *Poder político y educación en México.* D.F. México: UTHEA.

Peters, M., & Lankshear, C. (1994). Education and Hermeneutics: A Freirean Interpretation. In P. McLaren & C. Lankshear (Eds.), *Politics of Liberation: Paths from Freire* (pp. 173–192). London and New York: Routledge.

Peukert, H. (1984). *Science, Action and Fundamental Theology: Toward a Theology of Communicative Action* (J. Bohman, Trans.). Cambridge, MA, and London: MIT Press.

Piaget, J. (1995). *Sociological Studies* (L. Smith, Trans.). London and New York: Routledge.

Pippin, R. B. (1991). *Modernism as a Philosophical Problem*. Oxford: Basil Blackwell.

Pippin, R. B. (1997). *Idealism as Modernism: Hegelian Variations*. Cambridge: Cambridge University Press.

Plumb, D. T. (1989). *The Significance of Jürgen Habermas for the Pedagogy of Paulo Freire and the Practice of Adult Education*. Unpublished master's thesis, University of Saskatchewan, Saskatoon, SK.

Popkewitz, T., & Fendler, L. (Eds.). (1999). *Critical Theories in Education: Changing Terrains of Knowledge and Politics*. New York and London: Routledge.

Popkewitz, T. S., & Brennan, M. (Eds.). (1998). *Foucault's Challenge: Discourse, Knowledge, and Power in Education*. New York and London: Teachers College Press.

Preis, A.-B. S. (1996). Human Rights as Cultural Practice: An Anthropological Critique. *Human Rights Quarterly, 18*(2), 286–315.

Puiggrós, A. (1994). Historia y prospectiva de la educación popular latinoamericana. In M. Gadotti & C. A. Torres (Eds.), *Educação popular: Utopia Latino-Americanada* (pp. 13–22). São Paulo: Cortez Editora/Editora da Universidade de São Paulo.

Purcell-Gates, V., & Waterman, R. A. (2000). *Now We Read, We See, We Speak: Portraits of Literacy Development in an Adult Freirean-Based Class*. Mahwah, NJ, and London: Lawrence Erlbaum Associates.

Rahnema, M. (1997). *The Post-Development Reader*. London: Zed Books.

Rasmussen, D. M. (1990). *Reading Habermas*. Cambridge, MA, and Oxford: Basil Blackwell.

Rasmussen, D. M. (Ed.). (1996). *Handbook of Critical Theory*. Oxford and Cambridge, MA: Blackwell.

Rauch, L. (1987). From Jena to Heidelberg: Two Views of Recognition. In P. G. Stillman (Ed.), *Hegel's Philosophy of Spirit* (pp. 47–58). Albany: State University of New York Press.

Ray, L. J. (1993). *Rethinking Critical Theory: Emancipation in the Age of Global Social Movements*. London and Newbury Park, CA: Sage.

Rehg, W. (1994). *Insight and Solidarity: A Study in the Discourse Ethics of Jürgen Habermas*. Berkeley, Los Angeles, and London: University of California Press.

Richards, M., Thomas, P. N., & Nain, Z. (Eds.). (2001). *Communication and Development: The Freirean Connection*. Cresskill, NJ: Hampton Press.

Ricoeur, P. (1974). *The Conflict of Interpretations* (D. Ihde, Trans.). Evanston: Northwestern University Press.

Riegel, K. F. (1979). *Foundations of Dialectical Psychology*. New York: Academic Press.

Roberts, P. (1996). Defending Freirean Intervention. *Educational Theory, 46*(3), 335–352.

Roberts, P. (1998). Knowledge, Dialogue, and Humanization: The Moral Philosophy of Paulo Freire. *Journal of Educational Thought, 32*(2), 95–116.

Roberts, P. (2000). *Education, Literacy and Humanization: Exploring the World of Paulo Freire*. Westport, CT: Bergin & Garvey.

Rosenfeld, M., & Arato, A. (1998). *Habermas on Law and Democracy: Critical Exchanges*. Berkeley: University of California Press.

Sachs, J. (1991). Action and Reflection in Work with a Group of Homeless People. *Social Work With Groups, 14*(3–4), 187–202.

Said, E. W. (1994). *Representations of the Intellectual: The 1993 Reith Lectures*. New York: Vintage.

Sampson, E. E. (1993). *Celebrating the Other: A Dialogic Account of Human Nature*. Boulder and San Francisco: Westview Press.

Schipani, D. S. (1984). *Conscientization and Creativity: Paulo Freire and Christian Education*. Lanham, New York, and London: University Press of America.

Schutte, O. (1993). *Cultural Identity and Social Liberation in Latin American Thought*. Albany: State University of New York Press.

Schwenn, B. (1998). Reivindicar la modernidad a la posmodernidad en América Latina: El universalismo como base del relativismo cultural. *Estudios sobre las culturas contemporáneas, Época II/ Vol. IV*(7), 65–83.

Shor, I. (Ed.). (1987). *Freire for the Classroom: A Sourcebook for Liberatory Teaching*. Portsmouth, NH: Boynton/Cook (Heinemann).

Shor, I. (1992). *Empowering Education: Critical Teaching for Social Change*. Chicago and London: University of Chicago Press.

Shor, I., & Freire, P. (1987). *A Pedagogy for Liberation: Dialogues on Transforming Education*. South Hadley, MA: Bergin and Garvey.

Shor, I., & Pari, C. (Eds.). (2000). *Education Is Politics: Critical Teaching Across Differences, Postsecondary*. Portsmouth, NH: Heimemann.

Spring, J. H. (1994). *Wheels in the Head: Educational Philosophies of Authority, Freedom, and Culture from Socrates to Paulo Freire*. New York: McGraw-Hill.

Steiner, D. M. (1994). *Rethinking Democratic Education: The Politics of Reform*. Baltimore and London: Johns Hopkins University Press.

Strien, P. G. v. (1982). In Search of an Emancipatory Social Psychology. In P. Stringer (Ed.), *Confronting Social Issues, vol. 2* (pp. 1–26). London: Academic Press.

Stromquist, N. P. (1997). *Literacy for Citizenship: Gender and Grassroots Dynamics in Brazil*. Albany: State University of New York Press.

Strong, T. B., & Sposito, F. A. (1995). Habermas's Significant Other. In S. K. White (Ed.), *The Cambridge Companion to Habermas* (pp. 263–288). Cambridge: Cambridge University Press.

Sullivan, E. (1990). *Critical Psychology and Pedagogy: Interpretation of the Personal World*. New York: Bergin & Garvey.

Szell, G. (1985). Experiences de methodes en Allemagne et dans les pays nordiques sur la recherche des concernes. *Recherches Sociologiques, 16*(2), 293–306.

Tappan, M. B., & Brown, L. M. (1996). Envisioning a Postmodern Moral Pedagogy. *Journal of Moral Development, 25*(1), 101–109.

Taylor, C. (1975). *Hegel*. Cambridge: Cambridge University Press.

Taylor, P. V. (1993). *The Texts of Paulo Freire*. Buckingham and Philadelphia: Open University Press.

Thompson, J. B. (1981). *Critical Hermeneutics: A Study in the Thought of Paul Ricoeur and Jürgen Habermas*. Cambridge: Cambridge University Press.

Torres, C. A. (1976a). A dialética Hegeliana e o pensamento Lógico-estrutural de Paulo Freire. Notas para uma análise e confrontaçõ dos pressupostos filsóficos vigentes na dialética da pedagogía dos oprimidos e do pensmento freire-ano em geral. *Sintese, 3 (nova fase)* (7), 61–78.

Torres, C. A. (1976b). Servidumbre, autoconsciencia y liberación. *Franciscanum, 18*(54), 405–478.

Torres, C. A. (1978a). *Entrevistas con Paulo Freire.* Mexico, D.F.: Ediciones Gernika.

Torres, C. A. (1978b). *La praxis educativa de Paulo Freire.* D.F., Mexico: Gernika.

Torres, C. A. (Ed.). (1979). *Paulo Freire en América Latina.* Mexico, D.F.: Ediciones Gernika.

Torres, C. A. (1980). *Leitura critica de Paulo Freire.* São Paulo: Loyola Ediçoes.

Torres, C. A. (1990a). *Learning the World: Paulo Freire in Conversaton with Dr Carlos Alberto Torres* [videotape]. Edmonton: Access Network.

Torres, C. A. (1990b). *The Politics of Nonformal Education in Latin America.* New York: Praeger.

Torres, C. A. (1992). *The Church, Society, and Hegemony: A Critical Sociology of Religion in Latin America* (R. A. Young, Trans.). Westport, CT, and London: Praeger.

Torres, C. A. (1994). Education and the Archaeology of Consciousness: Freire and Hegel. *Educational Theory, 44*(4), 429–445.

Torres, C. A. (1995a). *Estudios Freireanos.* Buenos Aires: Libros del Quirquincho (Coquena Grupo).

Torres, C. A. (1995b). Participatory Action Research and Popular Education in Latin America. In P. L. McLaren & J. M. Giarelli (Eds.), *Critical Theory and Educational Research* (pp. 237–255). Albany: State University of New York Press.

Torres, C. A. (1998a). *Democracy, Education, and Multiculturalism: Dilemmas of Citizenship in a Global World.* Lanham, MD: Rowman & Littlefield.

Torres, C. A. (Ed.). (1998b). *Education, Power, and Personal Biography.* New York and London: Routledge.

Torres, C. A. (1998c). *A Pedagogia da Luta. Da Pedagogia do Oprimido a Escola Pública Popular.* Campinhas, SP: Papirus.

Torres, C. A., & Freire, P. (1994). Twenty Years After *Pedagogy of the Oppressed*: Paulo Freire in Conversation with Carlos Alberto Torres. In P. McLaren & C. Lankshear (Eds.), *Politics of Liberation: Paths from Freire* (pp. 100–107). London and New York: Routledge.

Torres, C. A., & Puiggrós, A. (Eds.). (1996). *Latin American Education: Comparative Perspectives.* Boulder, CO: Westview Press.

Torres, C. A., & Rivera, G. G. (Eds.). (1994). *Sociología de la educación: Corrientes contemporáneas* (3rd ed.). Buenos Aires: Miño y Davila editores.

Travers, K. D. (1997). Nutrition Education for Social Change: Critical Perspectives. *Journal of Nutrition Education, 29,* 57–62.

United Nations Development Programme (UNDP). (2000). *Human Development Report 2000.* New York and Oxford: Oxford University Press.

Van der Veer, R., & Valsiner, J. (1991). *Understanding Vygotsky: A Quest for Synthesis.* Oxford: Basil Blackwell.

Vygotsky, L. (1986). *Thought and Language* (A. e. Kozulin, Trans.) (rev. ed.). Cambridge, MA and London: MIT Press.

Wallerstein, N. (1993). Empowerment and Health: The Theory and Practice of Community Change. *Community Development Journal, 28*(3), 218–227.

Wang, C., & Burris, M. A. (1994). Empowerment Through Photo Novella: Portraits of Participation. *Health Education Quarterly, 21*(2), 171–186.

Warnke, G. (1995). Communicative Rationality and Cultural Values. In S. K. White (Ed.), *The Cambridge Companion to Habermas* (pp. 120–142). Cambridge: Cambridge University Press.

Weiler, K. (1994). Freire and a Feminist Pedagogy of Difference. In P. McLaren & C. Lankshear (Eds.), *Politics of Liberation: Paths from Freire* (pp. 12–40). London and New York: Routledge.

Weiler, K. (1996). Myths of Paulo Freire. *Educational Theory, 46*(3), 353–371.

Welton, M. R. (1995a). The Critical Turn in Adult Education Theory. In M. R. Welton (Ed.), *In Defense of the Lifeworld: Critical Perspectives on Adult Learning* (pp. 11–38). Albany: State University of New York Press.

Welton, M. R. (Ed.). (1995b). *In Defense of the Lifeworld: Critical Perspectives on Adult Learning.* Albany: State University of New York Press.

Welton, M. R. (1995c). Introduction. In M. R. Welton (Ed.), *In Defense of the Lifeworld: Critical Perspectives on Adult Learning* (pp. 1–10). Albany: State University of New York Press.

Wertsch, J. V. (1991). *Voices of the Mind: A Sociocultural Approach to Mediated Action.* Cambridge, MA: Harvard University Press.

Wertsch, J. V. (1998). *Mind as Action.* New York and Oxford: Oxford University Press.

West, C. (1993). Preface. In P. McLaren & P. Leonard (Eds.), *Paulo Freire: A Critical Encounter* (pp. xiii–xiv). London and New York: Routledge.

Wexler, P. (1983). *Critical Social Psychology.* Boston: Routledge.

White, S. K. (Ed.). (1995a). *The Cambridge Companion to Habermas.* Cambridge: Cambridge University Press.

White, S. K. (1995b). Reason, Modernity, and Democracy. In S. K. White (Ed.), *The Cambridge Companion to Habermas* (pp. 3–16). Cambridge: Cambridge University Press.

Wiggershaus, R. (1994). *The Frankfurt School: Its History, Theories and Political Significance* (M. Robertson, Trans.). Cambridge: Polity Press.

Yeatman, A. (2000). Who Is the Subject of Human Rights? *American Behavioral Scientist, 43*(9), 1498–1513.

Young, R. E. (1989). *A Critical Theory of Education: Habermas and Our Children's Future.* New York and London: Harvester Wheatsheaf.

Index

About the Authors

Raymond A. Morrow is Professor of Sociology and Adjunct Professor of Educational Policy Studies, University of Alberta, Edmonton, Canada. He teaches primarily in the areas of social theory and cultural sociology. Previous book publications include *Critical Theory and Methodology* (Sage, 1994) and (with C. A. Torres) *Social Theory and Education* (SUNY, 1995).

Carlos Alberto Torres, a political sociologist of education, is a professor in the Graduate School of Education and Information Studies, University of California–Los Angeles, as well as director of the Latin American Center. He has been a past president of the Comparative and International Education Society (CIES) and is a Founding Director of the Paulo Freire Institute in São Paulo, Brazil. Among his many books published in English, Spanish, and Portuguese are, most recently, *Democracy, Education and Multiculturalism* (Rowman & Littlefield, 1998) and *Education, Power and Personal Biography* (Routledge, 1998).